How
Remarkable
Women
LEAD

How
Remarkable
Women
LEAD

The Breakthrough

Model for

Work and Life

Joanna Barsh *and*
Susie Cranston,
and Geoffrey Lewis

CROWN
BUSINESS
NEW YORK

Copyright © 2009 by McKinsey & Company, Inc., United States

All rights reserved.
Published in the United States by Crown Business, an imprint of the
Crown Publishing Group, a division of Random House, Inc.,
New York.
www.crownpublishing.com

CROWN BUSINESS is a trademark and CROWN and the Rising Sun
colophon are registered trademarks of Random House, Inc.

Library of Congress Cataloging-in-Publication Data is available upon
request.

ISBN 978-0-3074-6169-8

PRINTED IN THE UNITED STATES OF AMERICA

Design by Donna Sinisgalli

10 9 8 7 6 5 4 3

Dedication was a challenging
task; what finally made it easy
was discovering the role love
plays in centered leadership and
for each of us.

So David, and Russell, and Anne,
this book is dedicated to you.

We are the lucky ones.

Contents

How

Remarkable
Women
LEAD

Introduction: Journey to the Center

Searching for the Magic

When I turned fifty, something happened to me. Nothing. Absolutely nothing. No sense of having reached a monumental milestone. No dread, no joy. And that sense of nothingness really bothered me. "You're just having an ordinary midlife crisis," I assured myself. "Go buy yourself some nice shoes or something."

Weeks passed and still the feeling would not let me go. On an early morning walk through Central Park, I shared my unease with my husband, David. Had I reached the pinnacle of my career, and if so, was this all there was? Other women surely had gone further, had done more, were happier. They were taller, more beautiful, more accomplished, had more sparkle—in every way, they were better at life.

There must be something they knew that I never learned. I wanted to meet them, and I wanted to know what they knew—not just for me, but for all the women asking these questions about what made other women so wonderfully successful as leaders. I was convinced that no simple skill-building formula existed, because if it did, I would have found it long ago.

There must be, I thought, something more, some kind of magic. If I could get my hands on it, I would go further, have a bigger impact, and feel fulfilled—just like them. What really got me jazzed was the idea that if I could bottle this magic, I could pass it on to the next generation of women, the ones who are on a path to leadership now—perhaps to my own daughters. Imagine what they could do if they didn't have to wait thirty years to find it for themselves. Imagine how many more women would make it to the top because these secrets would help them!

You could say I was driven by this idea, quietly obsessed. In the years since that walk with David, I have come to realize that this was a passion that had been waiting, dormant—a seed just waiting for the right conditions to sprout.

By any objective measure, my life at fifty was pretty great. We had two incredible daughters, healthy, doing well in school—as wonderful as it gets. My marriage was strong despite—or because of?—years of ups and downs. We had a beautiful airy apartment with light and color and a view. Every day we entered Central Park to walk with our girls to school. In a city crowded with buildings and noise, it doesn't get any better. On weekends we lived on a farm with rolling fields, ancient trees, wildflowers, and wild berries everywhere. We had fifty cows, thirty chickens, ten sheep, three donkeys, and a pig. This was as close to paradise as it gets.

I had all this and professional fulfillment, too. Despite my constant worries, I was a senior partner at McKinsey & Company, doing what I wanted to do, helping Fortune 500 clients transform and grow. There were times when I was madly in love with what I did. There were times when I dreamed of retiring. But for the most part—and despite frequent doses of anxiety—I was, as my beloved firm says, a partner in good standing. I was being useful, contributing, still engaged, still having fun most days. So, what was wrong with me anyway?

I thought about it, and it came down to this: I felt invisible. I was passing through life as an observer and had felt that way for a long, long time. So it should not have been a real surprise that I turned fifty without fireworks.

It hadn't always been this way. When I was a young woman, fresh out of school with two liberal arts degrees, I returned to New York as an independent spirit, ready to take on any challenge. My resumé then included waitress, usher, administrative assistant, and movie production "gofer." I took a job in retail—in management training, actually—and ran head-on into turbulence. Daily, my bosses called me on the carpet for a thousand mistakes—some real, some not—and I can honestly say I still don't understand why. (That was a big lesson for me: If someone doesn't want you to succeed, there are infinite ways to let you know, slowly erasing your self-worth.) So I became a young woman with unpredictable nosebleeds, in fear of my next mistake, too intimidated to quit. I finally applied to business school, more as a way out of where I was than to find a way forward. Not an auspicious start.

At Harvard Business School, I did well, finding the problem-solving fascinating, so much so that I returned to New York to do some more of it as work. Pretty quickly, I became a young woman going somewhere, working extra hard because I still feared the bosses who would find a thousand mistakes, who might call me in to announce that the biggest one was when they hired me.

Even at fifty I was waiting for that call. Funny how, when you lose a lot of weight, it can take years for your self-image to catch up. Likewise, after twenty-odd years of valued consulting and plenty of recognition, my self-image had barely budged.

So, during that spring of my fifty-first year, I waited and worked, fearing the call but hoping for some magic to appear that would transform me into the senior leader I wanted to be. And who was that? She was as calm and strong as a rock, as popular as Elvis, and as wise as a sage: a senior leader with supreme confidence, standing on a foundation of achievement, well-connected and content. Most of all, I wanted to be the leader who could look in the mirror and know that she had helped make a difference in the world. Where was she? Was she somewhere inside or nowhere to be found? That's what I still wanted to learn.

What I did know—and what I told my husband during that morning walk—was that waiting even one more year to find out would be a bad decision. I had to find what propelled and sustained the few women who made it to the very top. I wanted to document what it was that had made them successful in work—and in life. It would be an archive of conversations with women leaders. I wanted to archive their happiness. I couldn't wait any longer and I couldn't wait to get started.

As David and I walked and talked, he took my idea of an archive and made it big. That's why I love him—he dares to imagine, and there is no box that can contain him. He pushed me to scale up my ambition. His push was so big it made me uncomfortable. He said, "You're thinking of an archive? Great! Make it the biggest archive of women leaders in the world—something Steven Spielberg would be proud of!" Some combination of excitement and anxiety began to well up inside of me. He went on, "Video your conversations with a first-rate crew. And give the archive an important-sounding name. Call it something that men will find interesting." I was definitely leaving my comfort zone now. He went on, "Call it the Leadership Project! What are you waiting for? Who will you cold call today?" The professionals have a word for where I was headed—"The Panic Zone."

Panic or not, that's just what I did.

I've been at this a little over five years now. My exploration has taken me further than I ever expected. The Leadership Project has changed my own life through a new model for leadership that is the subject of this book. It has grown into a broad-based movement in our firm, involving women and men around the world who are growing as they contribute.

Looking back, I would have to say I was lucky from the start. Almost immediately, I knew that our interviews were tapping into something very powerful. Our women told fascinating stories, mesmerizing stories, stories filled with energy. They opened their doors to welcome me in and pour out their memories of love and success and joy—along with wrong turns and big mistakes and outright failures. They talked about their children, their health problems, their dreams for the future. They laughed and they told secrets. Some shed tears. They didn't hold back. They gave us their scarcest resources—time and energy—and they contributed real-life lessons learned the hard way.

Something was flowing through these conversations, connecting each woman to the next, to their work, to me. Each conversation was a gift—a little dose of optimism, a slug of energy, a practical tip, a story of meaning, an act of kindness. In their stories, I recognized little bits of myself. Unwrapping each of these gifts, I was filling up with gratitude.

My passion for the Leadership Project was delivering a sense of fulfillment that I had only occasionally felt in my work. Don't get me wrong. I absolutely love being a consultant—especially working with clients to make something happen, building teams and problem-solving with them on their way to action and results. And I absolutely love the moment of insight, the collective flash of understanding, the step toward impact. But my joy in work had had no permanence until now.

Passion unleashed, I felt good every day, and I could feel my outlines becoming visible. It was an unfamiliar sensation, a natural high that gave me the confidence and courage to take some giant steps forward. I was literally becoming fearless. It was time to speak up and step up.

No Going Back

In 2007 I crossed the line—in a good way. I began to take some professional risks to pursue my passion for the Leadership Project. I burned bridges to my old routines, shifting my time to work on this project more and more. Now there was no going back.

What's more, we elevated the Leadership Project from an under-the-radar labor of love to a serious professional development effort. Like so many organizations, our partners had worked hard to bolster the ranks of women in senior leadership. I was convinced that the stories of these women leaders contained what had been missing: a common set of beliefs, successful practices, and a way forward that would help our firm, and our clients, to accelerate the ascent of women to the top.

That's when a busload of talented women and men joined the expedition. Among them was Susie Cranston, a young McKinsey consultant based in San Francisco. Susie switched tracks for one year to become the point person for our research team, hunting down the academic and scientific knowledge to underpin what we were observing. We explored a wide range of fields—the leadership gurus and the experts on organizational development, the biologists and the neuroscientists. And we kept digging deeper, interviewing more and different kinds of women, looking for patterns. Together, with the practical real-life experiences of our interviewees, these academic theories could shape a teachable roadmap to leadership.

Before long, we found ourselves drawn increasingly to factors that lie beyond traditional approaches to management and professional development—to newer ideas about how emotional, spiritual, and physical well-being, a deep connection to the work itself and to one's colleagues—how joy—creates the conditions for successful leadership. Here were these women, leaders who had armored themselves to do corporate battle, voicing their passion—their feelings of joy and meaning without embarrassment. All those years of trying to hide my feelings melted away.

Another factor jumping up and down in front of us was our women leaders' optimism—no, make that extreme optimism. Many had overcome serious obstacles and painful setbacks. But they didn't spiral down when things went wrong, the way I did; they swung into action and kept moving ahead. They didn't get stuck at the bottom, replaying what happened in a closed loop. Instead, they were doers and fixers.

But how did they build and exude such contagious optimism? We found explanations in positive psychology, a discipline that focuses on what makes people flourish rather than what causes psychological and emotional distress. What we learned from the positive psychologists was that people who have a deep sense of meaning about what they do are happier and more energized and far more resilient. Our women to a tee: Each on a mission, serving some higher purpose than simply advancing their careers. They were changing the world, whether they were reaching five people in a start-up or five hundred thousand.

According to the experts, optimism can be learned. You can train yourself to be more optimistic and avoid getting stuck at the bottom of your emotional range. That struck a chord. I began to talk back to the tiny voice in my head that amplified the pain of every mistake. When something went wrong, I was learning to pick myself up more quickly and move forward. My worldview began to change.

We also learned about "flow"—the phenomenon that happens when your skills are well matched to an inspiring challenge and you are working toward a clear goal. I had experienced flow from time to time at work and always when I painted. When I'm painting, it's as if I'm outside my own body, experiencing the world without time and without physical sensation. Then I reemerge, tired but refreshed, and stronger in the knowledge of myself. Flow reinforces resilience.

We kept digging, collecting more input from women and men in our firm and developing our own survey research. One of the biggest questions about our women leaders was how they managed to pour enormous energy into their work and still shoulder the double burden that most women face as wives and mothers. How did they succeed at work without giving up on the rest? This was critical, because many women continue to opt out of careers or lower their sights when they feel that they can't do justice to their families.

Another revelation: Our women saw "work-life balance" for what it is—an unattainable goal. Instead, they have adapted to a life of managed disequilibrium—a fluid and dynamic approach.

They love their children *and* they love their work. There was no either/or. Accepting "and" filled them with energy.

Okay, but where did they even get the physical energy to have anything left at the end of the workday? That's what I wanted to know. I was the mom who rushed home to put her girls to bed, only to fall fast asleep right next to them.

We started looking for answers and found some right under our noses. As it turns out, the academics had already been at work on the question. They taught us that you can manage your energy by identifying what saps it and what recharges you and by making strategic adjustments in your environment and your schedule.

There were other factors, of course. These women had help on their leadership journeys. They were helped by everybody, but especially by senior men who stuck out their necks to create opportunities. They were plugged into the community, drawing strength from the connections. I thought back to everyone who had helped me. As I reflected, more and more faces appeared, and I silently thanked each one, including those no longer with us.

Unlike me, many women we met boldly proclaimed they were unafraid—completely without fear. That helped them regard opportunities as, well, opportunities—not chances to lose or fail. If they saw risks, they met those head-on. They were not held back by self-doubt, second-guessing, or perfectionism. This was another revelation for me, someone who had turned down many opportunities because of fear.

So, as 2007 drew to a close, our model for leadership took form. At its core were deep emotional connections: to work, to personal meaning and mission, to achievement, to nurturing instincts, and to a strong feeling of belonging. To joy.

This was certainly a new take on leadership for me.

We were weaving the threads of leadership, performance, and fulfillment into a system with behaviors, skills, and actions. It was something about purpose, because being a mother was so strong a pull. It was something about tapping into the deep well of positive emotion that coursed through the women leaders we met. It was something about action—helping women to push through fear, to act on their beliefs and their intuitions. It was also about choice, about personal ownership.

Meaning underpinned everything. It established the right motivation and helped women identify their direction. On top of this, we saw that there were three clusters of capabilities and tactics—framing and connecting and engaging—that led to sustained success and increased joy in living. Finally, we brought in "energizing" to fuel each woman's long-term journey.

Briefly, this is how our system lined up:

Meaning. The sense of meaning is what inspires women leaders, guides their careers, sustains their optimism, generates positive emotions, and enables them to lead in creative and profound ways.

Framing. To sustain herself on the path to leadership and to function as a leader, a woman must view situations clearly, avoiding downward spirals, in order to move ahead, adapt, and implement solutions.

Connecting. Nobody does it alone. Women leaders make meaningful connections to develop sponsorship and followership, to collaborate with colleagues and supporters with warmth and humanity.

Engaging. Successful leaders take ownership for opportunities along with risks. They have a voice and they use it. They're also able to face down their fears.

Energizing. To succeed long-term and to accommodate family and community responsibilities, women leaders learn to manage their energy reserves and to tap into flow.

Putting the pieces together created a silent boom, an "aha" moment. Our nascent leadership solution seemed elegant and simple, so much so that we had to sleep on it for a day, just to make sure. I looked for holes. For days, I looked for the holes. At night, I looked for them in my dreams. But all my anxiety and angst couldn't find much to quarrel with.

When we mixed the model's ingredients together, we created magic. The ingredients blend well and they reinforce each other. Think about it. If your opportunities are infused with meaning, you will also be energized. Optimism on its own is a good thing, but apply it to building relationships and you will find that your developmental network begins to thrive. Engage in a sponsor relationship and you can face setbacks more easily. Every one of these pieces fills up your energy reserves, and the more energy you bring to what you do, the bigger the chances of your success. Each concept builds on the others. In combination, they unlock tremendous fuel for performance and satisfaction—the keys to success. Figure 1 (page 12) shows the circular imagery we designed to illustrate our new leadership model. The circle is a female shape, symbolizing no single starting or stopping place—movement and rhythm, symmetry and beauty.

We started sharing our model with others. Some thought it

Figure 1.

Five Dimensions of Centered Leadership

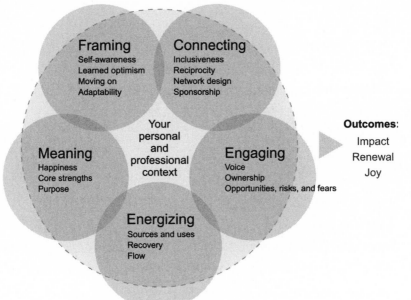

Preconditions:
Talent
Desire to lead
Tolerance for change

Framing
Self-awareness
Learned optimism
Moving on
Adaptability

Connecting
Inclusiveness
Reciprocity
Network design
Sponsorship

Your personal and professional context

Outcomes:
Impact
Renewal
Joy

Meaning
Happiness
Core strengths
Purpose

Engaging
Voice
Ownership
Opportunities, risks, and fears

Energizing
Sources and uses
Recovery
Flow

was too simple. Yes, the ingredients we used are available at any market; there are no special Chinese herbs or rain forest extracts. But we knew our recipe was challenging to execute. It might take a lifetime to build all the skills. Here was the magic—each step could be satisfying, reinforcing.

I realized that I had been absorbing these lessons and internalizing these behaviors. I wasn't second-guessing myself anymore. I wasn't confused and I wasn't unsure. David said it made him happy to see me so full of energy—joyful and unafraid.

Bottling the Stuff

At the end of the year, Geoff Lewis joined us. Geoff, a respected journalist and editor, helped us capture the recipe—to share the ingredients and how to use them, so all women could try it. We saw that this model had potential to sustain others on their paths to leadership, no matter what their starting points. They, too, could stand down their fears and gain the confidence and single-mindedness to lead, without losing their warmth, personal authenticity, or creativity.

We went to work on turning the model into learning programs. But what to call it? Centered Leadership fit the bill. We liked the imagery: It's good to feel centered. Feel the gravity beneath your two feet holding you steady as you stretch to the sky. Take risks and never lose your balance. Feel your spine lifting you up. Feel grounded, strong, and stable and, at the same time, lightweight, flexible, ready for what's coming at you.

All other things being equal (talent, education, drive), we now saw that it is the centered woman or man who sustains a successful leadership journey. These leaders thrive when things go well and adapt to significant change without losing their way, because they are centered—not just emotionally, but also intellectually, socially, and physically. A strong core gave our women leaders the courage to embrace new situations and adapt, to learn. A strong core helped them preserve and build physical energy. And the confidence that comes from a core belief in who you are and what is meaningful to you made them more open. They could listen to their social instincts. What's more, they liked themselves. Sure, they took wrong turns, made mistakes. But still they were happy.

We designed Centered Leadership especially for women, but not just for women. There are a few fundamental differences between men and women that the experts can agree on (beyond our obvious hormonal cycles and capacity to bear children). Women tend to experience emotions more at the extremes, and we are twice as likely to be diagnosed for depression. Women generally build deep relationships but have narrow networks, compared to men. Women tend not to raise their hands for new opportunities. Still, our research into the practices women and men deploy suggests there are more differences between individuals than between genders. So Centered Leadership can help men build needed leadership capabilities, too. We think they will want to, as Centered Leadership correlates with higher performance, greater success and more satisfaction at work. Who wouldn't want that!

That brought us to the last and most difficult question: Could Centered Leadership solve the shortage of women at the top? What was it that enabled some women to sustain careers that took them into top leadership positions in corporations, government, the arts, and other fields, while so many women stopped short, whether or not they literally opted out? With the same educational, social, and even athletic opportunities that have traditionally shaped male leaders, and entering demanding careers with the same drive and ambition as young men, why do young women continue to fall by the wayside?

Alone, Centered Leadership won't work miracles. Many environmental changes still need to occur before we see a level playing field. Many organizations have identified the gaps and continue to push for ways to fill them. Meanwhile, Centered Leadership complements that fine work; it doesn't replace it. From the perspective of my own journey, however, I see that it fills in a critical piece, and it is available to anyone who chooses it, regardless of where they work.

Of course, there will be skeptics. But as more and more people hear about what we are doing, the positive feedback overwhelms us. We have unleashed optimism and joy and love as integral parts of leading. The implications are far-reaching. Centered leaders would perform at peak and with self-renewal. Their organizations would model the behavior and perform at peak, too. Collaborative teams would come up with better, more creative solutions than those ground down by command-and-control leaders who use fear and doubt as powerful motivators.

No wonder the overall response has been overwhelmingly positive. Indeed, our new model of leadership is a positive contagion: At our own firm, colleagues who were exposed to it caught our enthusiasm and wanted to know how they could use it in their lives. Men and women I didn't know very well were there right alongside me. As it turned out, more than twenty-five years into my career, I belonged. I was no longer alone.

Now, Voyager

A final word about my own journey, which I'm happy to say is still ongoing. As Centered Leadership evolved, I chose full immersion. After all, if we were asking you to open yourself up to experience this new leadership model, I had to go first—to drink from that bottle.

And this drink contained some of life's biggest secrets. I could not have learned them from my wonderful colleagues or clients. My family and my friends were all too close to see it. Instead, I had to learn the secrets from a collection of strangers who opened their hearts to welcome me in. Thanks to them, and to these years of searching and dreaming and connecting, I realized that I truly liked myself and I really, really liked the centered leader that I was becoming.

The first half of my dream at fifty was to meet the women who understood. That became Centered Leadership, and I gave myself a big check mark for making that part of the dream come true.

But there was always more. I have two daughters who will grow up to be amazing women in their own rights, making a difference in the world no matter what they choose to do. The second half of my dream is to share the magic with them, and with daughters everywhere.

And that brings me to right now. To you. I want to pass that magic on to you.

This book is our way of doing that. You have what it takes: the brains, the desire to lead, the perseverance, the tolerance for change. You also have it in you to make your mark. It's your choice.

The magic is in here and you can unleash it through your own actions. But growing into a Centered Leader is something you have to decide for yourself.

Listen to the voice inside you—the voice of your dreaming— not the one complaining or critiquing or worrying or scolding. Give yourself permission to dream. Go ahead. That's where you'll start to find meaning, and that's the first step.

Read this book with your favorite pen in hand. We'll give you the room you need to write down your thoughts and ideas, the actions you plan to take. Better yet, buy an absolutely beautiful journal or notebook to record your reflections.

And as you read this book, welcome your heart and spirit into the act, too. This is not an intellectual activity alone—we want all of you.

That's because the most important part of our leadership project is you. Until you open this book, until you use it and experience it, we haven't accomplished a thing. Only when you begin to engage, when you open yourself to the tenets of what happens when women lead, can you bring it to life.

Are you ready? "Take the step," women leaders said. "What's the worst that could happen?" The upside is so great, taking that step is a must.

Are you ready?

We are. We know Centered Leadership is a lifelong endeavor. And we're here to help you on your way.

Let's go.

PART ONE

Meaning

CHAPTER I

It All Begins with Meaning

Sometimes I wonder if we're simply amalgamating and collating. On the other hand, I step back and think, "We have a responsibility beyond that. Raw data isn't enough for citizens, for governments. Anyone can give news, it's up to us to analyze its impact and bring out the pros and the cons of any action that can affect lives and to do it with integrity day after day."

Shobhana Bhartia, chairman, Hindustan Times

The late Katharine Graham, the first female CEO of a Fortune 500 company, once said, "To love what you do and feel that it matters—how could anything be more fun?" Mrs. Graham, who guided the Washington Post Co. for decades with her passion for quality journalism, was ahead of her time in many ways. But her insights about how meaningful work brings joy to life date back to ancient Greece. In the fourth century B.C., Aristotle wrote that people achieve *eudaimonia* (a contented state of flourishing) when they fully use their unique talents, thereby fulfilling their basic function in life. In the twentieth century, the psychologist Abraham Maslow restated the concept as "self-actualization," which he placed at the top of his hierarchy of human needs. Most recently, academics in the field of positive psychology have underscored the link between meaningful activities and happiness. Meaning is the motivation in your life. It's finding what engages you, what makes your heart beat faster, what gives you energy and creates passion. Meaning enables you to push yourself to the limit of your capabilities—and beyond. Without meaning, work is a slog between weekends. With meaning, any job can become a calling. By deploying your greatest strengths in service of a meaningful purpose that transcends everyday goals, you open yourself up to long-lasting happiness.

Meaning is a defining trait among successful leaders. When asked what the most important factors are in choosing a job and staying in it, women consistently cite the meaningful elements of the work. Women like Amina Susannah Agbaje, who started her own law firm to fulfill a childhood dream, have a profound belief in what they are doing. That leads to a higher level of commitment and gives you the courage to plunge ahead, no matter what the odds and no matter who says, "No, you can't." Finding meaning helps you set audacious goals and venture forth to meet them.

Everyone should dare to dream, even a young girl growing up in rural Nigeria. That certainly was the case with Amina, the eldest of seven children by her father's second wife. Living in two rooms in a large compound, they were not rich, but not poor either. There was a television in the compound, and every week young Amina would race home to watch a program called *Case File*. In each episode, two lawyers would square off, and the judge would decide the case at the end. Amina saw that a smart lawyer could keep an innocent man from going to jail or make sure a crooked one got his comeuppance. She was mesmerized—and inspired—by the show, drawn to the excitement of problem-solving and the thrill of arguing before the judge. Over time, this dedication became her purpose. That overarching goal was so big that it made decades of hard work worthwhile. "From primary school, I knew I wanted to be a lawyer," says Amina. "And I stuck to it."

Meaning seldom shows up as early and as clearly as it did for Amina. Sometimes it first appears as a small idea that expands over time. And often, meaning finds you (as opposed to the other way around). So if you plunk yourself down for the next hour to complete the vision assignment, you may be disappointed. Sometimes meaning hovers in front of you, hidden in plain sight. For some of us, it takes years to come into focus. You may be in a job for a long time before you realize that it's what you love—what you've been looking for—and what you wouldn't trade for anything.

That doesn't mean you have to wait. You can take steps and should, to find what motivates and rivets you.

Many women set out, traveling down academic and career paths, only to discover meaningful work after more than a few turns in the road. The zigs and zags of their career may seem inefficient (surely a straight shot to your goal would seem a better choice). Things are not always what they seem. In most cases, women leaders recall that these zigs taught self-awareness and those zags led them down the path to skills and experiences that opened a door. It was not time wasted. It was their time for discovering what they loved and learning new capabilities.

It does not matter when you find work with meaning or whether it has deep significance for anyone else. Once you recognize what is meaningful to you, you can marshal all your talents and capabilities for greater achievement and joy.

Meaning is a precursor to success because, psychologists say, recognizing and making it part of your life produces a sustained increase in happiness. Happiness is not just a nice-to-have goal. Emotional and psychological well-being are critically important to leadership for four very practical reasons:

- **Happiness is motivating.** People will expend extraordinary efforts when work makes them happy. "A business organization whose employees are happy is more productive, has a higher morale, and has a lower turnover," writes Mihály Csikszentmihályi, a leading expert in positive psychology.
- **Happier teams are more creative.** They approach problem-solving more creatively and often arrive at better solutions. Research by Barbara Fredrickson, a professor of psychology at the University of North Carolina, has shown that learning improves when students and employees feel happy; they are more open to new concepts and set higher goals for themselves.
- **Leaders who exude happiness are more effective.** A leader who finds true enjoyment in the work and is energized by it has a positive effect on those around her. Passion, enthusiasm, and energy are infectious—mutually reinforcing when the whole team feels them.
- **Happiness improves physical health, as well as stamina and resilience.** Studies have shown that happier workers have lower levels of stress hormones. Professor Jonathan Haidt points to a study of nuns that found that those who lived longest enjoyed a high level of happiness.

We underscore that happiness is not simply being cheerful or upbeat—or even brimming with passion. The happiness that comes from meaningful work is something far deeper and more sustaining. Positive psychologists define three forms of happiness, starting with pleasure (which is fleeting). Pleasure could be as simple as eating some delicious chocolates. Once the box is empty, the joyful moment is forgotten. (And those of us who have pursued happiness on these terms know only too well that an empty box can produce the opposite effect.) Next comes engagement—getting lost in the moment—clearly more absorbing than pleasure, but its effect, too, lessens over time. Just think back to a wonderful vacation, still enjoyable in the retelling. As time goes by, it's harder to recall the actual feeling, even though you still remember the story.

Meaning is the third level of happiness. It starts with engaging activities and then adds in purpose—for example, volunteering for a cause you believe in, active involvement in your community, working on a team with an important shared goal. Meaning is both transcendent and enduring.

That's why finding meaning trumps all other forms of happiness. Maslow's concept of self-actualization was based on the study of successful people (from Thomas Jefferson to Eleanor Roosevelt), who found pursuits that transcended the simple need for recognition and esteem. By fulfilling their "meta-needs," they found satisfaction on a higher level. Interestingly, Maslow also referred to self-actualization as the "growth need." People who find deep meaning in their work are satisfying these higher needs, and they develop a sense of well-being that sets them up to lead with confidence, to continually acquire new skills, and to persevere.

You can turn almost any job into your calling if it draws on your core strengths, engages you fully, and inspires you through a higher purpose. Martin Seligman, a professor of psychology at the University of Pennsylvania and author of *Learned Optimism,* cites the example of a hospital orderly. Most orderlies would tell you their job is to empty bedpans. This man saw his role as providing critical assistance to doctors and nurses in helping patients heal. As the researcher caught up with him, he was replacing a print on the wall next to a coma patient with another one from his shopping bag. When the researcher asked the orderly why he was bothering, he told her that when the coma patient regained consciousness, the first thing he would see should be something beautiful.

This transcendental nature of meaning is what sustained Amina Agbaje on her long journey to become a practicing lawyer. Like successful litigators everywhere, she loved winning cases and found that challenge very engaging. But without her deep identification with the underlying values of the legal profession, Amina would never have stuck it out—or even started on her remarkable journey. "My mother wanted me to become a nurse or a medical doctor, because when you look at the medical profession, they wear white. It's a symbol of purity," says Amina. "But lawyers wear black. That is a symbol of sin."

Amina was able to overcome her mother's resistance and applied to law school. "I think my greatest moment in life was the day I received the letter that I had been admitted into the university to read law," she recalls. "That was the high point of my life. I was going to school to read something I really, really, really loved." Eventually, her mother was proud to be called "Mama lawyer," according to the custom in northern Nigeria.

Meaning draws on your core strengths, which, in turn, increases your satisfaction. Everyone has core strengths to build on. Most of us seldom stop to think about them. For Amina, they include love of learning, problem-solving (using her creativity and ingenuity), and love of justice.

Amina's quest for meaning carried her through years of struggle, as she learned the law. Female law students were not unusual in Nigeria, but Amina's determination to stand up in court and argue the case was; most women law graduates wound up working behind the scenes, teaching or, more likely, settling into housewife and mother roles. Amina spent nearly two decades working for other lawyers, helping them prepare for trial, learning and watching. At one point she gave up, but her husband actually encouraged her to get back in the game with another lawyer, a senior advisor who demonstrated the values Amina believed in.

She finally got her chance in court, just like her heroes on *Case File*. But when the time came, Amina had to conquer her own trepidation. "The first day I went to court to move a motion, I was practically shaking before the judge," she recalls, laughing and beaming with pride. "I overcame my fears because I knew that I was doing something I was passionate about. That fear was a challenge before me. I needed to overcome it if I wanted to go by what my heart was telling me. So I told myself, 'Why should I be afraid?' It was then I became relaxed."

In 1999 Amina seized the opportunity to go out on her own, to run a firm and gain the flexibility to be with her three children. Today, Amina has five employees, and she dreams of a firm with twenty lawyers in offices in nearby cities, managed by other women litigators who share her vision. She looks ahead to grandchildren, and how she will tell them about her best cases—the times she found the arcane ruling that proved her argument or how she tricked her opponents to win. She'll tell them about the times when she lost, too, and how she pulled herself back together. "When I lose I have to pinch myself and tell myself the truth," she says. "I ask myself what went wrong and what I could have done differently, and then I head back to prepare to win again."

The fuel for meaning is your sense of purpose. Today, or perhaps at some points in your life, work is about having a job that pays the bills. If so, you will find satisfaction from the pleasures of time off and enough resources to pay for things you need. Perhaps work for you is more than a job—it's a career, the chance to build skills and advance to higher pay and more responsibility. If so, you'll find greater satisfaction from career achievement. At its best, your work can be a sustaining force at the center of your life.

Amina's work is indeed her calling. She treasures her paying clients and enjoys the cases they bring her. But she also represents indigent women and their children, pro bono. "These women cannot read, but more than that, they do not know their rights. It gives me joy that I'm able to help a woman like me," she says. "You find out that maybe a child is in prison for ten years. He's still awaiting trial. Maybe he got to prison at the age of fifteen. If he didn't know how to steal before he went into prison, by the time he comes out, you can imagine he does. I look out for those children. I tell the judge to give those children to me."

Amina's advice on meaning is drawn from her own experience: "Do you know that you are passionate about a particular thing? Challenge must be there. Obstacles must be there. You must be determined that, 'Look, this challenge is before me and I must cross over it.' So long as you do not cross over it, it will stand as a mountain before you. Tell yourself, 'I can do it.' And then you will find yourself doing it."

That's the acid test. Are you passionate about what you do, enough to give you the courage to face that mountain?

Close your eyes and listen to that voice inside, the voice of your potential. What is it telling you about your work? Do you feel, as Amina does, that you are in touch with your essential self—the person you were as a child—before "growing up" made you settle for all sorts of things that you were supposed to want?

Does your work itself make you happy, regardless of the rewards or the prestige?

Listen and reflect. Even if that voice is not yet loud enough to hear, or even if you don't feel much of anything, that voice will get louder, as will your feelings, if you continue reflecting as we go along.

Each in her own way, the women leaders who taught us attribute their success to finding meaning in their work. It doesn't have to be a giant, earth-shattering kind of meaning. The day-to-day variety—meaningful activities and interactions—are just as good.

It's never too late. Now's the time to begin questioning and exploring. You'll know when your passions are engaged, because you'll feel your heart race. You'll know when you've found activities that engage you and build on your strengths, because you'll look forward to them with anticipation. And you'll know when you've discovered your purpose, because it will just feel right.

In other words, you really can have your cake and eat it, too.

CHAPTER 2

Your Own Happiness Equation

I love when things are messy, when there's not just one, but many problems. Even when it won't be easy and it won't be fast, I love clearly seeing the pieces of the puzzle that have to move to fix the business. I love that initial intellectual challenge, and then, getting it done with people who didn't think they could do it. It's just awesome helping them see that we can do whatever it is—changing their mind-set to "There's almost nothing we can't do."

Claire Babrowski, COO, Toys "R" Us

Meaning starts with happiness. So, what makes you happy? When you were little, it was simple. Did you jump out of bed in the morning, excited about the day? Even if you didn't, chances are that you found something you loved to do and you just did it.

Then, life happened, right? Even as you were growing up, you were already moving away from your childhood self, as you worked hard to please your parents, then your teacher, maybe your friends, too. Over time, perhaps you rationalized choices like picking a college or a job, because someone told you it was the "right" thing to do. As you matured, maybe you worried about making your family happy. And maybe you forgot what really made you happy as you concentrated on pleasing others.

But what makes *you* happy? Most women struggle to answer that simple question. We don't even take the time to think about it—our lives are too crowded and complex and we're moving too fast to stop and ponder. When we do, it's entirely possible that we can say what others want us to be, but we no longer know what we want for ourselves.

But if you know what makes you happy, you've unlocked the door to your potential. It's worth finding out.

One of our favorite examples of the pursuit of happiness comes from a former colleague, a young woman who did all the right things to make her parents proud. Only when she was well on her way into a business career did she realize that her path would lead to success, but not to what she really wanted.

Georgia Lee Creates Her Happiness Spreadsheet

Sitting in the plane on her way back to New York from a client meeting in Paris, Georgia Lee remembers thinking, "Wow, at twenty-three years old I've made it. This is great. This is my life!" But the glow quickly faded. "There was this nagging feeling inside of me that said, 'This is great if this is what you want. But is it what you want? What is it that you want in life?' And that's when I started exploring."

That exploration led her from business into filmmaking. Ultimately it led to directing a feature film that won awards at the

Tribeca and Sundance film festivals. It seems like an abrupt change, but really was the result of a series of smaller decisions and steps. Only after completing a clear-eyed analysis of what would make her happy did Georgia take the flying leap.

The child of first-generation Chinese Americans, Georgia was torn from the start: "My parents' greatest dream for me was to become a medical doctor. So I studied math and science very diligently," she says. "They also encouraged me in the arts, never to be interested in it as a profession—simply to get the right resumé for admission to the right university."

Halfway through Harvard, Georgia discovered the art of film. She devoured the archives and learned all the great directors. A little fire had started. Still a respectful daughter, she put her interest in film aside. Georgia satisfied her parents with a degree in biochemistry, and then stunned them by signing on with McKinsey, turning away from a career in science or medical research.

Consulting life was great for Georgia. She was excited by the intellectual challenge and the opportunity to have influence. "I remember my first study. I had to present two pages to the client. I was very, very nervous, so I rehearsed the night before. And afterward, I realized, 'I did it. He's a CEO and I'm only twenty-one. But he listened to what I said and was thoughtful about it!' "

Georgia had mentors, an interesting circle of friends, money to buy great stuff at Barney's, and a clear path ahead to a Harvard MBA and business success. But movies kept taking up space in her head.

A year into her career, Georgia took the first step. She arranged a brief leave so she could enroll in a summer film course at New York University. In those five weeks, her life changed. "I still don't know how, but Martin Scorsese happened to see my first short film from school," she says. "I was very lucky." Indeed, he invited her to be an observer on the Rome set of *Gangs of New York,* just as she was starting her next year as a consultant.

So Georgia took another leave. "It was actually a very difficult decision," she says. "Most people might think it was obvious, but to me it was not, because the opportunity cost was advancing my career. I remember my parents saying, 'Martin who?' And they had just gotten comfortable with my career as a consultant!"

After Rome, Georgia applied to Harvard Business School, a natural next step. Accepted, she left after only a semester. By then, Georgia, who even now describes herself as "very risk averse," understood that the real risk would be to continue on a path that would not lead to fulfillment at work.

Like the business analyst she had trained to become, Georgia came up with a precise formula to weigh the choice—her own happiness equation—before pulling the plug on Harvard. "I did a very rigorous analysis of my happiness, or my utility," she recalls. "I created an Excel spreadsheet—a real McKinsey analysis." The key variables represented the things that were most important to her happiness—spending time with friends and family, maintaining a healthy life, achieving career happiness, intellectual stimulation, and so forth. "Then I created two scenarios. The best-case outcome from staying put was pursuing a business career and becoming a Fortune 50 CEO. The worst-case scenario was following a different route where I made little independent films as a scrappy filmmaker but never hit the jackpot."

Filmmaking was the clear winner. "I discovered something pretty shocking, which was that at the end of the day, my worst-case scenario in film was still going to make me happier than my best-case scenario in business. I'd rather be a scrappy filmmaker than a successful CEO. That's when I realized that Harvard Business School was great, but it wasn't for me. In my gut, I had known I wanted to be a filmmaker. It took me all these years to get the data to do that happiness spreadsheet—to realize that even if I analyzed it, I got the same answer."

Georgia moved to Los Angeles and camped out with friends as she finished the script for her feature, *Red Doors*. Her business experience paid off, helping her prepare a detailed plan to convince investors to fund the production.

Georgia won awards with her first feature film, but an award-winning movie is only a first step on the journey. What impresses us even more than her success is the courage it took to veer from a known path, with clear rules and milestones, to pursue a career where there are no fixed routes.

An intrepid explorer, Georgia looks forward, not back. "Ultimately you have one life, unless you believe in reincarnation. And it sounds morbid, but I actually think it's incredibly liberating to know that we all die. Once you do know that, you realize that you should just do what makes you happy. You could go tomorrow. You can go in thirty, forty years. How do you want to spend that time? Better be doing things that you like and with people that you love. That's what I believe."

Where Your Happiness Comes From

What would you put in your own "happiness spreadsheet"? First, come with us on a brief side trip to the sources of happiness with Jonathan Haidt, a professor at the University of Virginia and author of *The Happiness Hypothesis*. His equation is $H = S + C + V$. That is, Happiness equals

- Your genetic Set point band (the disposition you're born with) plus
- The Conditions of your life (gender, age, where you live, profession, relationships) plus
- The Voluntary activities you choose to engage in (that build on your strengths and give you satisfaction).

Your set point is largely an inherited trait, but you can gravitate to the top of your band. Or if you want to substantially change your set point, you'll have to look further. Psychologists suggest medication, meditation, or behavioral therapy.

For most, only a few changes in the conditions of your life can make a lasting difference. In one study, researchers tracked two groups who had a sudden change in circumstance: lottery winners and people who had suddenly become paraplegics. Within months, both sets of subjects returned to the level of happiness they felt prior to their life-changing events. That said, certainly you can and should do things to make the most of your conditions, like finding a shorter commute. Most of all, enduring and positive personal relationships can have a tremendous impact on your long-term happiness.

The variable with the most leverage in your own happiness equation is V—the voluntary activities you choose. You have the power to significantly increase your happiness in a way that is lasting through active ownership of what you do.

How can you locate the intersection between what makes you happy and realistic career possibilities? It will take some exploring and digging but it's there. Start by looking for ways to reconnect with what you once knew. "When I talk to young people, I always make them begin by telling me about their childhood," says Gerry Laybourne, the cable TV network pioneer. "People are so honest.

If you get them really thinking about what they were like, what made them passionate, and what they connected to, you can usually start getting them on the path to figuring out what they want to do as adults."

Another way to start is to identify more recent activities that gave you a tremendous sense of fulfillment. Think back over the past few years and remember the peak experiences you had at work. What were you doing? Who were you with? What was it about the goal that excited you? It's often easier (and more fun) to share those memories with a colleague who can help you understand what made you happy.

Remember, we are talking about an enduring form of happiness, which is different from pleasure. We're not against pleasure: We're against the "hedonic treadmill," a futile cycle of chasing pleasure and short-term emotional highs, a trap that many of us fall into. The pleasure quest has obvious implications—addictions and other excesses. Likewise, in the workplace you can fight all year for promotions and bonuses, only to find that the pleasure wears off within days or even hours, leaving you feeling low (even lower than before when the goal was ahead of you).

When Georgia looked into her own childhood for happiness clues, she recalled how much she enjoyed ice skating in particular. She remembered that her father was forever making home movies starring Georgia and her sister on the ice. It was not hard to make the connection. Indeed, if you get a chance to see Georgia's film *Red Doors,* you'll notice that Georgia included some of that home movie footage—homage to those early roots of meaning.

Many of the women leaders we met mentioned sports; a few were competitive swimmers as girls, for example. What these leaders treasured was the love of competition and winning and, even more, a love of being on the team. It was no surprise to find them leading teams, setting competitive goals, and searching for the natural high of victory.

A few who grew up in developing nations made special note of the thrill they got from playing games meant for boys. Looking back, they realized that what they really loved was the freedom they felt by being so spirited and independent. No surprise then that many have turned into pioneering entrepreneurs.

Others remembered accompanying their fathers to work, loving the early responsibility. Claire Babrowski, now chief operating officer of Toys "R" Us, recalled helping her father clean his medical office. She loved organizing all the small bottles on his shelves. Decades later, she marveled as she recognized this early sign of industriousness as a precursor to her passion for store operations.

Writing Your Own Happiness Equation

Spreadsheets are one way to get you to your own happiness equation. Making lists of what you love to do is another. Still another approach is to write daily pages, as prescribed in *The Artist's Way*, by Julia Cameron. She set out to help artists unblock their creativity and realized that the same techniques can help anyone unleash core talents. The exercise involves making time every morning to write in a journal, no matter what. And if that thought on top of your already busy day is unthinkable, start by setting aside time on the weekend.

Not yet ready for that kind of commitment? Then just scribble your recollections of childhood passions in the margin here. Set a date to do whatever you love to do. Finding the time just for yourself will help you get in touch with the voice and feelings inside.

Remember, reflections take time. Your first answer is not

always the one that will deliver real insight. Give yourself permission to spend more time. It's good for you and will probably be a remarkable change from always taking care of others. You'll be surprised how much *more* energy you will have—more than enough to compensate for the investment in yourself that you've just made.

With a clear understanding of your own drivers of happiness, you'll find some new paths and new goals along with the courage to stand down your fears, as Georgia did. You'll be inspired to break through barriers. Your hard work won't seem so hard and the long hours won't seem so long. You'll recover more quickly from setbacks and, what's more, you'll find more joy day to day.

So keep digging. You have the keys to connect to your own happiness—they lie deep in this data. And it's data that only you can provide.

CHAPTER 3

Start with Your Strengths

Definitely my sense of humor is a strength. When all else fails, I'll laugh. And optimism. I get up every day thinking today's going to be better than yesterday, and something wonderful is coming down the pipe. My other strength is the ability to recognize when I need to take a step back and think about where we want to end up. Then there's my fabulous team. I love working in teams!

Caryl Stern, president and CEO, UNICEF U.S. Fund

Even if your happiness set point is pretty high and you live in a palace, engaging in activities that provide meaning to you will give your life an amazing boost. And if you aren't starting out with the advantages delivered by birth, the activities you choose are even more important. So choose the activities that fire up your passions! Easy to say, but not so easy to do, especially if you're busy living your life and not really thinking about these things.

The surest way to the right activities is to focus on your core strengths. Most people spend their life shoring up weaknesses. Well-meaning parents and teachers point them out; performance appraisals do the same. Some days it feels as if the whole world is staring squarely at your weaknesses. Put aside your worthy plan to fill in critical development needs for now. Before you turn to them, know your strengths, and they will lead you to activities that offer you a chance at deeper meaning and fulfillment.

Time Inc. chairman and CEO Ann Moore is passionate about building on strengths and finding the job matched perfectly to them. It's what she did and why she found the courage to invest in, reshape, and launch magazines that are the company jewels.

Tapping Her Core Talents

Ann grew up as an Air Force child, attending six schools between Biloxi, Mississippi, and Japan before the sixth grade. Openness to change became a core strength out of necessity. And as the oldest of thirty-two grandchildren, another of her strengths was leadership: "I guess I was in charge from a pretty early age," says Ann. "I probably was influenced by my mother. She ran the household. She ran our family. She ran the school. She ran the church. She ran her local political committee. She was the most organized, competent juggler I know—and very skillful in getting kids to do what she needed us to do."

Ann's mother expected Ann to be a nurse, like every woman in their family. What Ann wanted was very different. "With three girls before the two boys, I think my father, who was very much a sports fan, resigned himself to the fact that he might only have girls. So he bought me a basketball for Christmas when I was in fifth grade. I wanted to be a trick shot when I grew up." Though Ann did not grow up to be a professional basketball player, sports played a very important role in her life. "I really think that basketball hoop was responsible for my whole career," says Ann. "When I got out of Harvard Business School, I took the job at Time Inc. because I wanted to work at *Sports Illustrated*."

Ann has cultivated her core capabilities and advises others to do the same. "If you are looking to have a career that has meaning for you, start by looking for all the clues. Number one, who are you?" she asks. "I'll tell you what I find odd: how many people who say they don't like numbers but force themselves into a career in finance. Why don't you play to your strengths? Stop obsessing over your weaknesses. You're going to go further if you capitalize on your strengths. Everybody has them."

Ann took her own advice, sticking to what she believed, despite career risks. "I turned down a promotion once, and top management was mad," says Ann. "But I made the right decision for me. It would have been a wrong decision to leave what I was doing and move to an area that I didn't really have an interest in. It was just the wrong fit. The odds were stacked pretty far against me and I paid the price. But that's what you have to do. Those bosses are not here now and I am."

Looking around at her friends, Ann observes that the ones who are happiest are those who have done the best job at self-assessment. "They know who they are," she explains. "They know what their value systems are, and they make their decisions accordingly."

Perhaps self-assessment is why Ann stepped up to launch new magazines out of keeping with Time Inc.'s portfolio of long-standing publications *Time, Fortune,* and *People.* Launching a new magazine is risky business, and besides fortitude, it requires creativity to spot unfilled consumer needs along with the advertising market's willingness to support another publication.

That's Ann to a tee. "When I got here, we only had five magazines, all targeted to men except for *People,*" she recalls. "Around 1984, I became a mother and my first launch was *Sports Illustrated For Kids,* because I was deathly afraid my son would never read."

The ability to place bets is a clear strength of Ann's, which helped her lead teams to innovate. For example, not everyone was convinced of *In Style's* business case at the start. Ann remembers: "Everybody laughed. Three years later, no one was laughing anymore." That's because Ann's team reinvented the beauty and fashion category, stealing the lead position. It wasn't that different with *Real Simple,* she says. "Everybody made fun of the first issue, and yes, it was terrible. But I said, 'I believe in this concept so strongly that I'll leave, and I'll buy it from you and relaunch it.' I knew we were rock solid. Women were completely stressed out and needed a magazine to bring order to their lives. The average woman in America spends fifty-five minutes a day just looking for things. Time is the most precious commodity I could give them." Within two years, *Real Simple* was on its way to becoming another star.

Ann's rise is built on a number of core strengths, including her ability to face the facts and make very tough decisions. "There was this unfortunate episode called *Makeover Magazine,*" she points out. "The idea seemed so good until we got into execution and learned otherwise. The women in our focus groups all said, 'No thank you. You can make over my hair, you can make over my makeup, but I like my life.' So I pulled the plug on it after one issue."

It takes time to find your strengths, and it takes even more time to turn them into capabilities. "I'm good at this job," Ann says. But, she emphasizes, it didn't happen overnight. "This is a marathon, not a sprint. Don't be in such a hurry to get to the top, because you won't be prepared." Twenty-five years into her journey, Ann moved into the corner office. Her other core strength?

Matching people to the best jobs for them, the jobs that deploy their greatest strengths.

Now It's Your Turn

Step back and think about what you really do well. What kind of work comes easily to you? In which work situations did time seem to fly by—and when did it drag? "Be honest with yourself about what you're good at and what you enjoy doing," advises Abby Joseph Cohen, the investment strategist and a managing director at Goldman Sachs. "I know it's called work, and you can't love every aspect of how you spend your day. But at the end of the week or the month or the year, there has to be a sense of accomplishment. There has to be a sense of satisfaction."

What strengths set you apart from others? Do others see these capabilities as a part of what makes you you? Are you excited and energized when you use them? If your answers are yes, then you have discovered your core strengths.

Many women we've met who are naturally outspoken seem to clam up when asked about their strengths. Modesty is a strength, but we wondered if there was something more going on. Using a premade list made it easier for women to spot themselves. That's why we turned to a strengths framework developed by positive psychologists Martin Seligman and Chris Peterson. They identified twenty-four strengths with universal application, based on an extensive review of societies across geographies, religions, and the ages. Their list may spark your own thinking on core strengths that can be building blocks to meaning for you:

- **Wisdom:** curiosity, love of learning, judgment, ingenuity, emotional intelligence, and perspective

- **Courage:** valor, perseverance, and integrity
- **Humanity:** kindness and loving
- **Justice:** citizenship, fairness, and leadership
- **Temperance:** self-control, prudence, and humility
- **Transcendence:** appreciation of beauty and excellence, gratitude, hope, spirituality, forgiveness, humor, and zest.

If you rank the twenty-four strengths according to how they resonate with you, you'll find which ones characterize you. Everyone has a Top 5 when it comes to personal strengths. What are yours?

One way to discover your own Top 5 is to ask those who know you best. Children, spouses, or friends may see you more clearly than you see yourself. What would a senior executive at work say? What would a customer say? What would your mother say?

Now, see how these strengths are used in your work. Think about a few experiences where you were a clear success. Dig deeper to understand why. Chances are, you'll find some core strengths at the bottom.

Of course, some jobs are genuinely the wrong fit. If your current job does not afford you sufficient opportunity to tap your signature strengths, think about what role might be more meaningful. Not sure? Talk to colleagues who seem turned on by their jobs; what do they love about their work? If, after several interviews, you don't recognize your own feelings in their descriptions, you may want to broaden your exploration.

But don't wait for a job change to start deploying your core strengths. For example, if one of your Top 5 strengths is kindness, choose to perform a random act of kindness daily. If a top strength is curiosity, exploring new problems at work should energize you. If that avenue is not open, use your time after work to continue to learn and grow. Try to steer what you do every day to your strengths. You'll be surprised at the positive results—energy, a feeling of lightness, satisfaction with work and with yourself.

Finally, remember that this is not a once-in-a-lifetime exercise. Your Top 5 core strengths change over time; that means you're growing. And with your new strengths, you've just expanded your capacity to lead.

CHAPTER 4

A Sense of Purpose

I see my dreams and I obtain them. People can tell me, "Congratulations, you are a very strong woman." But I don't do it because they tell me this. I do it because I want to be free. Sometimes I think, "I can buy clothes with $16 or I can buy a machine." And when I go to a store and find many kinds of machines, I want to buy them all! My company—it's my life.

Maria Esther Landa Chiroque, founder, Santa Maria Industries

Simply deploying your strengths in activities you choose out of interest will get you to a deeper satisfaction. That's engagement and it's good in and of itself. You can achieve this level of happiness at work or out of it. If you're a tennis player, you know the feeling. If you're not just a marketer but a great marketer, you also know the feeling.

Now add purpose to what you are doing, and you've got meaning. The women leaders shared their clear sense of purpose with us, offering us a lens into their personal journeys. Purpose is what drives you. It's the source of your inspiration and the compass that guides your way to making a difference, and at the same time, to the deepest level of happiness. And that's the real deal.

Some women know their purpose before the age of ten. Others only discover it after years of traveling down one path or another. It really doesn't matter. Gerry Laybourne, founder and former CEO of Oxygen Networks, is one of those who stumbled onto purpose almost by chance. It began when she met the man she would marry. Ultimately, Gerry switched fields, developed expertise in children's education, and turned her expertise into a passionate mission. After all, she was the driving force behind Nickelodeon and then Oxygen.

Gerry's Purpose in Life

Gerry grew up in a tiny town, the daughter of a businessman and a radio actress who retained her creative spirit. She was sandwiched between two dynamic sisters: "My older sister was beautiful and perfect, and my younger sister was brilliant and charismatic," she recalls. That left Gerry with few options to distinguish herself, until her father found one: "My dad took a look at me, and said, 'You know what? You're my business daughter.' He would take me to his office every Saturday and he would quiz me on stock symbols. By the time I was sixteen, I was running his office in the summers. He took me to meetings because he said I was always a better judge of character than he was. Because I was raised in business, I was very confident about it."

That said, Gerry chose to study liberal arts—actually, architecture. But it didn't take long for her to picture long years ahead, drawing plumbing fixtures before ever getting to design anything.

Inspired by her husband, Gerry finished a teaching degree and went to work at a small private school. But she saw how much satisfaction her husband derived from his work in inner-city schools, teaching how to make movies. These children, who couldn't read or write, found their voices. That was the glimmer of Gerry's purpose. And by the time she joined Nickelodeon (as the number three employee) in 1980, Gerry had become an authority on the way kids watched media.

She had also found her calling: "I really didn't care anything about TV. I just felt TV wasn't doing a good job for kids and that we could do better. Our ideas were radical—we didn't talk down to kids; we were entertaining in a respectful way." Gerry's path at Nickelodeon zigged and zagged as she pioneered children's cable television: "I got some things right and I got some things terribly wrong." One spectacular bump in the road proved to be an enormous learning opportunity. "I made a gigantic bet, the biggest bet, on a show called *Turkey TV*," she says. "The first thing I learned was, don't name your show something that people can make fun of, because the headlines aren't going to be pretty! The show was recycled comedy clips—Norwegian game shows, Italian game shows, advertising and comedy from all over the world. We had spent about a million and a half dollars on it, half our programming budget. When it arrived at our house on Memorial Day weekend, everybody sat down to watch. My son burst into tears, and said, 'Mom, you will never work in television again.' It was that bad. We called everybody back to the office and put people in edit suites. That bonded us. And in the scheme of things, we learned and we kept on going."

Gerry's aspiration for Nickelodeon was enormous—well beyond personal success. "I thought we could change the world, change the television landscape for kids, but I had almost no concern for my own career," she says. "I had almost no ability to even understand that stuff, because I was so driven to make this thing work." Not everyone shared this bigger purpose. Gerry remembers one woman on her team. "She came to me and said, 'Do you want to be a vice president?' And my response was, 'I couldn't care less. I want to make something great for kids.' And she said, 'Well, if you have so little ambition, I'm going to get another job.' And I said, 'You should do that.' I have plenty of ambition, but it's not a self-centered one. It's an ambition to actually change something. That was just unthinkable to her."

The path Gerry chose was unpaved, giving her the freedom (and the risk) as a pioneer in a new field. She felt lucky for the chance; no one was competing from the traditional, old boy networks. "A job in cable—people would look at you with sad-looking eyes, thinking, 'Oh, you poor dear. You're in a loser profession.' So lots of women got a break." And these women brought vision and purpose to the fledgling business. "We were passionate about something. Passionate about an audience, or passionate about a genre. And we were great explorers."

Today, Gerry worries about the new generation of women emerging from business schools, who start out without understanding their purpose. "Despite great educations, they get a little bit lost," Gerry says. "They think there's something wrong with them if they don't wake up thinking about business in the morning." To Gerry, they're clearly searching for why they're upset and what they're doing wrong. "They'll call me and say, 'Am I going to seem weak if I say no to this job that I really don't want?' I tell them, 'No. You're not going to seem weak. You should be going for the jobs you really want.' "

Gerry's perspective matches the research we've done. Meaning matters to men and women, but more women look for their work to be meaningful. "In general," she says, "men are much more concerned about who's on top. It's much more about 'somebody has to lose for me to win.' Women are able to think about the greater good. I don't think I'm unique among women. We really do, deep down, want to make a difference." On record as someone who loves men and loves working with them, Gerry sees valuable differences between the purpose men and women set: "I find men exciting, challenging, and their relentless focus—their drive to win—is really healthy in an organization."

For Gerry, women are hardwired to set and pursue goals with enormous personal challenge. "The great thing about women is we forget how hard it is. That's why we go back and have a second child," she observes. "It's why you can go back and launch a second network. There were times I couldn't breathe. There were times I felt exhausted. There were times I couldn't imagine how I was going to put one foot in front of the other. But I just remember the good parts. And you know what was interesting about my development? Everything sort of fits together. Everything has a purpose."

Purpose and Leadership

As Gerry's story shows, what makes you happy, what builds on your strengths and taps in to what gives you purpose, also makes you an inspiring leader. When you have a higher purpose in mind and it's shared by the team, leading is easier. You are not tripped up by the little stuff—who is ahead of you, or what department is outperforming yours, or a million other distractions. "Stop worrying about yourself, and start thinking about how you create an environment where you would like to work," Gerry advises. It was a breakthrough for her. "I went from taking the orientation of 'Everybody's being fired here and I'm going to be fired, too,' to, 'I'm the ranking person here, I'll take responsibility for making this a better place to work.' When you have your purpose in life, you're making a difference for the people around you."

With purpose, setting goals becomes easier. You find the courage to face new challenges. Many women leaders—like Gerry—found that setting goals impossible to reach in a few steps inspired them to greater heights. Indeed, taking a narrow view—staying in your comfort zone—usually leads to small goals and small achievements. Doing what you once thought was undoable is incredibly energizing. The classic example is the four-minute mile, a barrier that physiologists argued was impossible to break. But just two and a half years after Roger Bannister broke it in 1954, eight other runners matched his feat. Human evolution had not accelerated, but the belief in what was possible had taken a great leap forward.

So dare to dream a big purposeful goal. And as you work toward it, if you feel that you are serving your purpose in some way, you'll discover an enormous sense of fulfillment. "I like to think that if I drop dead tomorrow, would I think what I did was okay?" says Suzanne Nora Johnson, retired vice-chair of Goldman Sachs. "Did I touch the world and make it better in some way?" As a college graduate, Suzanne set out "to have a job where I could make a significant difference or change something about the world," she recalls. Her dream was to work in the World Bank, but her application was rejected. In time, she worked at Goldman Sachs, where she helped restructure Latin American debt. So did she fulfill her dream or change it? Upon retirement, Suzanne told us she was deeply satisfied, having touched the world in many ways, helping developing economies to create thousands of jobs. At the same time, she became one of the first women leaders at one of the most powerful firms on Wall Street.

But what if you haven't found your dream, or you're simply not a dreamer? There are other, more practical ways to discover what holds meaning for you. Psychologist Tal Ben-Shahar suggests making three lists. Start with the activities you enjoy and what you are good at. Then think about what is important to you. Gerry enjoyed artistic endeavors, educating children, and working with teams. Her numerous strengths included curiosity, leadership, ingenuity, and perseverance, among others. And it was important to her to make a difference.

As you reflect, look for patterns across your three lists. What stands out as a common thread? Gerry's thread was children's educational entertainment, and that led to deeper meaning over time. What could it be for you?

Next, compare those patterns to what you are doing today. See if you can find ways to adapt your work to fit your purpose. Or try talking with others—work colleagues—about their own sense of purpose. You may find that you share some of what drives them, making it worthwhile to join forces. But whatever purpose you set, remember, it's not just about the goal but about the journey toward it. The journey toward your goal provides happiness and meaning—more than actually reaching the goal ever can. The euphoria you will feel crossing the finish line dissipates all too quickly while memories of your trip last a lifetime.

Having purpose feeds your happiness all along the way. For example, when you know your direction, it's not necessary to keep your eyes glued to the map; you can stop and enjoy the scenery and breathe in fresh mountain air. Having a purposeful goal that excites you and pushes you to personal and professional growth can make the daily routine less draining: If you know what you want to accomplish in the next decade, you do not have to agonize over every little decision today. You can get lost in the moment.

You don't have to always be "right." You can delegate. You can be a better leader. It's all good.

Keep in mind that you are looking for a robust goal, meaty enough to sustain you for a while. Avoid the temptation to fixate on a particular position or timetable for your rise. That's distracting and self-defeating. We know plenty of people who set themselves up for big disappointments this way. Needless to say, they didn't enjoy the journey, either.

Research shows that goals that transcend the self—goals that serve other people, a cause, or a community—have the greatest impact on your sense of fulfillment. At the same time, to be meaningful, goals must be highly personal: They must inspire you to take on greater challenge and growth.

So why do so many people hesitate to search for true meaning in their work? Often, it's because it threatens the status quo or their sense of status. You know how this works. You rationalize, telling yourself that you can't afford the risk. Once you start asking questions, you find that what has meaning for you has nothing to do your long-held beliefs about what constitutes success. Deep down, you realize that those beliefs are based on expectations and values set by others. And you know the alternative purpose you yearn for takes you on a rockier and steeper path, surely a riskier one. Can you really turn your back on what you have?

Can you afford not to? Isn't the risk of being trapped in a career that has no meaning—with little source of happiness—greater than the risk of finding happiness doing something that doesn't impress everyone else?

If your answer is yes, take it step by step. Find ways to test the waters before making the jump, as Georgia did. You'll benefit on two counts. First, you can make sure your purpose is really right for you and a good fit. Try it on for size. Second, small steps help you manage risk. Just in case.

Don't worry about starting small in your pursuit of purpose. Your goal now may be a stepping stone, such as acquiring new skills. You may find that pursuit gives you a platform for growth that opens new doors, and those doors, ones you don't even know about today, tap a passion that is bigger than you.

Over time, your purpose will become clear if you continue the search. Just remember Gerry Laybourne, who started out in architecture, moved on to teaching, and ultimately found her calling in children's television (and launched a women's media company, too). If it sounds magical, it is, in a way.

CHAPTER 5

Dreamcatcher

At the time of our interview, Alondra de la Parra was just twenty-seven years old, but we think her story captures Centered Leadership: It shows that when fueled by your passion, when you are able to draw in others to share a goal imbued with meaning, when you take ownership and stay focused on opportunity, you can live your dream. For Alondra, that meant leaving home in Mexico to study conducting. Four years later, at twenty-three, she founded the Philharmonic Orchestra of the Americas in New York City.

Dreaming—and Doing

I was always in love with music, starting with studying the piano and then the cello. My parents loved music, too, and I would go to concerts with them. When I was thirteen, my father said, "Why don't you ever pay attention to the conductor?" I said, "He's not doing anything." And my father replied, "No, no, no, he is. He has to know the score better than everybody else. He needs to know everybody's part, and then he makes them come together."

Becoming the orchestra leader became my greatest wish, sort of a silent wish inside. I would think, "If I could pick whatever I want to do—if I could be anything—I would like to be that." It didn't mean that I knew I was going to do it. I had no clue how to become a conductor. But my father's a very sensitive man and a dreamer. Everything, since I was born, has been about dreams, fantasy, imagination. He is the kind of person who would never say, "That's not possible." He encouraged me.

So I thought, "Well, conductors must know a lot of theory," and I started studying a lot of theory. I thought, "They must know a lot of music history," and I studied a lot of music history. Then, when I was nineteen, I came to New York to learn. I thought, "What does a conductor need to know, apart from the musical side? I need to know how an orchestra works." I heard about an orchestra where I could be an apprentice. It didn't mean anything except setting up chairs and the stage, putting up the lights, photocopying. I did that for about nine months without getting paid.

Also, I made myself a challenge: Every time I went to rehearsal to do all this work, I would pretend I was a conductor, even though I wasn't conducting. I would learn the piece as if I was going to rehearse, and just sit silently after I had set everything up. I watched a lot of conductors rehearse. I thought, "I don't know if I'll be able to be a conductor, but I'll get to the point where there's nothing about an orchestra that I don't know."

Now that I think back, that was the key. I started filling in all the blanks instead of going directly to the goal. And later I understood that if you know how things work, then you can lead people to achieve the goal.

Maybe you can see that I'm obsessed with learning. Every day I need to learn something. I never want to feel that I've arrived somewhere. I'm always growing, I'm always in progress. I open my eyes and try to learn from everything. Also, I'm disciplined—not by nature. I made myself be disciplined, very organized. I also think I'm good at bringing people together. I like getting every-body's energy into one energy.

When I was first in New York, I was looking to apply for sum-mer conducting programs. I didn't have much experience, and for most programs you had to submit a videotape. I didn't have one, so I was hopeless. But a friend told me about a place in Maine where all you had to do is write why you wanted to be a conductor. I ap-plied and got in and then I was terrified. I thought I was going to a retreat with a bunch of Toscaninis. I thought, "I'm a nineteen-year-old girl spending three weeks with these fifty-year-old conductors!" I was super-intimidated.

This is where I met Ken Kiesler, who ran the program. The first thing he said when we gathered was, "I don't want to hear one word about career. I don't want to hear one word about any orches-tras you've conducted. I don't care. I just want to know who you are." And the minute he said that, I felt, "I have that. I know who I am, even if I don't have a career and I haven't conducted any or-chestras." It was totally disarming.

So I felt safe—until I got to conduct for the first time. That was frightening! But I remember the moment: Ken looked at me and he said, "You have something. You have a gift. And I'm going to help you." And I remember, I was bawling—I thought, "How can this man be saying that? I'm not even close to good." He gave me a hand and then told us something that has stayed with me: "The strongest one will be the one who's more vulnerable, the one who opens up and faces who he or she is, the one who just lets go." This is totally a paradox, right? Because you think, "No, you've got to be strong—you're the leader, you have to."

This was great advice. I learned very early that people connect to vulnerability, because we're all vulnerable human beings. It's not when you have everything perfect, everything under control, that you connect. They probably admire you and respect you, but it is when they connect with you that they feel empathy.

Later that summer, I got to conduct the Mozart Mass in C Minor, one of the most amazing pieces. I called my parents and said, "Okay, today I really need to tell you that if I die it's completely fine. Don't even be a little bit sad. I don't want to die, but it would be fine, because I have lived way more than what I ever expected of my life." I remember the feeling. I still feel that way. From that moment, I thought everything that comes to me is bonus, is extra, far more than what anyone could dream of.

Dreaming with Purpose

Ken became my mentor, and he told me from the start, "You have to have a purpose for why you do this. You have to think it through and write it down. And every single thing you do, you have to do it with that idea." It took me about eight months to develop. I would tell Ken, "My purpose is to make the best possible symphonic music for the audience." He'd say, "That's great, but is that all you want to do with your life?" So we kept going. Next time, I said, "I want to educate through music." And he said, "Oh, that's great." I finally got to a statement that works for me: "I am committed to being a growing source of inspiration for positive change to the world through music." I like that it's about growing—being a continuous source of inspiration through music for positive change. Everything I do I think about doing that way, and it just becomes bigger.

After that summer, I returned to my studies at the Manhattan School of Music. I began to notice the lack of Latin American and American symphonic music in general being played in the world. I thought, "Why is it not performed often? Wouldn't it be great to have an orchestra that would focus only on music of the Americas?" Those were just dreams I had. But one day I was called by the Consulate of Mexico and asked to make a concert of Mexican music. When I presented my plan for an orchestra of eighty musicians, they said, "It's way more money than we thought. We were thinking of a chamber group, something smaller."

But because I had already worked so hard, I thought maybe I should start looking for people who would want to make this happen. I learned about a festival where I could enter if I had the funds. Suddenly I am the conductor of this orchestra—if I have the funds. I didn't have an orchestra. I didn't have an administration. I basically relied on the good luck of having three close friends who were unemployed and smart. We were living in the same tiny apartment and working twenty-four hours a day on this. We put together a concert that was a success. So many things could have gone wrong, but they didn't. We figured out how to do absolutely every little detail.

After the concert, Ken asked me, "Do you think this is going to be it, just one concert after all you've done?" And then I told him I did have this dream of this orchestra. And he said, "Now you have to make this happen." I asked him, "How do you do that?" And he said, "You have to figure it out."

So I tried—and things started happening. There was another concert, and another. A lot of the people who came to the first concert became my board members. I said, "Did you like the concert? Great! Do you want to be a board member?" They were wonderful individuals—and very skillful. They helped me through.

Now I have been doing this for a while, but it's still an adventure. I do think that what I do in terms of music drives me—the compositions, the sounds, the textures, the combination of sounds made by different people. While I'm at work, that's my passion. I love the sound. I love touching the sound. And I love putting it together and mixing it as if it were colors. I enjoy life and I try to engage with every little thing that I do, as fully as I can.

Leading and Still Dreaming

Still, I have moments regularly when I just feel overwhelmed. I almost reached burnout more than once. I remember when I was in my piano undergraduate program. It required a lot of studying. I was doing that by day, and by night I was doing administration and fund-raising. It got to a point where it was either me or this project—I was going to collapse. I didn't have a life.

Then I figured out what to do. I say to the board, "Okay, either we raise enough money to hire an executive director, or that's it. I can't live like this." So they approve an executive director and off we go again! And when I'm at the verge of a collapse once more, then—boom—another musician decides to help. The project lives on its own, and it doesn't let me go. Still, you do have to protect yourself. You have to be sane. You have to be strong and healthy.

My mood changes a lot. I'm not always happy. A lot of times, I'm depressed. A lot of times, I'm feeling that I'm not good enough. Actually, most of the time I feel that way—that I may fail. What gets me out of it is when I think, "This is not about how I feel. And it's not about who I am." Kurt Masur, who was the conductor of the New York Philharmonic, said, "If you think they're going to love you, forget it—don't be a conductor. If you think they're going to praise you and say you're great, don't waste your time. Because if you're dependent on that, you're never going to get it." You have to be in the music. It's about the moment and engaging everybody.

Whenever I call my father and tell him, "Oh, this person, he is doing this and it's making me so insecure," he says, "That's great! This is the best news you could have given me today, because it means you're about to grow." When something's eating me up like that, the solution is to fix it. Don't let things keep going. If the other person doesn't want to fix it, then that's his problem.

A lot of the misunderstandings and problems in communication happen just because of perspective. As a conductor, imagine being in front of an orchestra, and you're rehearsing. You've never met these musicians before. And you see the third viola whispering something to the players around him and laughing. You immediately think, "They think I'm terrible." I've learned from many people—like my husband, who tries to look at the good side of people—not to assume the worst. I remember a time when I felt certain sections of the orchestra were resistant to me, questioning me. I didn't say anything at first because I thought, "They just don't think I'm good. And, you know, I'm not good, so they're right." It went on until one day I said, "That's it." I just took them aside and I said, "Can I talk to you? I feel you're not supporting me. I feel you don't respect me. Every time I want to tell you something, I feel that you don't want to hear it because you think you already know it." And they said, "We think that you don't like what we're playing. And so we don't know what to do, because we want to please you but you always look upset." If I hadn't approached them, that could have grown into a monster inside me.

Living the Dream

Here's how I look at it. You have to be good at the work. You have to be prepared. That's a given. You have to be on time. You have to be serious. You have to work. But the members of the orchestra want to see who you are as a human being, too. And the minute you share something like that, even if it's making a little bit of a fool of yourself, or sharing a little bit too much, when they see that you don't protect yourself and you're there for the good of the music—when you give yourself—then everybody likes that.

If the group loves the work they're doing and wants to do better and better, and if they see progress, then the group doesn't care about having a leader who's handsome or perfect. If they feel that when you are up there, they achieve more, they love you. But it's not about whether they love you. They just want to achieve.

The energy is the people. The sound is great, but it wouldn't exist if it wasn't for the people. When I connect with someone in the orchestra, I see his or her eyes and we're in the same place—for me, that's it. That's the best thing. You can tell that you are communicating with that person at a different level that is totally pure. It's not about who you are—it's about that moment of connecting. And when that happens with the audience, it's even better. When that happens in the whole group at the same time, that's when you really start to feel that music truly can change the world. There's nothing like it. What could be greater than that?

PART TWO

Framing

CHAPTER 6

A Matter of Framing

If you worry about everything that can go wrong, you would never do anything. You've got to be able to focus on the things that really matter and not lose too much sleep on the rest. No one is fully immune from what others say; we're all herd creatures. But in the exposure of national politics, if you got upset every time a newspaper columnist wrote something negative, or a voter came in to critique, or you saw a cartoon that made your nose ginormous, which happens to me every day of the week, if you're worried about that, then you wouldn't get through it.

Julia Gillard, deputy prime minister, Australia

We've described the tremendous fulfillment that centered leaders experience through work that holds personal meaning for them. A job well done is satisfying; work with meaning puts you in the psychological state to flourish—a deeper and more lasting form of happiness. Positive framing, like meaning, is a pillar of Centered Leadership, and as you will see, they reinforce each other.

Buddha said, "With our thoughts we make the world." In the

same vein, positive psychologists underscore that how we frame what we experience colors our reality. Same idea, different centuries. Since positive framing gives both the strength and clarity to keep moving ahead no matter what the obstacles, optimism correlates with success.

Make no mistake, this is not about putting on rose-colored glasses but actually seeing the world without distortion. The facts are the facts. Leaders who frame positively see the facts in the clearest light. What they don't do is let negative feelings distort their view of reality—exaggerating the dangers. So framing enables you to confront the harshest reality in a constructive way. It gives you both the clarity and the energy to face problems and find solutions. It gives you the strength to move on when you've done all you can; it builds resilience.

Positive framing leads to good things, too. For example, women who have a positive frame also have flexible mind-sets—they believe they are in control of their futures, that they can influence the outcome, learning and growing.

Simply put, optimism correlates with success.

Framing Is a Choice

Though reality may indeed be better than the way you see it, your unconscious emotional responses—triggered by anxiety, fear, and stress—can twist it into a different shape. When that happens, what you see looks very different to you, influencing your behaviors and actions. It makes life even more challenging when you face setbacks in the form of mistakes, wrong turns, and failure. You can find yourself spiraling down—taking the emotional plunge that robs you of the will and the energy to take action.

For some women, positive framing comes naturally. But for many of us, acquiring a positive frame requires unlearning deeply embedded behaviors—including snap judgments that constrain your views on situations, other people, and yourself. This ability to frame reality positively is a powerful capability and learning how to do it is part of your leadership development. And it has benefits for you that go well beyond work.

Positive framing is what made Emma Fundira dare to step into a man's world, challenging societal and industry norms in one fell swoop. Born in Zambia and now living in Zimbabwe, Emma grew up in a society where women have only recently attained basic rights, such as being permitted to own property outside of marriage. She also chose a career in the white man's domain. But Emma always believed that she could do whatever she set out to accomplish. Today she owns property and runs her own financial advisory business, living in a country struggling for stability.

Emma is the middle daughter and fourth of five children of a successful business man. "My father was very strict. He stressed culture. And he stressed ambition," says Emma. "He really wanted us to become somebody, but his focus was on my brothers, because in our African culture, somebody must carry on the name."

Even as a little girl, Emma wanted to be counted. "I always had to make my point. I had to be heard. I think I was a bit loud." At age nine, she was packed off to join her older sister at school in England. "When I got off the plane, I was scared," she recalls. "It was cold. It was wet. And I'm thinking, 'Oh Lord. What am I doing here?' I got to the school, and everybody was very different. My mother made me wear a dress and everybody was in jeans." Her sister had no time to look after a younger sibling, so Emma, the only foreigner and the only black student in her class, quickly learned independence. Her forceful personality helped. "I was always the dominant person there because I wanted to be noticed for the right reasons," she says.

Emma may have set out to please her father, but she learned her most critical ability—to view the world through a positive frame, especially in the face of adversity—at her mother's knee. When Emma was a teenager, her father divorced and left her mother to fend for herself. "My mother had absolutely nothing," Emma says. "But she was a survivor. She managed to set up a small transport business of her own and she bought herself property. She was an inspiration." Emma saw her mother quickly rebuild, moving on in a way any woman might envy. That experience instilled in Emma the importance of being self-reliant in order to succeed in a man's world. "I wanted to break the barriers," she recalls. "I used to think, 'What can I go into that men do—only men—and show them that I can do it?' I first thought of construction, but then I thought it would be too monotonous."

Summoned home by her father at eighteen to attend university in Zimbabwe, Emma trained to be a teacher, an accepted role. It became clear that her brothers were not going to follow in her father's footsteps. In time, Emma was determined to make her mark in a nontraditional way. So she quit teaching and took a job at Standard Chartered, the London-based banking giant.

The bank and the rest of corporate Zimbabwe were the domain of the white male elite. As a black woman, Emma was an extreme rarity. "I wanted to prove myself, prove to these people that I'm just as good as they are, if not better," she says. "And I wanted to show that I'm just as good as my male counterparts, the young black men. Just because I won't drink ten pints of beer doesn't mean that I'm any weaker."

With youth, gender, and race playing against her, Emma had a lot to prove. "You walk into a meeting, you're a black female, and these are white executives," she recalls. "They look at you and they think, 'She doesn't know anything. There is absolutely nothing she can help me with.'"

One client was particularly hostile. "He didn't relate to me very well in the meeting. But I just responded politely. After the meeting, he called and actually screamed at me over the phone, saying, 'You don't know what you're doing,' and calling me this, that, and the other. He was quite rude." But Emma remained cool under pressure and did not let him undermine her confidence. She went back to work on his behalf and did such a skillful job that the client eventually sent the managing director a letter, commending Emma for her calmness and her excellent execution. She even received an award from headquarters in London.

How Do You Frame What You See?

What about you? Consider the following situation: Your boss calls you in for an unexpected meeting. When you enter the room, you observe two other executives with her. They immediately stop talking and hastily put away their papers. They avoid looking at you as they leave. Your boss looks down at some papers and then back up at you. She doesn't ask you to sit.

What is your immediate reaction—your gut feeling? When discussing this scenario with a group of women, we singled out two who shared their top of mind reactions. "Oh, I must have done something terrible," the first woman blurted out. "I must be in danger of losing my job. I'm feeling a bit ill!" We turned to the second woman, who was smiling. "They were probably finishing up some other business," she said. "Who knows? I'll ask the boss what's going on!"

If you're chortling now, we are too. The divide between optimists and pessimists is so wide it's funny. The pessimist immediately turned the tables on herself—she assumed the worst and took it personally. Anxious, she began to worry. And while she was fretting, the optimist was imagining a brighter conversation and opening herself up for growth. In truth, neither of them knows what the boss is thinking, but the optimist automatically avoids the downward spiral just as the pessimist grabs hold.

Why did the two women react so differently? Martin Seligman spent years researching the answer and concluded that our optimism (or pessimism) depends on how we view reality through three lenses: permanence, pervasiveness, and personal control.

Think about a significant setback in your professional life (for example, a senior executive criticizes you, you receive a poor performance review, a severe business downturn results in your being laid off. How did you view that experience?

- Did you see the setback as temporary, or did you see it as **permanent**?
- Did you perceive the outcome as specific to the situation, or did you believe that it reflected a **pervasive** problem?
- Did you view the causes as external or did you assume that they were under your **personal** control—your fault?

For a pessimist, another executive's criticism is a personal assault; a bad performance review casts a shadow across other areas of her life and into the future. Worse, she is convinced that it's her own fault entirely—even a business downturn that leads to her layoff. Suddenly, her future feels much bleaker. Many pessimists, Seligman has observed, wind up exhibiting "learned helplessness." Believing that they can't improve the outcome, they stop making the effort, worsening their problems.

Optimists have a very different reaction. An optimist sees that executive's criticism as a helpful challenge; she doesn't let a bad performance review spill into the rest of her life, and she recovers more quickly from unavoidable setbacks. She is open to suggestions for improvement, investigates what went wrong, and takes action. So if a business downturn leads to layoffs, she is disappointed but able to recoup her energy and explore what's next.

Optimists and pessimists also react differently to positive news. Think about the last positive situation you experienced (for example, a senior executive complimented you, you got a promotion, your business unit beat its target). How did you feel? Here's what our pessimist might have said: "I was just lucky. It's unlikely to be repeated. After all, nothing is really different today than yesterday. I'm still the same!" Perversely, while the pessimist can take more than her share of blame for a failure, she minimizes her share of success. "It must be a mistake," she muses, "and when they catch on, I'll still get fired."

In contrast, our optimist might greet the good news by thinking: "I'm great! I worked hard to lead our business unit to success and it paid off. There's no stopping us now!" When good things happen, our optimist permits herself to enjoy the lift. Success propels her forward to seek greater learning and achievement. For optimists, great news sets up a great day and much more.

These are caricatures of extreme optimists and pessimists, of course. Most of us are somewhere in between and it's helpful to know your starting point.

When you understand how you characteristically frame reality, you'll be able to make a clear choice on whether to stay as you are or adopt new behaviors. Researchers say that as much as 50 percent of a person's outlook is genetically determined. Pessimists may not be able to—or want to—shed their frame entirely. But you can "learn" optimism by adopting some specific tactics. And optimists may find that they can apply their positive framing more consistently to help others see more opportunity.

Framing starts by first unlearning self-destructive habits—that downward spiral that often results in getting stuck at the bottom. In the next chapter, we'll show you how you can learn to view your situation more realistically, reframe, and turn setbacks into opportunities for growth. We'll walk you through the process of disputing the distorted view of reality that fear and anxiety produce and moving on to action. Sound like alchemy? It's not.

What If You Didn't Spiral Down?

Clearly Emma Fundira was an optimist. If she had spiraled down, it would have been entirely understandable. Many would not have worked through a rude client's upsetting tirade so quickly. Sadly, some women get hurt in a situation like this. They begin to ruminate, thinking obsessively about what happened and wondering what they did wrong. This can lead to mild and even severe depression.

Avoiding a downward spiral is a good thing in and of itself. But imagine an even greater benefit of learned optimism: experiencing positive emotions more intensely and putting them to work on your teams. Barbara Fredrickson has developed a theory called "broaden and build," which posits that people who experience emotions like joy, contentment, and happiness and have a positive frame are more likely to learn, develop, and explore. In her experiments, people who experienced positive emotions by watching uplifting and funny films showed greater creativity in problem-solving—and performed better—than viewers of upsetting and sad films.

Emma's experience certainly proves the point. With her positive outlook—fueled by the joy she derived from work—Emma never hesitated to pursue opportunities to learn and grow, aware and comfortable with the risks that came along.

One key opportunity presented itself when the head of project finance at Standard Chartered asked Emma to join his group. Even though she knew nothing about project finance, she jumped in. In turn, he sponsored her rise, taking her to meetings and soon letting her take the lead, sometimes shocking clients. "He'd say, 'Actually, you know what? Emma knows more on this topic than I do.' He always gave me the chance," Emma recalls.

When her sponsor moved to Barclay's, Emma followed and her career really blossomed. She was promoted to director with the prospect of becoming a managing director. Then a friend floated the idea of launching a business to counsel Zimbabwe's growing corporations about funding strategies. She was torn. By then Emma had married and was the mother of two young children, so giving up the security and prestige of Barclay's was risky. But a few months later, Emma jumped. "There was something in me that just wanted to try and go out there and do it for myself," she explains. "Something in you tells you it's time to move. If not now, when?"

Her timing proved anything but propitious. "Eight months later, our economy deteriorated," she says. "But not once did I ever think, 'Oh, I wish I hadn't left Barclay's,' or, 'I miss my salary check.' I was more focused on having to feed other families; we had to make sure our employees had a paycheck." Emma's optimism never faded. "It was definitely a challenge, but I always knew somehow I would sort it out," she says. "There's something in me that always tells me that I can do it. I will find a solution—I just need time to think about it."

This is not to say that Emma didn't feel the pressure. Regular physical exercise helped her regain perspective and work through stress. "I think, 'Let me go to the gym.' After that, I'll be able to think about it better," she says. "I don't get into panic mode."

Looking back, Emma's motivator early on had been to please her father. "He was so disappointed in my brothers. I wanted to prove to him that I could do it," Emma told us. But as she reflected on her development and success, she realized that framing had led to more than she could have imagined—changing her father's traditional mind-set: "He thrived on my success. He actually encouraged me to go further. When my father died, he died happy with me."

So positive framing is a powerful tool for change. But positive framing 100 percent of the time is not what we intend. Pessimism has to be in the mix when you face risky decisions—a big investment, for example. It's the lens through which you see the ugly details in the scenario and explicitly look for the worst case. One CEO told us that she looked to her CFO for pessimism; she knew she needed someone to help temper her strong optimism. So if you are coming from a position of pessimism, you can build on it as a strength. Either way, you'll be a more effective leader with positive framing in your leadership toolkit.

A Beautiful Mind-set

Emma's leadership journey is a great example of what happens when you have a flexible mind-set. She remained open to new possibilities and new ideas; she worked on the assumption that she was capable. At every age, people with flexible mind-sets continue to learn new skills. In contrast, people with fixed mind-sets tend to see their own talents and abilities as limited and are often threatened by fresh thinking that challenges their beliefs. You can see how these mind-sets relate to optimism and pessimism and how a flexible, growth mind-set fuels dynamic leadership.

Good things and bad things happen to everyone. What makes the difference is how you work with this raw material of life. Over and over, the women leaders talked about opportunities and how they didn't hesitate to take them. As we dug deeper, we discovered a recurring theme: These women approached new situations for their possibilities. When they had job offers in new fields, they leapt, believing that they could learn and grow.

And just as interesting, these successful women were not daunted by the risk—indeed, they found it exciting. When they were deciding on a new path, they would ask themselves, "What's the worst that could happen? Getting fired!" And when that happened to some, they bounced back, feeling lucky about their next opportunity. More than a few mused, "When one door closes, another opens." Their examples prove the point.

Now, consider how you typically think about things: Are you fixed in your thinking, or are you flexible? Are you happy to stick to your routine and uneasy when circumstances force you to change? Do you explicitly or implicitly limit what you are capable of? Or are you always open to new ways of doing things?

To test your mind-set, fill in the blank in the following statement:

I could be an amazing architect if _____.

If your answer was something like "if I could visualize spaces" or "if I could do math," you are showing a fixed mind-set, hyperaware of your limitations (real and imagined)—the reasons you *can't* do something. Typically, this is the response of someone who won't push herself to improve and, as a consequence, her ability to grow diminishes. She's judgmental about herself and probably about others.

If, by contrast, you filled in the blank with "if I wanted to" or "if I put my mind to it," you may have what psychologist Carol Dweck calls a growth mind-set. People with a growth mind-set believe that nothing is predestined; their own work determines their success. These are people who shape their futures by pursuing opportunities to learn and grow, absorbing the shocks along the way and turning feedback into blueprints for progress.

Look around you. The connection to success is clear—the happiest and most successful people are those with a growth mind-set. Wouldn't you rather have a growth mind-set that leads to a psychological resilience that can help you handle adversity? As Dweck writes, people with growth mind-sets can "look failures in the face, even their own, while maintaining faith that they [will] succeed in the end."

That's what we want for you. If you're starting out with a fixed mind-set, you can change it through conscious effort. Take a moment now to reflect on the career choices you've made and would like to make. Complete this sentence:

What I would love to be doing is _____.

Are you already doing what you love? If you aren't, what is in your way? People with fixed mind-sets can give a long litany of reasons not to try: It's not practical, there's too much risk, I don't have the skills, everyone will laugh—we could go on. Optimists don't waste their time and energy when they could be moving forward.

So let's stop right here and right now and be more like them: Choose to see reality without the distortions that chip away at your self-confidence and self-regard. Choose to feel in control, able to learn and fix almost anything with help from others. Choose to recover quickly from a mistake or even a colossal failure. If you look at your choices and don't like what you see, you can choose to change your mind-set.

Make Adaptability Your Skill

There's framing and then there's reframing in the moment, a related skill all leaders need. Today's pace of change, organizational complexity, and increasing specialization make adaptability essential for you. Given our multiple roles, women are masters of adaptability at home. Apply this capability in your work, letting go of the agenda when circumstances change. When the route you've chosen is not working, zoom out to see the bigger picture; you might just find a better way around the problem.

Emma was adaptable from the start, when she found herself at a new school, freezing in a light dress. She drew on adaptability when she entered the white male environment of investment banking. Leaving a venerable bank to be an entrepreneur once again required her to adapt.

We can all learn to reframe what we see in a more realistic, productive, and positive light. We know it's hard work, but you've already taken the first step in your journey by getting to know yourself better. And you know, the first step is often the hardest one. You are on your way.

CHAPTER 7

The Practice of Optimism

Most problems can be solved if we ensure that the right people with the right ideas are allowed to solve them. Most things that can't be solved are of a health nature or a loved-one nature. But if you get up early enough or stay late enough at the office, there's going to be a solution. That doesn't scare me. There's always a way.

Deirdre Connelly, president, GlaxoSmithKline North America

As Winston Churchill said, "I am an optimist. It does not seem too much use being anything else." The women we met, like Churchill, shared a common trait—a strong sense of optimism. They differed in every other way. So after reviewing the research on positive psychology and seeing links between optimism and success, we looked for a woman leader who was not an optimist.

We never found one.

But wait. You're probably thinking: Haven't many women who are not naturally inclined to view the world through a positive frame found success, too? Of course they have. These women power through and they prevail. But without the ability to deploy positive framing, they are less able to see truly creative solutions, less flexible in the moment, less able to sustain the resilience needed for the journey. They are talented, capable women, to be sure. We just want more, much more, for you.

Though born an optimist, Shikha Sharma, managing director of ICICI Prudential Life Insurance in India, made it through many small setbacks, relearning the lessons of optimism in her darker moments. And when she encountered one calamitous setback, she dusted herself off and got back to work, growing as a leader and as a human being.

Even Born Optimists Can Learn Optimism

Shikha considers herself privileged: Her parents were not wealthy, but they pushed their daughter to perceive her potential—and then work up to it. "My parents were incredibly supportive, very ambitious for me, even at a time when most Indian parents' ambitions were focused on the boys," she says. As a child, Shikha wanted nothing more than to excel at whatever she chose and stand on her own two feet. The oldest child, she got plenty of feedback from her father, a military officer. "If I came home and told my father I came second in class, I would have gotten a yelling. So I had to make sure I did well in school."

So coming in first was terribly important. Her ambition was put to the test. One day Shikha's teacher gave her a stack of report cards in grade rank order and told her to walk them to the principal's office. She reminded Shikha not to peek underneath the paper covering up the stack. "I remember I had to walk fifteen minutes to the office, and it was so tempting to slip the paper and see what the ranks were, and I was young at that time. That stayed with me. Do I have the discipline to not do that peeping? I was taught that if you promise something to somebody, you must stick by it." No, Shikha did not look.

She loved math and science at university but took her under-graduate degree in economics rather than physics on her parents' advice. In 1980 Shikha joined the development bank ICICI and never left. Why not? "It is a genuinely gender-neutral bank, be-cause of its leaders," she says. "And they know I love a challenge—something new, something uncharted is terribly exciting to me. Every time I've gotten anxious for a new challenge, it's been there. And I always had the belief that if I tried something and gave it my best, I wasn't going to make a mess out of it."

Shikha clearly views reality through a positive frame. At the bank, she gravitated to strategy development, with a strong belief that she could shape the future. Deploying framing skills for her teams, she found a formula for success: "Long ago, I led a team preparing a blueprint for what ICICI should look like," she says. "I remember we sat down to discuss what we should be doing. About 60 percent of the blueprint came from that day. It was a big lesson for me. By myself, could I have come up with a blueprint like that in one day? Of course not. I was elated by that experience."

But everyone has a first mistake. When she was head of the new markets division, their first major trading loss was a shock—and she needed some help framing. "It seems so trivial, because ob-viously you're bound to make a loss sooner or later," she says. "But at that time, we were a very bright bunch of young people making a lot of money. And then it hit us. Suddenly one day we're making a loss." For a few days, Shikha was afraid. "It was painful, but then our venture partner called me from Hong Kong to say, 'You've now become a good markets team. You would never learn some of the real-world stuff you need to learn unless you make a loss.' When he said that, I learned something about managing and leading. If someone has made a genuine mistake that results in a loss, it's important for leaders to show support. If traders lose their faith in themselves then they're finished. So that was quite a poignant moment for me—a little pain and embarrassment, but no disaster."

Shikha drew on that lesson later when her big mistake finally arrived. It took a good dose of positive framing and energy to turn this situation around.

It all began when an overzealous local manager in Shikha's insurance division came up with a new idea to meet his sales goals. Because every neighborhood office could run its own sales programs without approval, in 2005 this particular manager used questionable judgment in implementing a controversial concept: He declared that his sales reps were on a "jihad" to bring in sales, and each would be considered an "Osama bin Laden," who could "motivate" his team to get their numbers.

When the public saw the posters of Osama bin Laden that the manager had made up to urge his workers on, they applied judgment swiftly. Citizens stormed the office, and five ICICI employees, including the manager, were arrested. "Well, that hit media headlines and politicians started getting involved," Shikha recalls. "It got blown up out of context and proportion. But it was very embarrassing for me as the leader of the organization. Worse, it touched the credibility of the brand."

Shikha found herself on top of a national media crisis. "The first three or four days were awful; I was really stressed. I don't think I slept well, and I don't think I even had a normal conversation with anyone in my family. What I told them was that I was stressed out by this, so leave me alone for a while." Framing was what Shikha needed, and that was what she was doing—giving herself some badly needed distance from the situation and a bit of time to think. She began sorting out what she could and could not control and started making a plan. As she gained clarity about how to proceed and began to act, her stress level declined.

"The one thing my father taught me was that you can only do what you can do," she explains. "You are not always in control of the results, so don't keep thinking about it. How do you get rid of the pain and the anxiety and the stress of a situation that otherwise looks like you have no control over it? It feels like it's falling apart, but if you break it up into smaller elements and think, 'Okay, is there still a small piece I can be in control of and do something about?' Then you begin to claw yourself back, making small differences that can then snowball into big differences."

Shikha realized that part of her recovery plan involved making things right on the home front, too. Her two teenage children were shocked to see their mother on the front page of the paper every day. "But it turned out that talking with my children was a generally stress-free, relaxed time. Everything was so painful that I needed my family," she says.

Mostly, Shikha threw herself into doing the things she could to turn the situation around. She was in constant touch with the community, the media, the politicians, the police, and her own organization. "The people who were arrested and their parents needed our support, too," she says. Her challenge was to soothe the authorities and end the situation while protecting the company's image and, with luck, helping the employees bounce back. "This was our first brush with politicians, and I had a very honest and straight conversation with them," Shikha explains. "I saw that if you are honest and come across as honest, people are willing to listen to you. We had to let the law take its course, and at the same time we had to communicate with the rest of the organization to let them know that we were supporting the employees. You didn't want to kill the morale of everybody else who said, 'Well, if I make a mistake and get arrested tomorrow, the company will not come back and support me.' "

Shikha and her team did help the families through the trauma, and fortunately the employees were released within a few weeks. Some came back to work. After the crisis was over, Shikha called fifty senior managers to the auditorium and spent several hours talking about what went wrong, what they did right in terms of recovery, and how they could make sure it didn't happen again. "That was quite a good experience for all of us," she says. "If there is one common theme around how we managed it, it's about communicating. By talking with everyone all the time, we were able to find solutions."

Among the many resources Shikha called upon to reframe was her spirituality, which enabled her to put adversity in its proper context. "I believe in destiny," she says. "This Hindu philosophy, sometimes I think I understand it and sometimes I think I don't. You have to find what you were born to do, do it, and leave the results to destiny."

Shikha could not control the outcome when adversity struck. She could, though, apply the tenets of optimism she had taken for granted as a successful and high achiever. "Free will is in finding purpose in your life and choosing to go out and do it. You just keep doing what you believe you were born to do and forget about the results. The results will happen one day."

Now, that's optimism worth learning.

Stop the Spiral, I Want to Get Off

The fundamental belief of positive psychologists is that we can learn optimism. By understanding where pessimism comes from, you can learn how to avoid the emotional spiraling down and rumination that come so easily to pessimists. At its most basic, pessimism is an innate response to stress that, scientists believe, was hardwired into prehistoric human brains as a survival mechanism.

The species survived and evolved because humans developed a quick "fight, freeze, or flee" response to any threat. Those who did not develop this response were more likely to become victims of predators or other dangers. Those with finely tuned instincts survived and passed their capabilities to their children. The key to survival was remembering sounds and smells and events associated with danger.

Over the millennia, that basic instinct has stayed with us as a generalized response to stress. Our brains even evolved to create neural pathways that speed up the response. So when you feel stress, it immediately triggers memories of other situations when you felt stressed and threatened. Women are just more prone to spiraling down—their brains automatically dredge up memories of failures and emotional wounds and they miss the signal to take action.

Susan Nolen-Hoeksema, head of the depression and cognition program at Yale University and author of *Women Who Think Too Much,* has shown that women are literally hardwired to ruminate. In her research, she used scanning equipment to trace brain activity in subjects who were asked to think about negative information about themselves. In women, the part of the brain associated with rumination lit up.

Ruminating is not only unpleasant—the term was inspired by the way cows chew food they already swallowed—it's dangerous. At minimum, by spending hours and days going over what went wrong, you postpone, or even prevent, a meaningful response. It's easy to see that halting the downward spiral and avoiding rumination are an altogether better outcome.

How does the spiral work? Imagine that Joanna is experiencing an unsatisfactory meeting. Halfway through her team's presentation, she realizes something is not right. She has missed a critical piece of analysis and she feels her confidence slipping. She begins to tear down her own work. Then, an aggressive senior executive raises a question. She feels threatened and—like a "deer in headlights"—she blinks but cannot think of a single response. Soon, executives in the room are arguing and talking over one another. The shouting begins. Without a word, the CEO picks up his papers and leaves.

The meeting disintegrates from there. Joanna's downward spiral begins before she has left the conference room. She's reliving the painful experience. And the little voice in her head makes sure she sees it in the worst possible light: "You really blew that! It's clear the CEO is angry at you. And why shouldn't he be? You were unbelievably stupid to miss that analysis. You never think on your feet—you deserved it!" Humiliated, Joanna hurries away, not stopping to chat with the executives.

By the time she gets back to the safety of her office, Joanna feels physically exhausted. She "knows" her performance ruined everything. She's convinced that what happened was inevitable—it had to happen because down deep she also "knows" she said all the wrong things. She remembers all the other times she's blown it and begins to see a pattern of incompetence. Now she's thinking she'll probably get fired. In a nanosecond, she worries about an argument she had with her husband; he doesn't love her anymore. Next, she remembers her daughter's tantrum from the other day and adds being a lousy mother to her list of failings. Joanna begins to ruminate and rewind the tape in her head as the tears start to flow.

When you ruminate, your inner voice plays that tape in an endless loop, each time intensifying it, though you're wishing for a different ending. You feel terrible. But you can't seem to change the subject. That's the downward spiral/rumination cocktail and it leads to trouble. As Joanna ruminates, the grooves in her brain deepen and her negative feelings intensify. If she doesn't snap out of it soon, she'll lose the will and energy to remedy her situation.

Reframing: A Conscious Act

It doesn't have to be this way. You can stop the spiral before it drags you down. With conscious effort, you can build the capability to stop the spiral and get off. Let's start with two techniques: disputation (talking back to that voice in your head) and finding alternatives.

Disputation involves re-examining the situation and consciously separating how you experienced the incident emotionally from what actually happened. Start by refuting the emotional distortions the way a good lawyer would break down faulty evidence. Challenge the beliefs and assumptions implicit in your negative interpretation and re-examine the facts. Then try to understand the consequences of those beliefs. Finally, reframe: Take the undistorted facts and look at what you can do with them. How can you move ahead and address the real issues? Reframing and moving to action will energize you.

Let's look at how Martin Seligman's advice would work for Joanna's situation. She starts with that missing analysis. It's true that she saw the hole in the argument only once she started presenting. But that hole won't change her overall recommendations. In fact, filling it will probably strengthen the overall logic. How about that executive who asked a tough question? Putting aside his tone, it was a reasonable challenge. Had Joanna separated out the emotion, she would have been able to address it. That executive with the aggressive style was not really out of order. He was doing what he should in his role: challenging critical assumptions behind decisions that would affect his company's direction. His tone revealed his own anxiety. Thinking about the question with a bit of distance, Joanna agrees that further analysis is merited. Thanks to disputation, the voice of doom inside her head is growing weaker.

Finding alternatives is a second approach worth your consideration. It is simply looking for other explanations as to why the events unfolded in a particular way. In Joanna's case, incompetence may not be the best explanation for what happened. Why did the question lead to a barroom brawl? Joanna wonders if the guys were at odds over something else before the meeting started. And what else could have caused the CEO to leave? He might have been mad at the behavior of his team, or maybe he was just late for another meeting—this one had already run nearly an hour over.

Both of those approaches—disputation and finding alternative explanations—help Joanna stop the spiral. She's ready to start reframing and recovering: identifying actions she can take to rectify the situation. Reframing helps turn the situation from something that "happened to you" into the basis for a plan.

How can Joanna turn this event into a positive? First, she calls a member of her team to help her complete the missing analysis. Then, she calls the executive who asked the probing question. Now that she's no longer feeling so defensive, she's ready to address his challenge. If she can get him to collaborate with her on the solution, it could be a step toward getting his team to agree. After that, she'll get time with the CEO to learn what's on his mind.

The new analysis could mean refining the recommendations. That may take a lot of work. And it may not be so simple to find why the executives are resistant; it may take something short of a miracle to align them. Whatever is on the CEO's mind, she is eager and open to hearing about it. Joanna realizes she won't be fired, her marriage is strong, and her daughters love her dearly. It's true that she didn't do her best today. She can't change that, but she has a recovery plan. With a renewed burst of energy, Joanna gets down to work.

Sometimes, however, reframing doesn't help you fix the situation. Those are times when reality just bites. The facts add up to disaster, and the consequences of mistakes are real and enormous. You can't dispute these facts. There are no alternate explanations. Even an optimist will tell you there is no obvious solution. You're tired and you're going to need a lot more energy to get a handle on things. Your alarm bells are ringing, but you clear the decks and swing into action. You will just put your head down and power through it. Right?

Not so fast. Remember Emma Fundira, who said that when things get tough she heads for the gym? Remember how Shikha spends time talking and relaxing with her children? Those are displacement tactics, and they help you cope with severe adversity. Literally, you're putting yourself in a different mental place, diverting your energy and attention from the stress and negative feelings that lead to rumination and depression.

Even if you are coping, your brain and body need some relief during times of unrelenting adversity. You can practice displacement in many different ways. Physical activity is great; even a vigorous walk will do. You can remove yourself from the fray with any activity that commands your attention and changes the subject.

So, when stuff happens, remember to take time for a healthy distraction. You'll not only feel better, but you may find a creative solution to what seems like an intractable problem. A break often leads to a breakthrough, when relief from stress allows your sub-conscious mind to relax and mull over the problem.

And sometimes, you just need to move on. Displacement gives you the distance you need to be able to make that tough call, too.

Practice Reframing

Unfortunately, you can't wish yourself into a positive frame. You have to work at it. Start by recognizing when you feel the down-ward spiral begin, and take action. Nolen-Hoeksema suggests liter-ally thinking of a mental "stop" sign. You'll learn to recognize the warning signals and flash the sign. When you "see" it, consciously work on using positive emotions to replace negative ones. For ex-ample, when the executive challenges Joanna, she feels the physical manifestations of the spiral (the higher pulse rate and flush). The sign flashes; she takes a deep breath and smiles. Like Emma, she re-mains calm and asks a question or two, opening herself up to his ideas. In turn, this encourages the executive to lower his aggressive-ness and begin to work the problem with her. She thanks him for his input and, taking a step back, realizes that the group cannot achieve alignment in this meeting.

We can all be more like Emma. The next time someone who is quick to anger treats you in a decidedly negative way, pause before you respond. While it's natural to return anger for anger, getting upset may start the spiral. Instead, try forgiveness. Instead of wait-ing for an apology, your forgiveness has released your anger and put in its place a positive emotion. It may sound counterintuitive, but it's worth trying. See for yourself; you may find greater serenity and in turn, greater productivity.

Every woman leader we met was an optimist, and it really

doesn't matter who was born one and who developed the skill. With a little bit of practice, it will be your skill, too, and not just one to deploy at work. The benefits for you personally are enormous—success, happiness, even greater resilience—so consider optimism an extraordinary life skill and get going.

CHAPTER 8

Moving On

I was having lunch with my father in Jordan, when they announce the war on the radio. We jump in the car and drive to our home outside of Jerusalem. We're out of gas, and it's a full-scale war. Our house gets bombed. My father rents an ambulance and takes us to Jericho for safety. The bombing follows, and we spend the night in our orange orchard. Next morning, we need to move on, so we rent a Volkswagen Beetle with the driver, my father, my mother, my grandmother, and eight kids. Friends take us in when we make it to Jordan. That was my defining moment. At the age of fourteen, I became the strong one. You don't think at the time, you just do it.

Amal Johnson, CEO, Market Tools

Many of the women leaders declared themselves optimists—and realists—in the same breath. This distinctive blend of attitudes keeps them centered. They revel in the facts. So when they make mistakes, take a wrong turn, or experience failure, they are especially skilled in gaining feedback and using it to move on. It's what helps them transition from recovery to growth.

Does the prospect of receiving feedback raise your heartbeat and make you feel anxious? Our research shows that instead of listening for valuable information, many women hear only criticism and disapproval, tuning out everything else. It's hard to separate the message from the emotion. No wonder feedback often results in—here it comes again—a ride down the spiral.

Not all women respond that way: The women leaders we interviewed use their performance mistakes and feedback in a way that dazzled us—as a valued source of information and insight that accelerates their growth. They are lifetime learners. Believe it or not, they simply accept that pain often accompanies experience as they climb a steep learning curve. Learning from mistakes is their powerful engine.

Ellyn McColgan's story brings this insight to life. Until recently, president of the global wealth management business at Morgan Stanley and, before that, president of distribution and operations at Fidelity Investments, Ellyn built the very capability she needed for her long career: hearing the feedback, assessing the situation, and moving on to fix—and recover.

Facing It

Growing up in Jersey City, Ellyn remembers her grandmother as the one who first opened her eyes. "My dad was a steamfitter who worked every day and never took vacations. My mom stayed home taking care of us, doing laundry and ironing and cooking and cleaning," Ellyn says. "Their life was filled with work and obligation. But my grandmother thought that I hung the moon. She was my biggest fan and taught me to believe that I could do whatever I wanted to do. Mine is the American dream story."

Ellyn's family didn't have much money when she was growing

up. She recalls, "When there were field trips available in high school, to the Metropolitan Opera or something like that, my grandmother would always figure out how to get me the $20 for the bus money to send me off. Little by little, I began to see a bigger world out there. It also became clear to me that money and education were the two things I needed to gain access to that world." And that realization was the beginning of Ellyn's march to independence.

When it came time for college, she went to Montclair State College, a working kids' school where "everybody had a job." Upon graduation she took a job in personnel at a local department store. She earned enough to rent her own apartment—a first step toward independence.

Five years after college and a few jobs into her personnel career, Ellyn found herself working in HR at the Lifesavers Candy Company. She was lucky enough to have a boss who saw potential in her: "He told me, 'Read *The Wall Street Journal* for two weeks. If you're not sufficiently curious at that point, I'll leave you alone. But if you come to me with a whole list of questions, we're going to have to talk about your going back to school.' "

In two weeks she had a raft of questions. So, after taking one baby step—a semester at night school—Ellyn leapt. She quit her job to attend Harvard Business School, where her big dreams were born. "It was at Harvard that I decided I wanted to be the president of a big company," she says, laughing. "I remembered the president at Lifesavers. He was a very tall and handsome man, always well dressed. He had a car and driver and he had this great corner office. That looked good to me."

At Harvard, Ellyn shifted her focus from personnel to finance, from consumer products to financial services. She found this was the kind of work that really engaged her talents, and she loved it:

"All of a sudden, it became the formula that made everything work. I found I had a knack for it. But I also learned that I wanted to manage people; I wanted to manage an organization."

Taking the next few steps down that path, Ellyn joined the training program at Shearson American Express, and then became the chief operating officer's assistant for a few years. She parlayed her good work—and good relationship—into a transfer to a division in Boston that got her to her next job. She eventually moved to the Bank of New England to run custody operations and securities processing. It was a big organization—500 people—and so Ellyn started to feel that she was now in reach of her dream.

But life isn't always a fairy tale, and Ellyn's path turned bumpy. She had just bought her first home; she was thirty-five years old; and she was driven to prove she could do it all. "I had just signed the contracts to renovate my kitchen when the bank started to have trouble," she says. "I thought, 'Oh, gosh. I might lose my job. I just bought this house. And what am I going to do with the kitchen? The old cabinets are gone!' "

Her team at the bank got together and explored a few options, like selling the business to somebody else. Ellyn recalls, "We made a pact that we would help each other figure out opportunities somewhere. One by one, we found other jobs." Ellyn found her next job at Fidelity Investments. She spent seventeen more years building an extraordinary career—running every major distribution business, managing thousands of employees and clients.

Like other optimists, Ellyn sees opportunity everywhere. "It was 1992. I was asked to run the client services division for the 401(k) business, a business I knew nothing about at the time but it was growing like crazy."

Her job, as the "operations whiz kid," was to turn a high-growth business into a profitable one, with improved client service. "It required a massive reorganization of the functions, even geograph-ically. It was complicated," says Ellyn. "So I put a project team to-gether. We developed a two-thousand-step action plan. The thing was an unbelievable Gantt chart. We worked at it, and we worked at it, and we worked at it, and then we opened up our new opera-tions in Covington, Kentucky. Almost everybody had new jobs with new job descriptions."

You can guess what happened next: a hole in their path too big to transverse. They fell in. On the first day that the new organiza-tion was put into motion, all those new moving parts jammed. Nothing worked the way it was supposed to.

A few weeks later, Ellyn found herself on an emergency field trip to Kentucky with a contingent of executives from headquar-ters: "My boss's boss was with us. I overheard him asking a young woman who was doing bank reconciliations, 'How often do you do these?' She said, 'Every day.' Then he asked, 'And what happens if, when you get to the bottom, the debits don't equal the credits?' 'Oh,' she said, 'I put a journal entry in for the other side to match it.' Then he said, 'Do you go back and figure out why it didn't match?' She replied, 'I just put the journal entry in. That makes everything even.' Then the kicker came. He asked, 'When was the last time that the two columns matched?' Her fatal words were, 'Well, sir, I've been working here for ninety days and they've never matched.' "

The hole Ellyn was peering up from turned out to be very, very deep. Fidelity held a client conference and 500 unhappy clients showed up. Ellyn stood at the front of the room and said, "On be-half of the firm and all of our associates, we apologize. We have not been doing a good job. It is not worthy of our standard of care and I apologize deeply for that. In ninety days, we will have it fixed. I ask you not to make a change in your provider until then and to work with us to resolve your issues."

It was a huge failure for the operations whiz kid. Ellyn recalls: "It was terrible for me. It was awful. I thought my career was over. I didn't think I'd ever recover from it."

Ultimately, her team's model proved to be right but it took her four months to resolve the execution issues. Ellyn found out what she needed to do by going back to her team and demanding honest feedback all around—"getting naked," as she puts it. She told them, "We are lost and I took us there. We have to find our way again. What do we have to do to fix it?" And so they solved it together. Ellyn says, "People always rise to the request for help. I found strength in people I didn't know we had. I found strength in myself I didn't know I had."

At first, Ellyn fought a feeling of hopelessness. Fear can cloud perspective, and for Ellyn, it threatened at times. She feared losing what she most treasured—her independence. Fear drove her to work very hard, but it also lured her to the downward spiral. She remembers, "Of course, I had private moments, dark moments, when I wasn't out there in front of anybody, when I would think, 'Whew, this hurts. This really hurts and I might be wrong.' With a house, a car, and expenses, I was terrified that I would lose everything."

But her team stuck together, and she turned to a colleague who was "even more optimistic." Conversations with him helped her regain perspective: "I'd sit in his office and say, 'What are we going to do? Is this ever going to be okay?' And he'd say, 'Yes, it is. Here's why.'"

Thankfully, the scary time was brief. "Ninety days is not that long and eventually the processes worked," Ellyn recalls. "I began to get up in the morning knowing that I was going to get through to the end of the day. And we went on to build a wonderful business," she says now.

As things began to work, Ellyn's own recovery began, too. "I was in the doghouse for a long time," she recalls. "It was my dad who helped me understand why. I remember telling him, 'It wasn't my fault that it broke down. I had this project team and all these other people, and I wasn't managing bank reconciliation. Surely, nobody could hold me accountable for that problem!' And Dad replied, 'Oh, yes, they can.' He looked at me hard. 'Don't you manage that organization?' Yes I did. 'Then you have to stay and fix it.' So I stayed and fixed it. You know, you learn as much from fixing as you do from breaking."

Eventually, Ellyn gained an important perspective: With all that attention to the minutiae, her team had lost focus on the real issues. "Maybe I won't have two thousand action steps on the Gantt chart the next time, but I'll actually know how to take more risk," she recalls thinking. She also realized that her terror in the darkest moments was unfounded: "One of the things I'm passionate about now is saying to young people, particularly women, 'Go ahead. What is the worst thing that can happen?' You know what they always say? 'I might get fired.' Yes, you might. It's unlikely. You might be embarrassed. That's likely. You might go into the doghouse. That could happen. But you probably won't get fired. And even if you do get fired, so what! Go get another job."

Ellyn's optimism helped her move on, and eventually on to greater triumphs. But she still had to work hard to earn back the close relationship she had had with her boss. "Bob started to defrost after a year and we can laugh about it now," she says. "The connection I missed was that Bob knew many of these clients personally. He had brought them to Fidelity. He was so angry because they were being hurt by our poor service and he felt responsible for them. He had a right to be angry. I thought, 'Someday, he'll come back and talk to me, and we'll be fine,' which is what happened."

Ellyn learned many things from this painful experience, including that she could bounce back from the self-doubt that often accompanies setbacks. "I learned that it wasn't the end of the world. It was going to be okay," she says.

Today, Ellyn counts among her skills the ability to recover quickly. And, she says, that always starts with the team: "I take energy from everybody else. I'm happiest when I'm surrounded by other people, working together and getting things done. And I'm very loyal. I always know where my people are, always."

Ellyn draws on her optimism to pull through: "The only time that darkness arrives is when I'm without options. If I can generate options, then I can choose one. And once I choose one, I'll generate some more." She also perseveres: "I'm incredibly serious and I'm intense. I stay with things until they're done, no matter how ugly they are or how long they're going to take."

Ellyn finds needed strength in her values. "I believe that basically people are good and they want to do good," she explains. "Someday I will have to account for what I did and for how I treated people. I want to be at peace with that."

And finally, Ellyn's competitive spirit helps her rise to any challenge. Eventually, she led Fidelity's retail and institutional distribution areas and a good number of the operating areas.

But then it was time to move on, literally: "In 2007, after seventeen years of a fabulous career, I decided it was time to pursue other career opportunities and I resigned."

Thirty years into her journey, Ellyn continues to learn and to grow. She looks back on that business crisis and offers a profound insight. "You can't live your life from a place of fear. Live your life from a place of hope. A natural reaction to failure is to be afraid and to get smaller," Ellyn says. "But what you should do is get bigger. It's an opportunity to grow, not an opportunity to shrink. It might hurt while it's happening—all things that help you grow hurt."

Always, Ellyn looks forward, not back. It's a core strength that helps her recover. "I'm not sure what I need at this point," Ellyn says now. "My journey so far has been extraordinary. But it's not over yet! I'm still evolving."

Feedback Can Help You Grow

Optimists confront adversity directly, soliciting feedback and facing those facts. That's what Ellyn learned through experience. She faced her bosses, she faced her clients, and she faced her team. That said, many women find soliciting feedback uncomfortable—understandably. Feedback often triggers defensiveness and it's hard to check that response in order to clearly hear the facts.

You can wait and learn this skill in the moment next time you face adversity. Or you can prepare by simulating that experience. Here's how: Choose your own adverse scenario—your current project blows up, say—then predict all possible outcomes to it, writing them down. Assign a probability to each. In Ellyn's case, she could have predicted three outcomes from her poor performance: getting fired, quitting in anger, or accepting the feedback and working to fix the situation. When she really thinks about it (perhaps with help from a trusted colleague), she might estimate the probabilities as 5 percent, 15 percent, and 80 percent, respectively. This approach shortcuts the process of gaining enough distance to see things more clearly, without having emotions cloud your perspective. Talking through the analysis with others will likely uncover other potential outcomes that you may not have thought of. The very act of writing it down helps, too.

A second approach also helps you gain distance by writing things down. Here, your goal is to view the situation from different perspectives. Write down what actually happened in that adverse situation, including each element you can recall. Describe how each person involved is likely to have viewed it. Now, identify which observations are facts and which are your beliefs. Then, draw out the consequences of your beliefs. For example, had Ellyn put herself in the boss's shoes, she would have turned up a few more facts to challenge her original beliefs. Because she was feeling defensive, she was focused on herself and did not immediately see how others were affected by the same situation. It helps to reach out to others you trust and who have first-hand knowledge of the situation. They can give a more objective diagnosis. Ask them to read through your descriptions, adding to them or countering your version. If you don't have anyone to talk to, take a step back and look at the situation from all sides, assuming the perspectives of others who were involved. If you make this part of your routine, you will limit your exposure to rumination. Diagnosis and action will become your practiced response to adversity.

A third approach can be helpful in the moment when you are receiving formal feedback. If you know from experience that you tense up and feel defensive, prepare yourself ahead of time. Make sure you are well-rested and cool-headed; it's hard to remain open and flexible on limited sleep. Develop a few well-rehearsed questions that you're comfortable with, such as: Tell me more. What could I have done differently? What can I do to develop that skill? What did you do to develop that skill? You might even write yourself key words (e.g., "defensive" or "ask questions") on your notepad to remind yourself in the moment.

Feedback, including direct criticism, paves the way for growth. Time and again women leaders told us: Learn what you can from mistakes and setbacks. Sometimes you can fix the problem and recover. And sometimes all you can do is learn and move on. Around the corner, your next opportunity is waiting for you.

CHAPTER 9

Ready for Change

I sat in a room with all the lawyers and bankers and advisors. Me, who'd never done that before, I said, "Now we have to have a conversation about what we're going to do." And they all went blah, blah, blah, blah. Everybody wanted to have a say. I said, "Let's start again. I'll ask each of you, and you need to give me a very real answer about what you think we should do. Not the look back. How do we move forward?" Then it turned into a fabulous discussion.

Karen Moses, COO, Origin Energy

Successful leaders are able to inspire their organizations toward a shared goal that is infused with meaning. Everyone heads in the same direction, aligned. It's the same with a leader's personal goal: She sets off on a journey toward a brilliant place on a far horizon. And if this were a fairy tale, there would be challenges along the way, but she would arrive safely and live happily ever after.

But this is reality. Obstacles do stand in the way, and sometimes life just happens. Circumstances change. That's when the leader realizes it's time to adapt the course. This is the hardest thing of all: You must be singularly focused on the agenda and, at the same time, willing to let it go when it's no longer the right solution.

Adaptability is our next skill for you. We think women start with a natural advantage. If you're a mother, you're familiar with the need to make sudden changes. Anyone who has experienced her toddler's meltdown in a store knows the score. Anyone who has teenage children knows even better that every day you have to be ready to adapt to unpredictable requirements.

If you're not a mother, you've adapted in other ways. You've also had to make compromises between home and work. Simply by being raised a girl, you learned a lot more than your male counterparts about accommodating the needs of others.

So, why are we even worrying about adaptability if you are already conditioned? Many women leave this natural advantage at the door when they get to the office. The research indicates that in the face of challenges, we double down—dive in and work even harder to power through. You may prevail, but with tremendous frustration and energy depletion at the very least. Worse, you haven't looked for other options that might be more effective now. That's anything but adaptive.

You don't have to give up your sleep to fit everything else in when conditions change. You don't have to find the impossible compromise that makes everybody happy. In challenging work situations, doing the same thing more intensely may be the worst thing we can do (short of just totally losing it). What's called for is finding alternative solutions—a work-around or even an entirely new strategy—and quickly. That's adaptability. Think about what different course reveals itself in that moment, even if the course is just to take a break and reflect.

Adaptability is certainly a requirement for a leader like Christine Lagarde, the first woman to serve as minister of economy, finance and employment for a G-7 nation. Before that, she was the first female head of Baker & McKenzie, one of the world's leading law firms. Christine's experience as a new kind of leader underscores the impact of adaptability.

Working Through an Impasse

Christine says she knew she had the makings of a leader, even when she was a girl competing on France's national synchronized swimming team. "Soon after I became a swimmer, I became a coach of the junior team. And I just enjoyed it. I had the trust and confidence of others, which is a huge boost of energy," she says. "I think that I was always a leader in many ways. You have to take up that job if you have the skills, the quality, the inclinations—and what's more important, if people actually believe that you can help them. Being a leader has a lot to do with helping other people achieve what they can achieve."

When we met Christine, we asked whether her nineteen-year journey to the top of Baker & McKenzie was ever bumpy. She laughed. "It would be nice to say, 'Oh, yes, it was terrible. I had all those mountains to climb, and all those obstacles to overcome.' But no, it was a beautiful ride—a lot to do with the chemistry between my personality, my aspiration, and the values and principles of the firm."

That said, the firm was troubled as Christine assumed the helm. "We had just gone through a phase—it happens in all organizations—where budgets had been exceeded. It was during the burst of the Internet bubble. Management had been discredited and criticized," she explains. "There was a complete lack of trust in the governance of the firm. In consequence, self-esteem was low.

The major task that I set for myself and the team was to rejuvenate the firm while restoring confidence. We professionals are superb at either self-crediting ourselves or self-criticizing. But instead of having everybody look at their belly buttons, I forced them to take a client-first perspective. We reviewed the whole organization in terms of decision-making, practices, structure, and how we portrayed ourselves."

Christine faced broad resistance. "Few professionals can be more conservative than lawyers," she explains. "We are trained to be risk-adverse, and to change in a legal organization is probably the ultimate of change challenges." Her predecessors discouraged her from even trying. "They said, 'You will never make it. It's too hard. You're going to break your bones. Don't go there.' "

But she did, over the course of many years. Her chosen style was inclusive and adaptive. First she consulted with all the offices around the world because she knew that their buy-in would be critical. "I had to make sure everybody was together," she says. "We would take as much time as was needed. So we went through a process of analyzing, measuring, benchmarking, and taking advice. At the end of the fourth year, I thought that we were there. We had turned over every stone, covered every angle, and could put our ideas to the partners. We needed a 75 percent majority to move ahead."

Christine went to the partners' conference prepared to put the change plan to a vote. "There was a long session of explanation and discussions—think of a room with six hundred partners all thinking that they know better than you do, because they own the operation and they rightly want to say what they have to say. We talked until four o'clock in the afternoon and I thought that we had covered everything. I said, 'Let's take a vote.' The count was 72 percent in favor. At that point, I closed the meeting and we disbanded until the following morning."

What would you have done in Christine's shoes?

"You can imagine that during that night we worked hard, brainstormed a lot. I didn't sleep much," she recalls. "I was under huge pressure from members of the 72 percent majority as well as some of my predecessors to get it done. The way a majority vote had been achieved in the past was to twist a few arms during the night, work the corridors, and make sure that we could push it down the throat of the other 28 percent. I had a final session at six o'clock that next morning with the global executive committee. We discussed and decided what we were going to do."

If ever there was a moment to test a leader's adaptability, this was it. Christine walked into the plenary session with her six hundred partners. She recalls, "Most of them were expecting the revote on what we had recommended. I started by saying, 'This is what would have happened in the old days. There would have been arm-twisting and rehashing and pushing until it went through. But it's not the way I want this to happen.' "

To the surprise of the assembled partners, she told them, "We're going to take another year. We'll come back next year. We'll do whatever additional work is needed. But I want you to be happy with it, because it's your project, your structure, and our firm."

It was a tough decision to abandon her agenda, holding off on implementation for the year, but a watershed in the firm's history. "We came back the next year and the vote was 99 percent," she told us proudly. "Most people said we got that majority because of the way we handled the earlier vote, because I respected their views. It was very much in line with the values that the firm holds high—including respect, tolerance, and diversity."

Not long after that, Christine left for government service. As she tells it, it took one phone call—and twenty minutes—for her to decide on a new path. We love this story, too, because it highlights that adaptability and decision-making go hand in hand.

"I was in the middle of working on a merger of our New York office with another firm's New York office," she recalls. "It was a very exciting project that I had worked on for four and a half years." Back in Paris, though, things were moving on another front. "I knew that the French government was going through the exercise of forming a new team to be announced on Friday morning," she says. "On Thursday morning, when I got up, I found e-mails saying that the minister of finance wanted to talk to me urgently." That could only mean one thing—a request to join the new government.

She decided to stick to her plan to go to the gym. On the way to the gym and back, she phoned key partners and reached three. "I did not get counsel for myself," she explains. "I wanted to have their views about how the firm where I had worked for twenty-five years would fare if I were to leave it. If those three had said, 'Christine, we need you. You have to stay,' I would have stayed. They simply said, 'It is a call for duty, and you should put the country first. We will deal with the merger and get it done!' "

When she got back from the gym, there was a new message. This time, the prime minister wanted to talk. "So I called and had a twenty-minute conversation with him. I asked him the questions that I wanted to ask," she says. "There was a silence after that. I said, 'How much time do I have to think about it?' He replied, 'As long as you want. But I'm not putting the phone down.' " So with the good wishes of her partners, Christine left the United States that evening and landed in Paris the next day as Madame Minister.

How was Christine able to make her decision that fast? "I trust my gut feeling. I make mistakes, I know," she says. "But I check with the family—my two sons. They were critical voices that I listen to. I thought hard about the firm because I was giving up a lot. But the firm was fabulous about it."

Cool Under Uncertainty

Harvard professors Ronald Heifetz and Marty Linsky contend that many leaders fail to meet adaptive challenges because they cannot make the mental leap of faith to pursue a new course that does not have a guaranteed outcome. For example, developing a new business, reaching a new customer base, and pushing any kind of innovation are all adaptive challenges—and they're all a bit scary. In each case, you don't know what is going to happen. You can't see far down the road. It's more than getting comfortable with ambiguity; it's getting comfortable with uncertainty, too.

Heifetz and Linsky use a compelling metaphor for leaders facing adaptive challenges: Think of yourself "on the dance floor and on the balcony" at the same time. When you're on the floor you're interacting with the people around you at close range, but you can't see past them to the rest. You may even get lost in the moment yourself. You're feeling what others are feeling but have no distance or perspective.

Now switch. Picture yourself on the balcony, looking down at the dance. You can see patterns—what's happening across the entire space. Reframing to see this broader view can help you identify new directions or breakthroughs.

It's one thing to imagine that out-of-body experience on the balcony, floating above the fray, but it's another to do it in the heat of the moment. What you're confronting on the dance floor is a rush of emotions from those around you and emotions you may be feeling, too: possibly anger, confusion, anxiety, fear, or frustration.

Many situations, not just major changes, provoke these feelings. You're facing off against a bully. Your team is dead set against moving in the direction you've committed to. Senior management is criticizing the plan you've invested six months developing. Customers turn you down. You're in the thick of it, and that may make you feel a bit like a boxer in the eighth round—weakened, your perspective gone, and wishing your opponent would just give in or put you out of your misery. So what do you do and how do you do it?

Here are a few ideas for regaining your balance in the moment. Say you're in a meeting and things are not going well. You know the signs: Your heart is beating fast, you're interrupting and talking too quickly, you feel defensive. That's the signal to step back. Remember mankind's three reactions to danger: fight, flight, or freeze? The ancient part of your brain is hijacking you, but you can override it.

First, just breathe deeply and count to ten—enough time to set the restart button. Now you've got some choices. If you can, literally step out of the room for a few minutes to review what's really going on. Get the physical distance you need to see the bigger picture. If leaving the room isn't an option, imagine that you're an observer at the meeting and do a quick "reality check." Step into the shoes of somebody else, perhaps even your opposition, to get a different view. At the very least, stop talking and focus on listening, trying to understand what's behind everyone else's comments. Ask questions to probe underneath their statements. If you're the leader of the meeting, ask for a recap—going around the table and listening to the current view of each participant. With cool reflection, you might see the situation differently.

When the challenge does not require immediate adaptation, reach out to mentors and sponsors for a more detached perspective. These senior people won't be as distracted and can help you understand the bigger picture of the organization. You might also reach out (discreetly) to people who are in the thick of the process with you. How are they really feeling? Take them to the balcony with you. Who is supporting what you're doing? Who's opposed? How is the process really going?

Watching from the balcony is not enough. Having both perspectives is enormously helpful, particularly when the environment is changing quickly or significantly, when people are anxious and don't know what will be expected of them.

So don't linger too long on the balcony; sense when it's time to rejoin the dance. Asking the hard questions can help you get some perspective. It's also a superb tactic to gather vital intelligence. Think of those long-gone TV detectives, Columbo and Kojak. Columbo, in his battered old raincoat, politely asks a lot of questions; sometimes, on his way out the door, the question he asks cracks open the case. In contrast, Kojak swiftly demonstrates his superior logic in an intimidating way. Columbo is the expert listener, Kojak the expert talker. Be more like Columbo when you need to be adaptive.

In particular, find allies who can support, protect, or strengthen your cause. But reach out to the opposition, too. Knowing the objections of your adversaries and addressing their challenges will make your plan better.

On the dance floor, you can also be a powerful role model. That's what Christine did when she faced her partners on the second morning. She was living the value of mutual respect. It's no surprise that they came on board the following year.

But as much as many women work their hardest to be liked, don't expect everyone to like you. When you're leading change in your organization, there will be casualties. Everyone won't go along, and some will try to block you. And as they show their displeasure, you may encounter resistance from a new face—you. Facing your own fears first will make you a better leader.

Staying Adaptive

Remember, zigging and zagging on your leadership journey is not only fine, we expect it. Every woman leader we talked to had to adapt to twists and turns in the road as new opportunities, new adventures, and new challenges presented themselves. When we don't adapt professionally and personally, that's when we lose perspective and become rigid, letting the world get to us and letting our emotions run amok.

From time to time, consciously reframe: Think about your goals and whether you should change them. The formula that worked for you in the past may no longer fit the circumstances. And when you see (or feel) the signs that you are locking in, take a deep breath and head for the balcony. We don't want you to ever change being open to change.

CHAPTER 10

The Journey, Not the Destination

Optimism has guided Eileen Naughton through turns in the road, through highs and lows professionally and personally. With a flexible mind-set, she regularly reached out for the next opportunity to explore her passions: as a reporter, a tour guide, a magazine executive. A few years into her dream job as president of Time Group, Eileen was laid off. Today, as Google's director of media platforms, she's still on the journey, still an optimist, and a Renaissance woman.

Journey's Roots

My father was an immigrant from Ireland who worked for the New York Telephone Company. My mother had her hands full, raising the six of us. We were expected to be good students, respectful of teachers. We had a lot of rules in our house—getting things done on time, having a neat room, eating with the proper fork and knife, never back-talking to our parents, going to church. I'm an orderly person, but I'm also an explorer. Confidence and self-reliance were part of my makeup.

Something early on connected me to words and expression. I remember that in the fourth grade, I had my first poem published in the local newspaper, and hey, I liked that: an ode to the shoe-maker who had a shop in the front of our apartment building. It probably instilled in me a lifelong love of shoes! Then in the sixth grade, I got an award from the Daughters of the American Revolu-tion for an essay on Thomas Jefferson. I had to read it in front of blue-haired ladies at their favorite restaurant. My little knees were quaking because I'd never spoken in front of a group before.

After college, I had two job offers. One was to work at an in-vestment bank in a trainee program on Wall Street, and the other was to be a writer for a newspaper syndicate. The bank would have been a more lucrative career, but I knew I liked writing. And so I came to New York to cover everything from travel to home im-provement and fashion shows. My boss was intense, and after a while, I just had to quit. I wanted to go back to Europe, I spoke two languages, and I figured working as a tour guide was kind of a paid vacation.

After two years of fun, it was time to get serious. I worked at MasterCard International in New York as a communications man-ager in PR until I figured I needed an MBA. I went to Wharton, met my husband, and we moved to Europe.

The start of our real careers came in 1989, when we came back to New York. I could not have imagined staring at a trading screen on Wall Street day in and day out. That would have just deadened my soul. I knew enough about what I liked to steer the prow of my ship toward publishing. You know, I've always followed my tro-pisms. Serious journalism was one.

So it's probably not coincidental that I sought an opportunity to work at Time Inc. I started working in the manufacturing divi-sion—not very sexy and not where MBAs went! That didn't matter to me. Working at Time Inc. did. And after eighteen months, I was asked to become *Fortune*'s editorial business manager. I remember a colleague's warning: "You're making a big mistake. If you want a career in finance, edit is not the place to go." But I was going to learn how a magazine was made.

I loved it. Our business was booming, and I got an incredible opportunity to help reorganize *Fortune*'s whole business structure. I was eight months pregnant with our second child. Things were fantastic!

The Single Biggest Challenge

Then one day, it all stopped. We had an appointment with a geneticist. We got the dreaded news that our young son had a disability called fragile X syndrome and that he would never live independently or lead a normal life. There was also a one in two chance of passing on the gene to my unborn baby.

I learned all this on Tuesday at 3 p.m. The next morning, I was one of three featured speakers at Time Warner's annual management meeting. It was being broadcast to all the offices for the first time. Our chairman would be sitting in the front row. Of course, it was a huge honor to be singled out. I remember returning to the office from Mt. Sinai to finish the gosh-darned slides and figure out what I was going to say.

Usually, I would be nervous speaking in front of so august a crowd. But when I woke up that next day, I realized that the worst thing that could ever happen to me just did. It was liberating. I don't even think I realized that morning how profound his disability would actually turn out to be. Because I was stunned.

So I got up there and did a fine job. And I realized I never had to be afraid of anything again. I was going to be fine and so was my kid. We'd figure this out.

That moment freed me in a way. I knew I had to work to pay

for support, but I also knew that work would be a wonderful anti-dote to the pain. It put the rest of life into context. Some things that might have seemed heavy or important didn't belong in the heavy and important bucket anymore. I learned to embrace differences and to be less harsh.

No, I didn't spiral down. I do remember early on having one good heaving sobbing session before my second baby was born. It was just so sad and frightening to consider whether she would also have fragile X. But I had my daughter, who is perfectly healthy, and went on to have a third child. You never know exactly what your future holds.

I think my husband and I both picked up and moved on with a vengeance. I became an expert on fragile X, and we got my son a lot of treatment, because for the first few years you believe you can fix it. And then you accept that you can't. But by nature, I'm optimistic. It's hard to keep me down.

We put Patrick in a special boarding school in Boston. It was a tough decision. His life is not what we would have hoped for him, and it's been hard on us to raise a child with a profound disability, but there's no shortage of love and joy in doing so. We speak every night. When Patrick first went to that school, he couldn't eat properly with a knife and fork. Now he's accomplishing huge things. He's six foot three now, a happy, funny kid.

And when, one day, our CFO tapped me on the shoulder to talk to me about shifting roles to lead a cost management program, I knew the company needed to do this and I couldn't say no. I worried about my popularity but I trusted in the system—and it worked out really well. It was a great way to get to know Time Inc. and its management. And nobody hated me!

Then, in January 2000, they announced that Time Warner and AOL were merging. There was dancing in the halls. Our stock was at an all-time high. Conceptually it was brilliant—but as it turned out, the AOL business was not all it was supposed to be. I was tapped to work on the integration—another growing opportunity. Then, that summer, Time Warner's head of investor relations left, along with her deputy. There we were, a public company with no investor relations function heading into a very complex merger. The chairman of Time Warner asked to see me, and he told me that I was the hands-down favorite to run IR. I thought, "Huh? How could this be?"

I knew IR was an assignment that took so much personal stamina that I could only do it for a few years. But I also thought, "How much fun to have a seat at the table at the merger of these two giants! This is going to be one ride." And it sure was. When I look back, I think it was my own personal Baghdad!

About eighteen months later, I got a call from Ann Moore, who's now chairman of Time Inc. She said, "Eileen, I have a very interesting assignment to talk to you about." And I thought, "Oh glory, I get to go back." I let her spend two minutes describing the *Time* magazine assignment before I jumped in and said, "Why wouldn't I do this?" I was scared but I had wanted to work at *Time* all my life. Never in my wildest dreams did I think I'd work there as president. There had only been three or four presidents of *Time,* and none of them female. It was my dream job come true.

During that part of my life's journey, I think I became a good leader. I was able to grow into one because I was very connected to the temperament and the culture and the work environment. First and foremost I learned to establish trust. You have to demonstrate that you're willing to make tough decisions: You cannot tolerate poor performers; you have to have a team that will walk through a hail of bullets with you. And you have to be willing to do it for them. I think building a great team is the most important characteristic in a leader—the ability to touch people, give them a vision toward a higher goal, show them the path, and reward them when they do it, whether they do it with big steps or little ones.

Also, I noticed early on that I was one of the more outspoken people there. I'm polite, I have good manners, but I don't bite my tongue. I don't say stupid things, but I call a mistake a mistake if I see it. It's not personal, it's business. I don't think I'd be respected if I left a problem to fester or had the wrong person in the wrong job for too long and didn't address it. It's important for me to have these decisions be transparent, to be fact-based or business-based. That matters more to me than being liked. With experience, you exercise that muscle of decisiveness more. I have three kids, I have a husband, I have a job, I have a life. And I don't have time to waste.

Dream job or not, by early 2005 things were not going well for the company. The consequences of the AOL merger were certain: Time Warner would continue to operate in a straitjacket of financial underperformance. At the same time, the print model was under assault with high input costs; paper, ink, transportation, postage were out of our control. There was widespread flight of readers to the Internet. *Time* was in the crosshairs of this profound change. We had had our best year in 2004, and deep down I guess I knew that we couldn't repeat that year, maybe ever.

So by late 2005, Ann Moore made the decision to do a layoff. In order to save the company, she had to purge a lot of costs—and the first place she looked was the most senior people in the division. On December 13, 2005, there was a wholesale purging, about sixty-five people.

Ann came to me—her voice was quite unsteady—and she said she had made some decisions. She had eliminated my boss's job and my job. After she left my office, I called my husband and said,

"Honey, my job's been eliminated." As my voice started to crack, he said, "That's fantastic! You've just gotten a hall pass!" My entire staff took me out that evening and got me pretty loaded with vodka. I only remember getting into a black car and saying, "See ya, guys," and going to bed.

In a way it was a great relief. In the last year of my tenure, I had absolutely limited choice, limited investment, limited discretion over what we could do. And the company was operating in a cloak of suspicion and lack of trust. It was not an environment I could thrive in.

But then it settled in. The first day I was still stunned. Next, I got mad. It didn't feel very good for the next month, because I'm used to having control in my life. I spent it doing yoga and I took care of my home and my family. It wasn't until May that I got it out of my system.

I wanted to work. And it was very clear to me that I needed to have three conditions in my next place of employment: One, it must be based on a fully digital business model; two, the prospects of forward growth must be visible and clear; and three, I needed a leadership team that had demonstrated a core set of principles and values I could connect with.

So I turned down publishing jobs, and the more I looked and researched and spoke to people, the more clearly it appeared to me that Google fit all my criteria. I reached out to a headhunter, who said, "Well, Eileen, I do have something there, but I don't know if it would be something you'd consider." Here I was, coming from the president of *Time* role, and this was a director of advertising and media sales for Google in the New York office. I asked, "How big is the business?" It was $400 million or more. That's big enough, I thought. A real business.

I met with folks at Google here in New York and had an offer, third week of June, something like that. I took the summer off and started in September.

I brought a lot of skill and experience to Google, but I also had a lot to learn. The nature of the work drew me in immediately to be at a cutting-edge kind of company. I loved the consumer reaction to Google. And there's cool stuff here—technology innovation not only around the ad space but around how you retrieve information and make it useful in your life. That's exactly analogous to why I was attracted to Time Inc. in the first place. It's also very different. It's team-based, a very flat culture, nonhierarchical. I happen to like that.

I have zero regrets for having stayed at *Time*. Well, I'd say one regret may have been staying too long when the writing was on the wall. I think back to spending seventeen years at Time Warner and what I might not have been looking at and how I might not have been keeping my eyes peeled around me out of fierce loyalty.

I think I was lucky in a way, too. There are all sorts of blunders and difficult corporate scenarios coming to light across this country. It's got to be an unhappy time for many people in many industries. We just happened to have an earlier dose of it at Time Warner. So, my advice is: Take care of yourself. Indulge yourself a little. Be mindful that there is no such thing as perfection and perfect balance. I used to be a perfectionist. I mean, I made all my own baby food! I look back and wonder, what was I thinking? Forget perfection and balance! The best you can hope for is organized disequilibrium. Sometimes it feels like chaos, but it doesn't keep me up at night. I know that the best thing I can do when something hasn't gone just right in a day is get some sleep and think it through in the shower the next morning.

I have drive and ambition, but in some ways I have had zero expectation. I was always looking out for the next interesting, stimulating, cool thing to do. It didn't really have much to do with status and pay. Focusing on the journey instead of the destination is a beautiful way to describe managing your career.

Recently, I found something I'd written in Italy when I was twenty-five years old. I was cleaning a closet. It was a list of "things I want to do in life." I wanted to learn Italian. Done. I wanted to play guitar. Haven't done that. I wanted a beautiful garden. Done. I wanted to raise children. Doing. I had a yearning to work at *Time* when I was nineteen years old. Did that. I'm grateful for the opportunity.

I still have many years of working left in me. I want to look back and be able to say, "Wow, we lived a great life. And it's been hard at times, but it's been thrilling. It's been interesting."

PART THREE

Connecting

CHAPTER 11

A Path to Belonging

We don't accomplish anything in this world alone. Whatever happens is the result of the whole tapestry of one's life—all the weavings of individual threads from one to another that create something.

Sandra Day O'Connor, former U.S. Supreme Court justice

Those threads that retired Justice O'Connor refers to are your connections—the relationships you build along the way. Virtually all the women we talked to in our project concur that connectedness has been essential to their rise but also to their sense of deeper fulfillment. The data show that people with strong networks and mentors enjoy more promotions, higher pay, and greater work satisfaction. In particular, women leaders benefit from professional development and active career support. And when they lead, they often achieve higher team performance because of their ability to connect.

So, building relationships is part of your day job. It's not just about advancing; it's a part of maintaining your well-being and that of your teams.

Connectedness is core to Centered Leadership because it addresses a deep human need. A leader with strong connections to colleagues and team members can share her sense of meaning and mission—inspiring others to make extraordinary commitment to the work, too. She can also draw wisdom, energy, and joy from those whom she connects with. Xerox CEO Anne Mulcahy told us, "One of the most important ways to be successful is actually to create an army of people who are rooting for you. It's nice to have the support of the person you work for, or a board, but the most important support you can get is from the troops."

The Science of Inclusiveness

Women are naturals at relationship-building. Evolutionary biologists trace this capability to women's prehistoric role, which was to increase the chances that their offspring and the tribe would survive. So, while the male brain continued to react to fear and stress by fighting the threat, fleeing, or freezing, prehistoric women learned to work together and help one another to protect their children and survive. Thus, women developed "social" hormones such as oxytocin, which are released in moments of stress and suppress activity in the amygdala, where aggression originates. This is why, when things go badly in the workplace, men are more likely to start shouting at one another, while women try to smooth over differences. Our ancient survival instincts are kicking in.

In many ways, women benefit from this hardwiring. You're probably better than the men around you at "tending and befriending"—the modern manifestation of our prehistoric survival mechanism, which compels us to take care of the group and look out for its welfare. Clearly this tendency toward inclusiveness can help make you an extremely effective leader, capable of mobilizing talent and inspiring commitment.

Amanda West is the chief innovation officer for the recently merged Thomson Reuters (the marriage of the financial information company and the storied wire service). She depends on strong internal and external networks to succeed and is a natural connector on many dimensions.

The Art of Relationships

For Amanda, connections were a childhood survival mechanism. Early in her life, her family moved to Africa from England, and she went from being a proper English girl to "an African wild child, bare feet running through the bush," she says. "My younger brother and I spent most of our time hanging out, running in circles in the middle of nowhere. I was a keen explorer, even then."

That idyllic time ended abruptly two years later, when Amanda was sent to England for boarding school. "I can remember having to talk myself into the fact that this was a good thing," she recalls. On her own, Amanda found that her happiness and success depended on creating the right relationships. "It's how I survived, having to make my own connections at a very young age. Flying from Zambia to England on my own, staying overnight in Heathrow and then flying on somewhere else." Her return to England did not last. "England didn't work out for me—I was too African by that time. Then I went to this amazing boarding school in Swaziland. That school was my community. You'd probably find a common skill among us—how to become a team."

Amanda's connecting skill helped her much later on. Early in her career, she led a team developing a new business concept. It was a challenge, managing an eclectic collection of talented—and decidedly independent—experts. Used to individuals with individuality, Amanda recalls how she forged "one mission and joint success." She remembers: "We reported to our CEO every quarter, which my team found both terrifying and inspirational. Tom was brutal if he didn't like the direction you were taking. First, it would just be me in front of him, but bit by bit, the whole team joined me; I made sure we had a collective voice. We delivered that project six to twelve months earlier than planned because we were so connected as a team."

Amanda says she never loses the thrill of making new connections. More recently, she reached out to IBM's top R&D executive, who arranged a briefing for Amanda's team. "It was giving me a bad case of butterflies, trying to sort out what we'd talk about for eight hours. I was thinking, 'Why did I do this?' But we got started and the time flew by. These scientists were fabulous! I'm always astounded by the fact that if you ask, most people will actually talk to you," she says. "It reminds you that there are no boundaries, only the ones you make yourself."

Just how does Amanda manage to build strong and powerful relationships with so many men and women? "Listen, listen, listen," she told us. "It's about getting to the point where you have some understanding of what motivates the other person. It's not about what motivates you. Women are naturally better at this, I think. Guys are hunters. We're not. We're nurturers. I know this sounds terribly simplistic, but I do think that's a big part of building relationships."

Long ago, Amanda learned the art of reciprocity—making the first move and offering assistance, to start a two-way connection. "The relationships just formed," she says. "Some of the people—who actively mentor me and who I look up to—are really quite bossy about keeping in touch. I appreciate it hugely, actually, to have people outside of your life bringing perspective to your effectiveness and your impact."

Why We Need Network Design

The downside of our natural connecting abilities is that the way we like to connect is not always the most effective way to network at work. Because women take the time to build relationships, most of us are inclined to keep a small number of deep relationships with like-minded individuals. Men, on the other hand, tend to build broad and shallow networks, giving them a wider range of resources for more career opportunities. This puts women at a disadvantage in the corporation: The typical male executive has a network many times the size of a woman's at the same level.

So, while men are comfortable with transactional relationships, women continue to look for sincere friendship. Some women don't believe in networking because of this very different context. Even if they do, many simply don't have the time to enrich their networks. Often, that's because of trying to get home for the second job (parenting and housekeeping), while men continue relationship-building after hours. Whatever the reason, many women do not allocate the time it takes to build professional networks.

Let's be clear: This part is not optional. You really do need business networking and connecting skills to be an effective leader. It takes a well-populated and balanced network, whether you are corporate or decidedly not. And whether you need to develop closer relationships with senior people or you need to get farther outside your close professional circle, we want you to think about network design explicitly. This is not about meeting strangers in a forced situation. We're talking about the real kind of networking—

creating and maintaining connections with colleagues, customers and clients, mentors and supporters, and friends who help us develop and have positive impact.

At the time of our interview, Amanda was ten days into her new job in the newly merged company. She could not be certain of much—almost everything was changing or new: the company culture, her direct reports, the nature of her job. Amanda was not expecting smooth sailing in the short term. She did not know her new colleagues, and she did not know if her role and skill set would be appreciated by the acquiring Thomson organization, with its heritage of pragmatic, financially driven management. Reuters' culture was more open to experimentation and blue sky ideas. "I think it will take a while. The Thomson businesses are huge and successful in their own right," Amanda says. "I have to strike up relationships that are credible and useful, and hopefully over time, the Thomson executives will learn what they can get from us." This is network design by someone who knows what she's doing.

Clearly, keeping her network fresh is another of Amanda's strengths and one of the things she likes most about her job. "You really have to work at it. These relationships don't come for free. Every week in my diary, I have an entry that says, 'Call people.' I block ninety minutes. I've had some astounding breaks this way, just from nurturing my network." It provides Amanda with fresh ideas, help in getting her projects completed, and ongoing counsel.

At the Core of Networks: Sponsors

That last point is important: Amanda gets protection when she needs it because she develops relationships with sponsors—senior mentors who have the power to make things happen. Yes, you can rise to the top without one, but your journey will be easier—maybe faster—and certainly more enjoyable with someone helping and supporting you. Sponsors are far better than mentors, although you should have both kinds of senior people in your network. Women with mentors are more likely to advance at the same rate as men.

But a sponsor is even more valuable. Your sponsor believes in you and so is willing to stick his or her neck out to create opportunities and to protect you when the chips are down. They don't help you just because it's part of their performance review. You help your sponsor succeed, too, but he or she gets a lot out of the relationship. This makes a sponsor relationship much more gratifying: With a sponsor on your team, you're never really alone.

In retrospect, Amanda's first boss was also her first sponsor. This boss saw something in Amanda and took a chance on her. "He was the guy who pushed me to extremes," she says. "I remember him once giving me some particular business to look after. I really screwed it up—I didn't mean to, but it did not go well. It wasn't a huge piece of business, which was just as well. But I drove my husband absolutely mad at the time because I was distraught about what was unraveling in front of my very eyes." Amanda pleaded with her boss to take her off the assignment. He stunned her by refusing. Then he explained: "You're learning all sorts of things that, frankly, I needed you to learn. This is working out very well."

Amanda found her third (and current) sponsor in the CEO Tom Glocer, who holds the same title in the merged company. She had been asked to present to the board on innovation. "I had to go quite a long way out of my comfort zone to write a persuasive board paper," she says. "And when I presented it I ended up telling Tom, 'We're going to do this and you are going to lead it.' And I'll never forget that he turned around and said, 'Why?' in a rather gruff way. And I thought, 'This isn't going so well.' " Amanda plunged ahead and explained exactly why she believed that only the CEO's visible leadership and involvement could make the innovation effort succeed. "I think that formed the right relationship," she says now. "He knew that I was going to go a bit further than the average person. And I did."

Tom encouraged Amanda to step outside the box, which she did quite happily. Amanda says, "Then he let everyone know that's what we were doing so that we didn't get the business orthodoxies tripping us up." Still, bold ideas have put her close to losing her job more than once. That's when having a sponsor really mattered. For example, she met a wave of internal opposition when her team floated a plan to develop a business to supply localized weather and commodity price information to farmers in India via cell phones. If the plan worked, Thomson Reuters would own a huge and valued information business in India, replicable in other markets. But no one had ever created such a business for this kind of customer. "Now that's really quite risky," says Amanda. "When we sat down and wrote the business plan two years ago, I could see this huge opportunity and along with it huge uncertainty. Everyone in the company who opposed it would make that blindingly obvious statement: 'If you give me the money, I'll make the company twice as much tomorrow.' Many thought we were absolutely mad."

But Amanda knew that Glocer had challenged her team and would back her, too. That made all the difference. "I had come through some pretty rocky moments just prior to that, when we were putting forward these ideas. Very senior people were saying to me, 'There's no way we're doing that. So you better go and sit over there in the back.' And I just kept thinking, 'Ooh. Okay.' They were quite certain I was on the wrong track. I was quite certain that I wasn't. Ultimately, it was only because Tom backed it that we went anywhere."

By now you may be saying, "So, how do I get a sponsor? Who is the right sponsor for me and how do I make that happen?" Further on, we'll show you how to pinpoint who is best suited to help you develop and what you can do to cultivate him or her. If you're well along your own leadership journey, we'll help you to become an effective sponsor. Our feeling is that any company interested in cultivating women leaders would do well to invest in developing an army of sponsors to bring the next generation along.

CHAPTER 12

Your Organization as Family

How do you unleash fifty thousand people to get the job done? It goes back to how do you let them help. We changed from, "Let me tell you the answer" to "What do you think we ought to do?" Did we make them feel like they were worthwhile, or did we make them feel like they weren't at all? So, underlying the change was that fundamental element, and it did, in fact, make it happen.

Brenda Barnes, chairman and CEO, Sara Lee Corporation

When we asked women leaders about connections, almost every one of them spoke about her team and the people in her company as much or even more than about her senior sponsors. They talked about the magic of teams and their pride in seeing the organization pulling together. They reported the same satisfaction from watching their people grow that they derive from their own families. Indeed, they often described their organizations as families.

While it's hardly a breakthrough discovery that inclusiveness is a valuable leadership trait, the emphasis that our women leaders placed on it was too strong to ignore. As we learned, women are biologically primed to seek out and nurture relationships. The ancient reflex to "tend and befriend" survives today, passed down through social hormones that still influence our survival—and our success.

A great example is Xerox CEO Anne Mulcahy, who joined Xerox in 1976 fresh out of college and never left. Her instinct for tending, befriending, and including has shaped her leadership. Famous for its exemplary corporate citizenship, in 2001 Xerox was caught up in an SEC investigation involving accounting abuses that caused the company to reverse $6.4 billion in reported revenue. The stock went into free fall. In stepped Anne, who led Xerox to a remarkable recovery, made possible because everyone pulled together with her. Her style as CEO, as it turned out, was exactly what Xerox needed in that moment for survival.

Family Model

Anne recalls her childhood as simple, normal, very nurturing. The Mulcahys were unusual in one way: They treated Anne, the only girl, exactly the same way they treated their four sons. "Expectations were as high for me as they were for my brothers," Anne says, "so I feel quite blessed that I grew up in an environment with a ton of support, both from family and friends."

Anne chose Xerox to begin with because she prized its reputation for values, like inclusiveness and social responsibility. Once inside, she found it to be a nurturing environment. "For the first maybe twenty years of my career, it was all about enjoying what I was doing, feeling that I was valued, making a contribution, and not a lot more than that," she explains. It became a family of sorts for Anne, and many of her colleagues felt the same connection.

She started in sales, because she liked the focus on quantitative results and financial rewards. It was still early days for women in corporate America, but she trusted in the values her parents had taught her: She could accomplish whatever a man could, if she did the work. It only occurred to her when she didn't move up that there might be unseen factors working against her. "I remember interviewing for sales manager assignments after a few years and not being terribly successful," she says. "One of the great things about my upbringing was that I never really thought when I didn't get an assignment that it had anything to do with being a woman."

Anne pushed and finally got that management assignment— for a team selling to the state of Maine—not exactly a booming opportunity. On top of that, her team members were very senior men who had been in place a long time. The deck was not stacked in her favor. Would you take that bet?

She did! The assignment was a turning point for her. "It was one of those great experiences where, when you give people a chance and you get to know them, and you actually work together, people step up to the plate," Anne recalls. "All of a sudden, they begin to aspire to do more than they would have under normal circumstances." She learned that you can sometimes accomplish great things when it doesn't seem possible—through teams. She also loved bringing out the best in people and realized she had a knack for leading.

Anne kept taking on larger challenges until she was running New York City, the best territory in North America. She was ready to move up into corporate management, but with young children at home, she had other priorities, too. In what seemed to her friends like career suicide, she turned down a promotion to run the corporate quality initiative and report directly to the president of the Xerox U.S. division. She said no thanks; it would have meant moving her family to Rochester for the role.

Even then, it was not a hard decision for Anne to make, she says. Instead, she took a marketing position that ultimately led to a job in human resources, an area that had never been on her radar screen but wound up providing her big break. "It was a time when the company was going through radical change, and the HR job was enticing because it was about change management and organizational effectiveness," she explains. "HR became an enabler for the company's future, and I was excited by that." That job turned out to be pivotal in her learning about leadership. "I really enjoy fixing things, whether they're people problems or business problems," she says. "With enough smart people around you and energy against a problem, it's solvable."

Along the way, Anne has maintained her connections across the organization with a host of people who have contributed to her success. "I don't think there's anybody who's been more helped than I have," she says. "Keeping in touch with and having those connections to the people on the ground is so valuable, in terms of having knowledge that allows you to provide direction to run the company. I am just an extraordinary beneficiary of a very, very large cadre of people who have been supportive and wanted to help. It is truly the success factor here."

The reach and depth of her connections proved enormously helpful to Anne when she became CEO and faced the challenge of turning the company around. From the outset, she approached the task as a team effort on a company-wide scale. "I think if you let people know they really are the keys to the kingdom, they feel that," she explains. "Xerox people knew that I recognized that the only way to get things done here was to have their hearts and minds. That was invigorating and motivating for them."

Many CEOs don't get the results they want because they don't have that kind of connection, Anne says. "I've watched really smart, brilliant leaders who just don't have followership. If you can have only one thing, focus on followership. There are lots of smart people who can make decisions and help run companies, but followership truly is the key for big companies, where alignment is everything. That's how you get things done. I think the employees knew that I believed in them, that I cared, that I recognized the power that comes from the alignment of people around objectives. And if that's visible, then I think they'll kill for you here, and they did."

Broad connections throughout the organization also impose a new set of responsibilities on the inclusive leader. "They come to expect something of you, they know who you are," Anne says. "The need to continue to make sure that you don't disappoint them or the external world is the most significant set of pressures you have as a CEO or as a leader in anything. The one thing you never want to do is let people down. So, you have to make sure that you continue to live up to the expectations and the privilege of having a job like this." This level of inclusiveness means establishing and maintaining trust—something that you can do only if you are true to yourself.

When community develops in the workplace, it makes the job rewarding and it helped Anne through the difficult times. "It's about relationships and experiences. It's an emotional bank that you build up. It compounds over time," she says. "I don't know how people could do these jobs in a clinical way. It's got to have emotion and passion associated with it to really bring out the best in a company. It's unmatchable here. Maybe women are a bit more comfortable talking about companies using words like *love* and *emotion* and *passion* than men are."

For Anne, love and inclusiveness go all the way back to her

family. And she carries it forward every day in the way she leads. It's one and the same.

Letting Instinct Guide

Anne Mulcahy has flourished by listening to her instincts. By following her impulse to tend and befriend, she truly included a broad swathe of the Xerox "family" in her network. And nearly every woman we met who talked about her team echoed Anne's sentiments. Are you seeing parallels in your life?

Think about how important social and professional groups have been to women. History is filled with examples of women's groups that survived for generations and provided unique comfort to their members; for example, suffragist groups achieved victory through group action and support, and women's political forums exist even today. Or think about the informal groups—the sewing circles our grandmothers joined or the bridge clubs that many of our mothers love. You may be a member of a book club today or a group filling a similar instinctive need for belonging.

Wanting to belong is also a trait that can help us lead and connect with a wider world of women in our chosen fields. For example, the Stanford Graduate School of Business creates groups of women who meet weekly during the two years they are at business school. These groups, called Women in Management, often survive for years after the women graduate. Many women cite that experience as one of their most memorable in business school.

And if our instinct for membership helps us achieve progress through connections, it also helps us convert a hostile environment to a more open and safer one. We can prove this, but we don't have to; if you have ever worked in an all-male environment, you know what we mean. Women are skillful group builders. Leaders using inclusiveness create a better environment for everyone around them, setting off a virtuous cycle of positive energy and the new ideas that come with it. As Anne showed us, when female leaders cultivate and care for the members of their teams, they discover that employees become determined to do the most amazing things they are capable of. Then, when one team succeeds, its success makes it easy to extend the experience of inclusiveness to more teams, leading to more success for the organization.

Practicing inclusiveness has related benefits for leaders, too. Leaders who cultivate the people around them are able to read their emotional cues. It's no wonder that many women are great at EQ (emotional quotient)—gleaning insight from more than what words alone tell you. Numerous studies have shown that women understand more about what's going on in a given situation than men. And having these additional sources of information makes you a better decision-maker. You can prove it to yourself. After a meeting, ask the women who attended what happened. Then try that with the men. In most cases, the women will remember much more about the meeting, and will mention emotional cues that passed the men by. What's more, some of those cues may explain mind-sets and behaviors not spoken, and those will influence your decisions in some cases.

It gets even better. Though we're often told we should tone down our emotions in the workplace, using our instincts and capabilities—seeing the emotional truth of a situation and spending time nurturing to bring out the talent in others—can make us extraordinary leaders.

Put Your Instincts to Good Use

You may already be an inclusive leader. If you're not there yet, you can draw on instincts to become one. Think about it. What draws you to connect with others? How does it make you feel when you're leading a group versus when you're working on your own? Take a moment to reflect on how others have nurtured you. Remember the times when you needed an open door so you could say what was on your mind? What about the times when you didn't know how to proceed and looked to a senior colleague for some guidance? What may have helped you then—a clear road map, a great idea, assurance, or even a gentle shove forward—could be the very things you can use to help others.

Even if you're a passionate competitor, you may still feel more satisfied being part of a team. For many women, belonging is a very real source of fulfillment. So if you're not part of a group today, think about how you could change that. Is there one in your industry or in your company that you could join?

Could you form a group—bringing together women with a shared commitment? Look beyond the office if you can. It can be refreshing to be part of a group where the dramas of your company are not known. You can get a fresh perspective and meet people who value your contribution to the group, regardless of what's going on at work.

Once you have unleashed the power of inclusiveness for yourself, applying it at work becomes easier. Start, as many women leaders do, by making sure that the members of your team are individuals you believe in. Once you're surrounded by talented people, you'll want to develop them, care for them, and give them credit. The more you crow about them, the better you'll feel.

Men are coachable, too, so don't exclude them! Your gift of

reading cues (it comes from mothering infants who communicate through facial expression) will be of great value to them. Many men just miss these clues. But reading emotional signals is a skill that can be learned and taught.

Inclusiveness—cultivating team success and feelings of belonging—is one of the advantages that women bring to leadership. Deploying this skill helps not only us but the people and organizations around us, too. The positive cycle you create leads to greater success than you could have ever imagined. So take the advantage and run with it.

CHAPTER 13

Reciprocity Forms Relationships

I was chatting with an executive in one of our portfolio companies, and I asked him for counsel about my young son, who likes computers so much it's a little distressing to me. Well, he turned to me and said, "Don't limit him. Let him play as much as he wants. When I was growing up, my parents decided to let me go crazy on my computer. That's why I'm the kick-ass engineer/product guy I am today!" I thought hard about that. At the end of the day, that's how you build relationships. It's both sides sharing.

Patricia Nakache, partner, Trinity Ventures

Building relationships is something that women excel at, right? We're hardwired to build them; we reach out to others almost instinctively. But relationships at work are another story altogether.

It's something that men do, and they do it well. Their approach to relationship-building starts with their own hardwired social instincts. How is it that men can walk onto a basketball court and pick up a game with total strangers? Why do many men enjoy sitting with forty thousand other fans in a stadium? "If you make a list of activities that are done in large groups, you are likely to have a list of things that men do and enjoy more than women: team sports, politics, large corporations, economic networks," psychologist Roy Baumeister writes.

More important, because these networks are based on the most casual connections, they can be overtly transactional. At the same time, the connections can be extremely powerful, because both parties see the potential to benefit. That's reciprocity in a nutshell. Both parties benefit. It's that simple. And it's why broad and shallow networks dominate most corporate workplaces—and why they remain overwhelmingly male.

With an inclination to want deep relationships, many women are put off by the instant bonhomie they see when men gather in groups. Men often say it's all about the adage "You scratch my back and I'll scratch yours." That's a surefire turnoff for many women who experience negative feelings from this show of reciprocity in its rawest state.

The idea of cultivating someone for the sole purpose of trying to get something out of them just doesn't feel right. Women give many reasons for not making the first move: It's presumptuous, the other person is too busy, the other person will reject them, it's crassly commercial, and so on. Interestingly, women who routinely practice reciprocity with their spouses, children, and friends are less likely to reach out in professional contexts.

Well, it's time to reframe. Remember that reciprocity is the essence of the Golden Rule: "Do unto others as you would have them do unto you." Reciprocity is what Jonathan Haidt calls the "glue that holds societies together," which is why it is enshrined in nearly every religion, from Buddhism to Zoroastrianism. Not only is reciprocity important for our success as citizens and human beings, but it also builds our professional success: What you give to others when you provide help or encouragement, you will also receive. And it doesn't mean relinquishing our gift—and desire—for making deeper connections.

Learning how to reciprocate helped Denise Incandela, president of Saks Direct (Saks Fifth Avenue's Internet business), turn the start-up into an ongoing entity. Denise planned Saks Direct when she joined in 1999, launched it soon thereafter, almost lost it when the Internet bubble burst, and then nursed it back to health. Reciprocity in her relationships made all the difference between failure and success.

Before and After Reciprocity

Denise arrived at Saks fresh from a five-year consulting career. It was not an easy transition, she notes. "When I first took the job, I was building this website that was very vague as to exactly what it was going to be. I was building an organization, too, but I had no experience running one. Those early years were tough. I was working terribly hard. It was very stressful building the skill set I needed, and I made lots and lots of mistakes."

Saks.com launched at the peak of Internet euphoria. Denise and her colleagues built an infrastructure and organization to support a $100 million business, believing that sales would quickly grow to $500 million. "In our first year we only reached $14 million in sales," Denise says. "Imagine the devastation. We lost way too much money and I had to lay off 40 percent of the people I had just hired. I didn't have a safety net; I didn't have a contingency plan. I didn't say, 'We are going to slowly build this as we earn our way into it.' I was naïve. I thought it would work out and it didn't. It was emotionally horrible."

In hindsight, Denise sees clearly that the core problem was not just the overly ambitious business plan and subsequent over-building. What sandbagged her as a leader was what she didn't do—her start-up lacked important connections to experienced executives across the business who could have helped Saks.com and Denise.

How could this have happened to someone so capable? When she joined Saks, Denise thought she was smart enough to just roll up her sleeves, work sixteen hours a day, and get it done. But that wasn't enough. "What I didn't realize is that I needed to build relationships and that I was never going to succeed on my own," she says now. "I was only going to succeed by having other people vested in the business's success." When the business failed, she says, "I had a moment where I realized that no one else really cared whether my business succeeded. That was entirely my fault. I needed to take accountability for that."

Denise found herself alone and in low spirits. "I closed off for about six months. I was just coming to work and going home," she recalls. "But I didn't want to go on in that permanent state of despair, so I told myself, 'You either have to find something else to do or you have to make this work. You have so little precious time on this earth—why would you want to waste it living like this?' It was my wake-up call. I told myself, 'You either get excited about it and make it profitable, which is what you should've done in the first place, or you go.' And then I realized I could turn this thing around and get it back."

With an improved outlook and critical support from her boss, Denise set about curing the business. Her boss helped get her moving by giving her the tough-love feedback she needed. "I had made a bunch of relationship bungles, and he came and told me what I did wrong," says Denise. "Then he talked to the people that I made mistakes with and said, 'We need to give her a second chance. She's learning. She gets it.' The one thing I would also say that's been very helpful for me—more so over time because it comes with maturity—is being able to take feedback."

Denise knows that she was lucky to get that second chance. "Frankly, most people who had that type of experience launching Internet sites were laid off." So, she started over, this time putting reciprocity first. "I began by thinking through who was important to the success of the business," she explains. "The way I approached these relationships was not about what I was going to get out of them but what I could do for this person. How do I get this person vested in this business? The way that I'm going to get them vested is not just by pitching myself or talking about what the business needs, but by actually coming up with something that I could do for them. A big part of my relationship-building has been thinking about the business, not just from my point of view but from other points of view, and about what this business could do for other areas in the company—like driving traffic to the store and featuring brands they were investing in."

Slowly but surely, Denise built bridges. One of her biggest challenges was winning over a particular senior executive who clearly resented the newcomer Denise. "She must have thought, 'Here comes this young whippersnapper with a Wharton MBA and all these ideas on how to change things.' That's not how she thought things should be done, so she was a deterrent, a real naysayer," Denise says. On the advice of another senior colleague, Denise took the executive to lunch and confronted her. "I told her, 'We started out on the wrong foot, and I get the feeling you don't like me and don't respect me, and I'm very sorry for that. What can I do to mend this relationship? It's really important to me that we work well together.' She was completely shocked. Sometimes being confrontational in a professional way is necessary. Within a year I had built a very solid foundation of relationships, to the point where there are cheerleaders now throughout the organization. That executive and I became much, much closer."

Forging strong relationships—with peers, senior executives, and her team—made the difference between failure and success for Denise. "I have a fabulous team that I've built over the years," she says. "Working with really smart people who are passionate about what they do certainly energizes me." Sharing the success with people she cares about and learning from them has made Denise a stronger, more confident leader, too. "At some point, I started realizing that I was getting good at what I was doing and I loved going to work," she says. "I still have lots to learn, but I know the people side has probably been one of the most important lessons for me in my career."

Looking back, Denise says, "My first baby was Saks.com and my second baby was my daughter. I don't think my daughter would be happy to hear that—or my husband—but it's really true!"

Forming Relationships

The best connectors know that relationships start when you offer something first, well in advance of when you may need help in return. But what if you're not sure of what you have to offer a senior colleague or boss? It's there waiting to be discovered.

When people receive something, they feel an obligation to reciprocate. This is true regardless of your culture or home country, because reciprocity is deeply ingrained in human behavior—our ancestors learned early on that if they shared food when they had plenty, they would receive food when they needed it. Today, the pre-emptive gift has become a proven sales promotion, used by everyone from marketers with free samples to charities with tokens. We naturally feel obliged to give after we've received.

You can deploy reciprocity for a better purpose—to initiate a relationship with someone you don't know or don't know well. In this case, an exchange of information may be a very fair deal. One high-profile woman leader told us about two candidates she was considering for an assignment. One called and asked for the job directly. That's fine initiative. But the other called to say that she had been thinking about the challenge of the work and offered her thoughts in a white paper, which the leader found helpful. Which candidate do you think she chose?

If you still find the idea of reciprocity a bit alien—start off small. Try sending an article that you think might be of interest to an executive you worked with recently. You'll be surprised how pleased most people are to hear from you. And pay attention—often people give you clues that make it easy to get a reciprocal relationship started. They talk about something they need and it turns out it's something you can give. Other times, you need to do a little homework and brainstorming. Start by finding out more about the person you want to get to know. Now, think of the gift you can give that will help.

Here's a starter list of what you already have to offer:

1. **Your own know-how.** You may have relevant analysis or access to knowledge that is of value to the person you'd like in your network. If you want to find a way to be helpful to someone who is senior to you, think about what information she might need to know and the best way to get it to her. For example,

perhaps you could find the information on a podcast and load it onto an MP3 player, which you could lend. Alternatively, read a relevant book and send a summary.

2. **Your network.** Often you know people who can help those you want to know. Even for people more senior than you, chances are you know someone who could be of assistance. Look through your address book for ideas about people your target might find interesting or helpful to meet.

3. **Your radar.** Sometimes the most important thing for the other person is to learn what people in the organization think. A senior executive does not have the same access to the grapevine that you have; she rarely hears the unvarnished truth. Compile what you've heard, synthesize the message, and present it fairly.

4. **Your time.** It's worth more than you think. Whether you're taking on tasks from an overloaded colleague or helping someone get more done, your gift of time will be remembered. Start by volunteering to help with a project close to the person you want to get to know.

5. **Your ear.** You can be a good listener and a sounding board. As one woman leader told us, she prizes hearing honesty, a scarce commodity in her organization. As she rehearses for an important meeting, she wants people to tell her exactly what they think, as long as they communicate with kindness.

6. **Family assistance.** Most people's first priorities are their families. Think about what you might do to help out a child or spouse of the person you are trying to get to know better. Maybe her spouse is trying to learn more about an industry and you have relevant contacts. It would be easy to arrange an introduction and start to build a relationship.

7. **Your questions.** Asking good questions may turn you into someone's valued counselor. This is not simple. You have to do

your homework to figure out what kind of questions would help the other person advance her thinking. "What if?" types of questions often come in handy.

8. **Your resourcefulness.** Let your imagination roam. Where could you find an opening with someone you want to know better? A woman leader we know became friendly with a junior colleague who volunteered to revamp her presentations with better designs. Delighted, she then helped the helper.

9. **Your open offer.** Even if you don't have something specific to offer now, letting the other person know you are available to help is a form of reciprocity, albeit one that comes at a price to the other person. You are forcing her to do the upfront work—giving you a task—which makes your offer less compelling. Use this approach when you're out of other ideas. But it never hurts to offer.

Connecting is also a matter of chemistry and disposition. Outgoing people love the thrill of meeting new people and seem to meet them everywhere. But if you're an introvert, just the thought of walking into a roomful of unfamiliar faces can give you agita. Putting yourself out there makes you feel vulnerable, and that feels risky. But give yourself a big reason to meet those people (your career, your happiness), and you'll soon find you are engaged and enjoying yourself.

Use Reciprocity on a Regular Basis

Whether you think of reciprocity as a trade or something more meaningful, we strongly believe it's an indispensible tool for leaders—on their way up and when they're on top. You may still be uncomfortable with making the first move. But remember, that man down the hall doesn't hesitate to reach out and offer assistance—with the clear goal of one day getting something back. So please take those first, uncomfortable steps and give yourself permission to reach out regularly.

Don't think of reciprocity as mechanical: perform a favor, wait, receive something in return, repeat. Keep in mind that you're building a capability. The time between giving and receiving could be years, so reciprocity ought to become your regular habit. Sow those seeds today.

Finally, don't keep score. Not everyone will reciprocate in exactly the way you want. Sometimes you may never know how the gift is repaid. There will be people who take without giving; if you come up against a serial taker, just move on. For everyone else, you'll enjoy the good feelings that come with helping others. That is a gift, too.

CHAPTER 14

The Tapestry You Weave

We are all human beings. If you are open-minded and you send out positive vibes that you are willing to learn, if you open yourself rather than close in, you will have other people walk into your life.

Carol Shen, managing director, Estée Lauder Companies China

Forget those chilly hotel ballrooms. Forget your elevator speech. Leave your business cards in your bag. We're about to go networking, and none of those items will be necessary.

The fact is you already have a network but you're probably not cultivating it the way you should. We'll show you how to use it to help you grow professionally. That's not all your network can do. It can help you make a difference in the world. And it does one more good thing. Imagine the environment where you most want to be. Then fill it with people, each of whom offers something special. Now place yourself among them. Feel the warmth? That sense of belonging you feel is a basic human need and it's what network design is all about.

Designing your network can be an exciting adventure, even for someone who is naturally shy. Carolyn Buck Luce has made networking one of her top skills, despite her reserved nature. Today, she is global pharmaceutical sector leader at Ernst & Young LLP and a well-known voice on women's issues.

The Road to New Destinations

At the age of eight, Carolyn set her sights on becoming a world leader. "I had really big ambitions as a little girl," she says. "I was very captivated by John F. Kennedy. He said we could go to the moon and I believed him. He said we should volunteer for international service. I heard him. I really responded to that call for service."

Carolyn sees herself as the combination of her mother—an outspoken champion for reform, overcoming intense shyness to run for judge after working for twenty-five years as a lawyer—and her father—also a lawyer, with a big personality and an appetite for risk. "As the middle child, it just seemed that I was always trying to climb higher, or run faster, or jump into the lake when I couldn't swim," she says. "I always felt on the edge, trying new things. I have a natural question that's always in my head, which is 'Why not?' I have always hated to be boxed in."

Coming of age in the late 1960s, Carolyn admits that perhaps she tried too many things. She was rebellious and decidedly not a good student. "No one thought I would be able to accomplish anything," she recalls. "I was experimenting with all the appropriate and inappropriate social norms of the times. But I learned that I had the control to know when enough's enough—that no matter what people said, only I could know what was right for me."

Suspended from high school in her senior year after organizing a walkout and teach-in about the invasion of Cambodia, Carolyn failed to get into college at first. She wound up at Ohio State, because it had rolling admissions. Once there, Carolyn "knew" exactly what she needed to do: transfer to Georgetown, where she could pursue her ambition to lead. Suddenly, she had to get straight A's. Done. Next, she switched majors from Romance languages to Russian and Business (doing four years in three). Done. Then she decided her next step would be landing a job in the foreign service. Done. Carolyn was on her way.

Posted to the Soviet Union, Carolyn got a crash course in connecting and networking—to survive. "I was stationed in Tashkent, Uzbekistan, Azerbaijan, Baku Azerbaijan, and then Moscow, in a hostile environment," she says. "Because I wasn't a native speaker, people weren't going to believe what I had to say. I needed to be able to reach that crowd and relate to them in a personal way, so that on both sides we could leave our suspicions behind. During eighteen months of focusing on how you establish relationships under really difficult circumstances, I learned the importance of being other-centered, the importance of understanding someone else's agenda. I learned to understand not only what they were thinking but what they were feeling, and I learned to take responsibility for that."

Life unfolded, with ups but also downs, and they spurred Carolyn to action. She would set her next long-range goal and then explicitly redesign her network to help get where she wanted to be. She started with people she already knew and from there got help meeting new ones. "I'm a big planner," she told us. "I've always set out my ten-year goals and then tried to get here from there. Part of building my plan was to include five interesting destinations that I knew nothing about. I'm not talking about physical destinations.

I'm talking about 'What do I want to learn because it's important to me to know?' "

She really honed those skills in her forties, when her marriage ended and the demands of a decadelong career in banking were too much for a single mother. "I left banking when I was getting the divorce," she says. "Then I had my own broker-dealer, but financially it was too much pressure to build my own company with children to support. I wanted them to know that the most important thing was supporting them."

So she set out to find her next career. "Once you choose your destinations, you have to ask, 'Who do I need to meet?' You have to be very focused on meeting those people." Carolyn recognized she needed different types of relationships, each with its protocols. "I actually created a board with different colors for each destination and began to map my network," she says.

She took each destination and identified the first two or three people to meet. Once she learned about them and shared her interests, she asked for recommendations of people they thought she should meet. In turn, those people helped her expand her thinking and, importantly, her network of relationships. "It's a great satisfaction being able to create your constellation of relationships, and to see how they grow," Carolyn observes. "All of a sudden, you realize that you're in the middle of it. People are coming to you and you can help them. That's how I got to Ernst & Young. It wasn't on my radar screen."

For Carolyn, strategic alliances are the essence of her network: "Who's in your network? How do you know when you can help them and when they can help you?" Also, she stresses the need to be diligent in network building—size does matter. "For every sponsor, you need five mentor relationships," she says. "And for every five mentors, you probably need twenty-five strategic alliances. Men do this extremely well. But too often women say, 'I have a mentor. I'm done.' Did you know that up to 50 percent of a company's intellectual capital is the company's relational assets? Well, probably 75 percent of an individual's capital is relationships."

Carolyn is great at all the mechanics of building a web of strategic alliances and counting how many mentors, allies and sponsors she needs. But the real secret to Carolyn's networking success is her empathy and warmth. "I'm very shy by nature, but I have a natural bent for wanting to know people." she says. "Left to my own devices, I'd never go to a party. But once I'm there, I engage. And I'm always very interested in who they are, what they're thinking, and what they're feeling. I've rarely met anyone I didn't like. There's something to like about everyone. A related lesson for me—and I still work on it—is: The best way to learn about others is less about me and more about them."

Carolyn used the same exercise again at fifty: "I knew that by the time I turned sixty, I was going to want 'optionality' and to be in a position to make a difference. So I picked a political party to help. At that point, I'd never done fund-raising. I picked a university. At that point, I was not a published thinker, nor was I engaged in teaching at a major academic institution. I asked, 'How do I do more on women's leadership outside of work?' Then, I picked foundations. I also picked pharmaceuticals as a new area at work."

Her advice is to get focused early and spend the time to plan your network. "You can't build a network when you need it," she points out. "Then, it's too late. You have to have built it before. It sounds very 'planful.' It's more like dreaming."

In her role as teacher and mentor, Carolyn has given a great deal of thought to why some of us don't deploy our natural connecting instincts more successfully at work. "We build relationships based on getting to know each other personally," she says. "But when we come to work, we feel we've got to turn that relationship-building ability into business. That feels like imposing, and women don't impose on their friends; women help their friends. We have to recognize that building a network is not an imposition, particularly if you're focused on how you can help.

"Women have the formula backward. Here we have this natural ability to give and we aren't giving. My idea of strategic alliances unblocks that. You're initiating a valued exchange. I'm interested in what you're doing. You might be interested in what I'm doing. Let's share information. You never know when we might need each other."

Today, Carolyn's latest destination map has given her many new connections in business, academia and philanthropy. She also has what she calls her hand-picked board of directors, a half-dozen individuals whom she regards as her role models. "They've had very successful careers and have become the people I would like to be," she says. "I met them over the years and asked them one by one to be board members. Each has a purpose and a skill I value. They know each other, because they're all friends of mine, but they've never met as a group. The push me to make sure I'm doing the right things for the right reasons. When I want to be reflective, these are the people I trust. The board is not just around for professional issues. I use them to reflect on the really important parts of my life, including my jobs as a parent, a daughter, a spouse."

For Carolyn, connecting with people via destinations is what helps you define meaning in life. "Nothing holds you back except your own mental models," she says. "If everything you have is folded up into one thing, your job for example, then you're not living life to the fullest. To me, discovering and creating meaning is about having a series of important projects that you're working on at the same time—the community project, the friend reclamation project, the learning-a-new-skill project, the giving-back-to-your-family project, whatever it is."

You're Connected

For many women, networking is like eating your vegetables—you know it's good for you, but you'd rather not. And it's easy to find examples of bad networking—someone feigning interest in whatever the most important person in the room is interested in, blatantly out for herself. No wonder many of us prefer not to go there.

Networks are not about politics. They're about reaching out, showing interest in another person, offering help. They also happen to be a key to personal and professional growth. So let's reframe networks in a way to entice you: A developmental network is all the people who take "an active interest in—and action to advance—your career." Now that's something to get excited about.

A good place to begin your network design is to take inventory of who you know who can help you grow and succeed. Here's what we suggest: List everyone in your network today who meets these two criteria: (1) people you have worked with, either directly or in sufficient proximity, in the past two years; (2) people you had moderate contact with over the past two years. (You may want to go back further for individuals who had extensive exposure to you in the past.)

Next, think about how influential each person is in your career. How influential are they in your organization? How connected are they? Now, consider the type of relationships in your network—think carefully about who you know in different organizations, industries, roles, and social groups. Do you know senior executives outside your firm who could provide guidance or even be a sponsor—creating new opportunities for you? Don't forget to consider the relationships that give you a sense of belonging and meaning. Those people may be further afield from you professionally and you may not be thinking of them as part of your network.

Once you have listed the people in your network, you're ready to place your relationships in the network design map. The horizontal axis pinpoints how comfortable you are working with each individual. The vertical axis pinpoints that person's power. Use the exhibit below to guide you.

Who's in your "sweet spot"—the upper right quadrant? If there are many individuals in that box, you're in great shape. That's where you'll have, or be able to cultivate, your sponsors. If no one's there who fits the bill, that's perfectly normal. Having used this exercise with hundreds of young women, we know that most women need more names in that box. Indeed, you may find that the most

Network Mapping Exercise

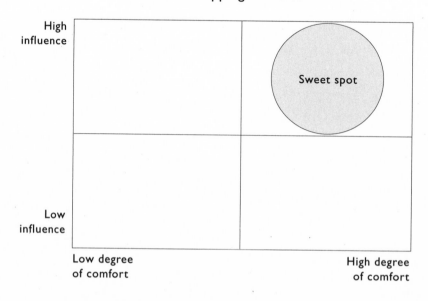

crowded box is the lower right—populated with colleagues whose friendship means a lot but who don't wield the power and influence to further your development. Part of Carolyn's strategy was to fill that box—a great idea to jump-start network design. But don't stop there.

Take a look at that upper left box—the influential people who are not yet pulling for you. Is it because you haven't stepped up to get to know them? Often, those influential people seem unapproachable, intimidating. Maybe the gossip about them has colored your view. One senior woman told us that she avoided working with a certain senior executive early in her career because of what she had heard. When she ignored it and approached him, she found it was fun to work together. Eventually, he became one of her most important sponsors, a relationship that lasted many years. Remember that what you hear in the hallway is not always true. And even if it is, it may not be true for you.

As you look at your network design, draw your own conclusions. How balanced is it? Where do you need to invest? And is it time to go out into the world and find more people to get to know?

Become a Connector

Our essential network advice in a word? Diversify! As Carolyn teaches, think well outside your own business unit, division or even company; don't limit your potential. Each organization represents a unique social system. More systems create more possibilities. Also, a diverse network improves your knowledge by increasing the breadth of information you pick up and providing alternate viewpoints.

It's particularly important when you're thinking about a significant change. People who know you are conditioned to think about you in one way. They're unconsciously biased. In addition, people in your company and your profession may be blind to opportunities in other fields. If you are planning a career transformation, access to new connections will be extremely important. During such times of transition, sometimes a little creativity can open new doors, but it takes a fresh pair of eyes to see opportunity. Even if you're settled in, remaining open to new connections and ideas is never a bad thing. It keeps you growing.

Another way to think about your relationships is in the context of formal and informal networks. In your organization, are senior mentors assigned for your development? Programs like these are established with the best of intentions. But, for our money, they don't match the power of informal networks. Informal networks are the ones you weave. They develop organically, based on shared interests and mutual affinity. As you can imagine, they are significantly more influential to a career than the formal kind. So travel beyond your assigned advisors. This is one time when going far afield is a good thing! And look behind you to bring along younger colleagues, too. They're already looking at you as a part of their network. It's never too early to lead.

How can you get started? As Carolyn suggests, set your long-term goals and identify five destinations that really excite you (making sure only one of them is connected to your work). We agree on the number five and strongly encourage you not to stop short. It helps to put several irons in the fire, particularly at the start of an adventure, when you don't know what (or more aptly, who) you will find.

Then, using the "six degrees of separation" rule, figure out who you already know who could help you take the first few steps toward those destinations. Five people you know can connect you to more; relationship math is exponential. Ask your colleagues if they know people in other companies who would be interested in meeting on a topic you are pursuing. Use a broad checklist to brainstorm all possible connections: family, friends of friends, members of professional organizations, customers and clients, neighbors, classmates, and employees.

You're on your way! You'll soon be meeting thirty or forty or more new acquaintances across your five destinations. It's a joy to stand back and see what you've created—a community of interested and interesting people who have already supported you by sharing something of value.

But we're not there yet. Remember, like other living things, networks decay over time without active care. After all, it's not just about the people you know, it's about the quality of your relationships. You can buy a special software program to keep track of your network activity, but we're fans of plain old pen and paper or a simple spreadsheet to track which relationships you're cultivating and how often you reach out. It takes several interactions before people start to know you.

We love Carolyn's wall-size people map with colors and network lines, because it's fun to create and, once it starts to fill up, it's satisfying to use. You'll find interesting patterns on it. Another way to enrich your network further is to broker introductions within it. Become a connector.

And stay focused on personal development—yours and everyone you've placed on the map. After all, the more you help someone, the more likely they are likely to help you, and the better you'll feel. Reciprocity in action again!

One day, like Carolyn, you may see that what you have really created is a life map. "I looked across my destinations to find common themes, which in turn helped me shape a vision of my purpose: to help women and children who can't help themselves," she says. "I've been able to connect that purpose with my responsibilities as a mother because I've taught my own children how to get the most out of life. I'm their counselor on destinations and networks. And that's been more important to me than making the best peanut butter and jelly sandwich."

CHAPTER 15

On the Shoulders of Sponsors

I attached my star to probably the most powerful and thoughtful person in the city, David Rockefeller. I thought, "I can be the mechanic who uses and leverages his power and his commitment to New York City to get these neighborhoods rebuilt." Now, that's the magic.

Kathryn Wylde, president and CEO, Partnership for New York City

Do you have someone at work who "has your back"? Someone who makes sure you receive the recognition and success you deserve? Someone who creates opportunities for you to shine? That's a sponsor. If you have one, treasure this relationship. Make no mistake about it: Almost all the successful leaders we know had sponsors who assisted their ascent.

Not yet on your way? We'll show you how you can cultivate a sponsor. And if someone is your sponsor already, we congratulate you and hope that you'll become one, too. You'll be paid back in joy for your generosity of trust, time, and effort.

Ruth Porat is a vice chair of Morgan Stanley, a mother of three, and a breast cancer survivor—not once but twice over. Ruth has cultivated sponsors and relied on them throughout her career, from early on, when she was one of the rare women in investment banking until now, as a senior player. Her sponsors help her thrive on the work she loves.

Ruth's Story

Ruth taught us the distinction between a mentor and a sponsor. There are two key differences. First, mentors dispense wisdom whereas sponsors get involved. Second, a sponsor believes in you; a mentor may not go that far. As you read this story, watch for the signs of both.

When she was a second-year associate, the chairman of a consumer products client called one of the managing directors of Ruth's firm to say he expected a woman to lead the board presentation; naturally, his consumers were all women, and a woman's viewpoint was essential. So the managing director called Ruth in and told her she would present. "I'd never been in a boardroom, let alone made a presentation to a board," Ruth says. "I was petrified. And he said, 'Sink or swim. You're in. Go.' "

She swam. "It was awesome," Ruth recalls. "I can, to this day, remember the mistake I made. But I can remember it was overall good. He took a risk on me." Ruth's perseverance and determination are a part of her makeup and why she found herself on Wall Street to begin with. She was born in England, where her father was at university with the dream of bringing his family to America. He had fled the approaching Holocaust, realizing that the only way to get to America was to solve a need that somebody had. He taught himself physics and when Ruth was three, he secured a teaching job at Harvard. The family moved to Massachusetts, then to California, back to England, and finally settled in California for good when Ruth was ten. It's no surprise that perseverance, learning, and risk-taking are a part of Ruth's makeup.

Hard work is, too. Ruth's mother was also a professional, a psychologist who always worked. "When I got home from school, nobody was ever there. I had to do everything on my own," Ruth recalls. "To me, it was obvious that I would work."

So Ruth studied economics at Stanford and moved to Washington, D.C., to work for the Department of Justice. But Ruth didn't stay in that field. "When I was in business school, all of a sudden I realized there was this thing called mergers and acquisitions; it fascinated me because it had a little bit of strategy, but then you actually could implement a transaction."

In those days, Wall Street had three white-shoe firms, and Morgan Stanley was at the top. Ruth found its people, ethics, and culture to her liking, and so joined the M&A department in 1987—just in time for the crash. She remembers thinking, "What have I done? Where's my career going to go now?"

Drawing on her strengths, Ruth worked hard and remembers enjoying the work. "You counted the number of what we called round-robin trips—running home after you work all night, taking a shower, and coming right back. But it was just one of the most exciting times, because all the deals we were doing were on the *Wall Street Journal*'s front page."

M&A gave Ruth lots of exposure to experienced people early in her career. "At a pretty young age, it gave me the opportunity to see how you should conduct yourself at a more senior level. I worked for Wall Street legends!" Ruth named seven. Understandably, she calls herself lucky; apprenticeship was her first step to finding a sponsor.

Indeed, Ruth's clear advice to us is to be very conscious about finding one: "It's your responsibility to find him or her. If you're working for someone who isn't going to take a risk on you, get out because you're not going to change the person. That is a dead-end approach to a career. I've worked with men—I've always worked for men. As well meaning as someone may want to be, biases are deep. So you have to tell yourself, 'I'm not going to have the same opportunity unless I change bosses.' One of the biggest problems women have is they work really hard and put their heads down and assume hard work gets noticed. And hard work for the wrong boss does not get noticed. Hard work for the wrong boss results in one thing—that boss looks terrific and you get stuck."

Cultivating potential sponsors to help you is the very next step. It helps to recognize which of your strengths your sponsor can leverage. You know Ruth's—among them, perseverance and industriousness, judgment, integrity.

From the start, Ruth understood that her sponsor needed something from her, too. "I wasn't stupid enough to think, 'He's just doing this out of the kindness of his heart,'" she says. "I helped his career and there was no question I was giving him a lot of support. But it was more fun to work around the clock and actually spend time with clients, so it was a good bargain for me."

When one of her mentors left Morgan Stanley for a rival company in 1992, Ruth followed. She ran the financial sponsors group at his new shop for two years. "When I was thinking of leaving Morgan Stanley with him, I don't think I was as clear as I should have been with the people running the firm about why I was leaving and what I was concerned about with staying," she recalls. "My father even said, 'I don't understand why you're leaving. It's such a high-integrity place and you've always respected that.'"

As soon as she left, Ruth regretted it. "If I had put all the issues on the table, I bet they would have been addressed. I didn't really want to leave," she says. "Having invested that many years at Morgan Stanley, I think I owed it to myself and I owed it to them to be very direct. And you know what? They may have said, 'We can't meet the expectations and you should leave.' Probably they would have realized that I had some reasonable expectations. If there's one big lesson, it's if you're thinking about leaving you'd better put all the issues on the table so you don't kick yourself later."

Despite her strong relationship with the sponsor she had followed, Ruth didn't like the work or the culture of the new firm. She recalls thinking, "Oh my god, I've completely messed up my career. I want to go back and I won't have the option."

Two years in, Ruth did get the option to return to Morgan Stanley, but only if she took a step down, reentering without the title of managing director. That was tough to swallow because all her peers were MDs. She remembers telling the head of the firm: "Are you making me eat dirt? I'm very concerned. I don't want to be made an example of. I don't want to come back and then have people say, 'See, if she'd never left she would have had a great career.'" She remembers, though, what the CEO told her: "Don't worry about it. It's going to be a tough year. But in two years, you're going to look back and I assure you, you will be thrilled that you made this decision."

She took him at his word, as a personal guarantee. They both knew there was risk, but Ruth chose to trust him. And with that trust, she found other sponsors, too. A number of managing directors assured her that they would provide air cover. "They told me, 'We know it's hard to reenter.' It was the right decision."

A few years later, Ruth was diagnosed with breast cancer. "What's great is that I was able to look back and say, 'I'm actually very proud of what I've done professionally. I am absolutely thrilled that I got married and had kids. Everyone has to make her own choice about how to fill out her life, but I'm glad I had something more than work,' " Ruth says. "I bring this up because one in three of us will have cancer in our lives. Everyone's going to have to deal with somebody going through this. You might not have as much time as you think. So make sure that you're as well-rounded as you want to be, as early as you can be."

Sponsorship has been a critical factor for Ruth in coping with cancer. She recalls that when she was first diagnosed, the global head of investment banking (another sponsor) told her that he assumed work would probably be a part of her recovery. "He wanted me to know that when I came in it was for me—and not for Morgan Stanley. I thought that was a great message. He knew how much I loved work," she says. "I want to continue doing it as long as I possibly can, and hopefully that's another couple of decades. For me, having the professional richness along with the personal richness is so important."

Better a Sponsor than a Mentor

Do you have mentors? Mentors draw on their experiences and wisdom to guide you with sage counsel. It's good to have mentors, and the more the merrier.

But mentors don't change the trajectory of your career. As Ruth explained, a sponsor makes things happen. He or she works on your behalf, getting involved in your career. That could mean opening a door to opportunity. A sponsor also protects you when the chips are down or when you've made a mistake. You still have to deliver the results, but you're no longer alone.

Sponsors do good in many not-so-obvious ways. For example, your sponsor can help you when you're not in the room, by battling gender biases that unfortunately still persist. We all know certain behaviors that work for men often backfire for women. When a man is aggressive, other men may not take offense. When a woman comes on strong, she can get a reputation for being difficult. Similarly, a young man can blow his own horn, but when a woman does it, she's seen as pushy. And, perversely, male colleagues often disdain a woman who doesn't demand recognition, concluding that she's not ready for leadership. Sounds like a no-win situation, doesn't it? Well, sponsors toot the horn on your behalf and speak up if you are being evaluated unfairly.

Because they've gone before you, sponsors can be expert guides around the booby traps and dead ends that exist in any organization. A sponsor can be invaluable in setting you straight about organizational politics, cultural norms, and acceptable ways of gaining visibility and leading. These are subtle issues that a senior advisor with your interests at heart can help navigate.

Finally, a sponsor can be your best source of feedback and can help you maintain your emotional well-being when you face development issues. You trust that she really does have your best interests at heart, so you are primed to open up and hear the facts. You're in it together.

Finding Your Sponsor

So where are all these sponsors hiding, when they could be helping you develop and advance?

Few people are fortunate enough to enter an organization with a sponsor in hand. If you haven't found yours yet, then it's time to invest the effort to get one. If you're just starting out in your career, talk to colleagues to understand how they found good people to work with. Often, sponsors bond with less-tenured people over a common interest or a passion for a certain kind of work. Many are eager to pass on their expertise and respond well to someone who shows genuine enthusiasm for their work. Informal relationships can often blossom into sponsorship if and when you get the chance to show what you can do.

So take some time to think about your strengths and your passions. Remember the "six degrees of separation" rule and identify the senior leaders who operate in the area of work or discipline that interests you. Reach out and let them know your interest (deploying reciprocity).

Another good idea is to look for potential sponsors among the "usual suspects": the men and women who have been sponsors before. While many senior executives don't have the inclination, those who derive satisfaction from it tend to remain sponsors over time. So find out who has been a sponsor in the organization. Leverage the informal networks your colleagues are connected to, or simply ask more senior women who helped them along the way.

Of course, others may have identified the same sponsors, and there may be a long line of people ahead of you, many of whom share the same passions as the man or woman behind that door. Not to worry. Your next move is to find someone who has the makings of a good sponsor but isn't the center of attention yet. You may be able to coach that leader to become your sponsor.

As you begin to list potential sponsors, improve your odds of success by getting to know more than one. Then, as you become more familiar with the strengths and knowledge of your potential sponsors, step back and reassess. Do you share a passion for specific work interests? Is the person in the best position to meaningfully influence your career? Do you feel comfortable talking to the person about both personal and professional issues? Not every potential sponsor will have the right chemistry with you. That's fine. Keep looking until you find the right match; it's worth the time.

While we've met women leaders who have succeeded without a sponsor, there is no doubt that having a sponsor on your team is a huge advantage. A sponsor will almost certainly accelerate your growth, increase your feeling of belonging to the firm, and help you find meaning in what you're doing.

It's not a one-way street. The giver gains fulfillment from her acts of kindness and giving. Sponsors may see you and others as their legacy to the firm. Or they may simply enjoy these personal relationships. Some start sponsoring at an early tenure, because there are always talented folks coming up behind them.

And that's why we hope you'll become part of the circle, reaching out to sponsor the next generation of women, too.

CHAPTER 16

Member of the Tribe

Shirley Tilghman is a molecular geneticist and the first woman president of Princeton University. Like many women leaders, she had two wonderful parents who always told her she could do anything she wanted. And what she wanted was to be a scientist. That might have been the end of it, but Shirley was fortunate enough to find and cultivate her talent for connecting with others. It took her out of the lab and on to a leadership path.

Role Model Mentors

I'm often asked, "When did you know you wanted to be a scientist?" And my answer is always "When didn't I want to be a scientist?" I was always in love with numbers and puzzles. From my earliest memories, I was encouraged in this interest in mathematics, and never for a minute thought that this was inappropriate for women. I always had a fair amount of self-confidence, and that leads to a lot of very positive things. It allows you to be outgoing; it allows you to feel comfortable trying new things, unafraid of embarrassment. I think I was pretty courageous as a child thanks to this sense of absolute security in who I was, and this was because my parents gave me a sense of my true worth.

But it was a history teacher in high school who truly altered my worldview. He was the first teacher to see that although I was a very good student and a model citizen, I was, essentially, less intellectually engaged with the world than I could be. Instead of saying, "Oh, what a good girl" and "Nice paper," he said, "You need to be using your brain more. You need to challenge yourself more. There is so much more happening in the world than what is in your ken in Winnipeg, Manitoba. And here's what you need to do to engage." It was a critical moment. He opened my sights through his after-school History Club. One year, we investigated every religion within a hundred-mile radius of our town. Another year, we just explored political institutions. It was an extraordinary, mind-opening experience, and that teacher has always been a model for me.

I've been very lucky in the mentors that I encountered along the way. In my third year at Queens University in Kingston, Ontario, Professor Brock told me that I was never going to become a great chemist! I was a good student, but he fundamentally understood that I was succeeding through exceptionally hard work and not because there was something in me that understood chemistry at a visceral level. Sometimes, it's as important to understand what you're *not* going to be good at as it is to find out what you will excel at. And he cared enough about me to have this very hard conversation.

Fortunately, I was ready for it. I was already beginning to think about other areas of science where I could perhaps make a greater contribution, and though difficult, it was a conversation that led me ultimately to molecular biology—the field where I was going to be able to have an impact.

Why did chemistry fall flat for me and molecular biology do the opposite? As I got further and further along in chemistry, it became more abstract. To many people, the field grows more fascinating as the chemistry becomes less concrete, but I found it less and less intellectually engaging. I wasn't interested in chemistry that was primarily a lot of equations on a piece of paper. What absolutely enthralled me about molecular biology is that the questions you could ask allowed you to imagine that there was a potential benefit to someone, someday, if you could only answer them.

From the day I entered the laboratory of my Ph.D. mentor, he treated me like a colleague. He expected me to have ideas, and he expected me to argue with him; to propose alternatives to what he was suggesting. The way you treat people has a tremendous influence on how they feel about themselves, and both of these men treated me as a serious scientist. So, in consequence, *I* thought of myself as a serious scientist.

My inclination was to be outspoken, but even that requires encouragement. In my first year in graduate school, I went to a seminar that my eventual Ph.D. mentor was teaching. I put up my hand and said, "I may not have completely understood what you said, and I could have gotten this completely wrong, or maybe I didn't hear it, but . . . ," and then I asked my question. I still remember that Richard Hanson came up to me after class and said, "Don't you ever ask a question that way again. There is no reason for you to be apologetic about your question." As it turned out, it was a good question, on the minds of lots of others, too.

Sponsors Who Open Doors

You can mentor someone by simply being a good role model or by being a good teacher. Sponsorship, however, is a different thing. It means recommending your students for positions, mentioning their names when people are trying to put together speaker lists, nominating them for prizes, and, in general, promoting their careers. I was lucky enough to have in Phil Leader an extraordinary sponsor. A lot of very good things happened early in my career because he told others about my contributions in his laboratory.

There's a stereotype about scientists that I have to dispel, that we are loners, hidden away in a dark lab, in lab coats with pocket protectors, not communicating or networking. Nothing in my view could be further from the truth. To be successful in science, you must first and foremost do good experiments. But it's really critical that you also go to meetings and give seminars and talk about your work more broadly than just simply publishing papers. In the beginning, that's often a very hard and very painful thing to do. You're going to meetings and you don't know anyone and no one knows you. You have to initiate all the conversations. It's a skill and a trait that you need to develop for it really serves your science well to have it more broadly discussed. And at those initially awkward meetings, you're also taking in an enormous amount of new information. Science in my view is an extremely social activity.

I can remember very clearly going to meetings early on, forcing myself to sit down next to someone and introduce myself, explain who I was, and ask questions. When you are introduced into a new community where you have to prove yourself, it takes courage, but by the end of that conversation, you're usually saying to yourself, "Well, that was easy. Why did I think this was going to be so difficult?"

When opportunities present themselves, it's important to seize them, and I'm grateful that my sponsors opened such doors to me. Relatively early in my career, I was asked to serve on a National Institutes of Health study section. These are review panels for grants. It was in the early 1980s, when the government agencies involved in science were told that they had to find more women. Had I been a man, I would not have been asked. So I was faced with the choice: Do I say no, because the only reason they're asking me is that I'm a woman? Or do I say yes, because if I join that panel and do well, it will make it much easier for them to think of women in the future as wonderful reviewers and not simply to fill a quota? I accepted the offer and eventually chaired the study section. Of course I was nervous at the start. A lot of people who had been my heroes, who I revered, were working alongside me.

Later on, the distinguished scientist Bruce Alberts asked me if I would be willing to join the National Research Council's committee to study the possibility of sequencing the human genome. This was a committee made up of Nobel laureates, the greats of twentieth-century genetics, and I was the only woman on the committee and certainly the youngest. And I knew perfectly well why I'd been asked to serve.

A lot of what we did required scientific judgments, and at the end of the day, this was a political decision about whether to invest billions of dollars in sequencing the human genome. I loved that committee; it was one of the most intellectually stimulating things I've ever done. And I learned a lot by watching Bruce chair it. He had a style that saw us through all kinds of conflicts. Gene sequencing was a contentious issue, and this was not a shy group, nor did we start with a consensus view. We had many heated discussions, and one of our members actually resigned in protest. But at the end of the day, it set in motion the Human Genome Project.

After that, I found myself pulled more and more into the Washington policy world, often because of Bruce, who became indefatigable in asking me to do things. I think that was the beginning of the path that ultimately led me to my present job.

Leading Through Others

I've been very lucky that I have spent my life doing what I love and what I love is science. I wouldn't change a single thing about it, except maybe some of the failures, but the choice to become a scientist, that I wouldn't change.

The way I ended up as president of the university was by agreeing to serve on the search committee to identify Harold Shapiro's successor. About four months into the process, the committee chair asked if I'd be willing to step down from the committee and become a candidate for the job. That was perhaps the biggest surprise of my life. Frankly, it had never occurred to me to do anything but make sure that we had a president who supported life sciences.

I would be the first president in modern history who did not hold a Princeton degree, but I think the chair saw that I was deeply devoted nonetheless. We talked about what Princeton is, and what it isn't, its strengths and weaknesses. And it may well be that he saw, in my own expressions of those things, both someone who understood the university well—which I didn't, as it turned out—and someone who saw the university without rose-colored

glasses. I think he saw in my attachment the perspective of someone who could also see that there was much good work yet to
be done.

One of our trustees once described me as having the ability to
imagine myself in somebody else's skin. I think that I am empathic
and that's very important when leading a place like Princeton,
which feels so much like a family. The other important thing is a
respect for and a pride in what we're doing. I get up every day feeling as though what I'm doing is important. I'm proud of my institution and want it to always do the right thing. I also have a deep
respect for ideas, for the life of the mind, for the freedom of expression that universities embody. And then there is the zest that
comes from doing things you feel passionately about. I can't imagine what it is like to be in a job where you punch the clock and
really don't care what happens next.

When I have to, I can really be decisive and make a call, and
live with the consequences, some of which are very painful. I'm
prepared to do that, but hopefully with understanding how it's
going to feel to the person on the receiving end of the harsh
decision.

The responsibility of my role is enormous. I feel it acutely,
literally every day, as I make decisions that affect the university.
This is a great and beloved institution, and the notion that something really terrible would happen to it on my watch is an awful
thought. On the other hand, if you are completely risk averse,
you will never propel your institution forward. Therefore, you
have to weigh the costs and benefits of each decision and try
to follow a path that will continue to advance the mission of
the university while minimizing the risks to its reputation or
to its students, faculty, and staff. Bringing others into this

deliberative process can be extremely helpful and, at times, essential.

Two years ago, we were faced with the risky choice of eliminating early-decision admissions. In the early 1990s, along with virtually all of our peers in higher education, we had adopted a system in which we had two admission processes—fall and spring. The early process was intended largely for students who had been born knowing where they wanted to go to college. That system morphed into a very different one, largely used by students who had many advantages. Good guidance counselors had figured out that the chance of being admitted early was greater than the chance of being admitted through regular decision, and as a result, we had two different applicant pools, and we were giving the advantaged a further edge.

And so, about five years ago, we began thinking about eliminating early decision, because it seemed to be inherently unfair. When we decided to do away with it, there was only one other university, Harvard, that had made the same decision, literally the week before. This was a risky decision because it absolutely could have affected our ability to attract very good students. So we based our decision on an enormous amount of data, and we went to the Board of Trustees for their support because of the risk. We spent a good three hours discussing the issue, together.

The most important aspect in that particular decision was bringing the right set of people together and moving their thinking forward. That included the dean of admissions, for we couldn't make a major decision of that kind unless she supported it. And the undergraduate dean of the college and the other senior administrators within the university were going to have to support the decision. In short, we needed to build consensus.

I hate stereotypes, but as I have watched female and male leaders, it seems to be the instinctive preference of women to bring everybody along. In this case, it helped that we didn't have a lot of strong voices in opposition. We were all intensely concerned about maintaining a level playing field, and I think that what was required was not so much patience as testing our ideas, over and over again, with increasingly large numbers of people, and listening to their reservations, thinking about how we would ameliorate both concerns and risks.

Sponsoring Tomorrow's Leaders

One of the most important things leaders can do is give women responsibility early, allowing them the opportunity to realize their potential and their talents. Women come to leadership with perhaps a little less self-confidence than men. So if you can give them opportunities to demonstrate their abilities early on, you will grow leaders much more often than if you keep them on the same time line as men. It's as much about convincing them that they have the potential to succeed, as it is about convincing people in the organization of this fact. We find that women don't know they're ready when they are. They hold themselves back.

I was very lucky to be given opportunity early, to have the backing of incredibly supportive people, but not all women scientists have been so fortunate. I know lots of extraordinary women scientists who've had to fight for every single achievement, held back by mentors who were anything but mentors, who resented their success. It's a tough world out there.

So if you are really committed to seeing women at the top of your organization, you may have to do things slightly differently with respect to men and women. Beginning, I think, with my predecessor, women have really been successful at Princeton and have risen to very senior leadership positions. We're sending great women leaders out into the world, and I'm extremely proud of that.

PART FOUR

Engaging

CHAPTER 17

Crossing the Line

I was in high school when one in twenty-seven girls played sports, and I wanted to be on the tennis team. There was only a boys' tennis team, so I told the coach I wanted to play. I thought he was going to have a heart attack, but he said, "If you want to play, I'll let you try out." I had to play against a guy I really liked. Sure enough, I won and the coach signed me on. Now, if I didn't make the team, would I have come back? There's no doubt I would have.

Donna Orender, president, Women's National Basketball Association

Engaging is where it all comes together—when you choose to cross an invisible line from being a person to whom things happen to becoming a person who makes things happen. It literally means breaking the bounds that circumscribe your career and your life. Making the commitment to do so is one of the best things you will ever do for yourself. It takes courage. It takes a willingness to fight for what you want, even though you may, in fact, be fighting your own resistance and fear. It releases unbelievable energy.

Let's make it actionable. Engaging means: standing up to be

counted, owning your development, choosing to act on opportunities that carry risk, and facing your deep-seated fears. Now that's a tall order, and once you commit, there's no going back.

Among the women leaders we know whose lives changed when they seized the opportunity to cross the line is Dame Stella Rimington, Great Britain's first female Director General of Security Services, better known as MI-5. Coming of age in the 1960s, Stella entered a professional world that was not welcoming to women. Her first job was as an archivist, organizing parish and village documents for historians to use.

When she got married and her husband accepted a post in India, she closed that door, only to open another. "I gave up work altogether to go with my husband to be a diplomat's wife," she recalls. "But quite by chance, I got recruited to join MI-5 at a cocktail party. I joined at the height of the Cold War, and India was at the forefront really—East met West in India. There were spies all over the place, and you had this real sense that you were at the heart of a mysterious world. So I joined, thinking, 'Gosh, this is fun'—a kind of James Bond-y sort of attitude, I suppose."

As it turned out, Stella was rather good at this work. In her twenty-seven years with the agency, she was among the first women to advance from clerk to analyst, into the field onto supervisory roles, until she reached the top. "Once you've done something, people's preconceived ideas about you tend to change," she points out. "Instead of thinking, 'She's a woman, she can't do that,' they think, 'Hang on, she's just done that. Maybe we can have her doing this.'"

Standing Tall

Despite being an anxious child growing up in wartime Britain, Stella found her voice early. "I had a determination to do something. I wanted a life with excitement. People used to ask me, 'What do you want to be when you grow up?' I told them, 'I want to be an airline pilot.' Now, women couldn't be airline pilots in those days, but I thought, 'That sounds like an exciting job, and I want to do it.'"

Engaging starts with finding your voice—literally. That's easy for some women to do, but for many, speaking up is daunting. But to lead you must be heard. You must have presence. You must put yourself out there; it lets people see how you think, how you interact under pressure. Some tough love for you: Start working on this today. The longer you wait, the harder it gets to speak up—and the easier it becomes for people to overlook you.

A senior woman in investing told us how she learned to speak up. "Every Monday, we had a senior management meeting. In the beginning, I just listened. I learned from the guys because they were all there. After a while I started to speak up. You don't want to say something stupid, but you did the work, so you've got to talk about it!" What was her secret? Practice. She started by relaying analyses she had done. She observed her role models and learned from them. And over time, people looked to her for her opinion, too.

Take it step by step, as Stella did. Returning to England in the 1970s, Stella continued to work after her maternity leaves, but at a desk job. "The theory was that women could deal with the papers and some intelligence analysis," she says. "That is very important, but it's not the 'sharp end' intelligence work. It's not being out in the street, recruiting the human sources and running them. I would describe it as being in a glass box, hemmed in on all sides."

So Stella and some female colleagues spoke up. "We women—and there were quite a few of us by then—sort of ganged up and said, 'Why is it that we have a completely different career from men who are exactly like us?' For the first time, the powers that be started to scratch their heads because they had to find an answer. Their situation was exacerbated by the fact that sex-discrimination legislation was just coming in." Stella recalls, "In the end, they decided that they would have to promote a few women. Of course, the women who did get those jobs did them quite well. Now women are doing very well in even the most dangerous areas."

You can learn to speak up for what you want, too. It takes knowing what you want. Surprisingly, the secret to success is usually just asking. Your own preconceived notions may be limiting our definition of what's possible. Afraid of rejection, some don't ask. Sometimes we're afraid we're not ready. Maybe some of us are afraid to win. But by not speaking up, no one knows what you want. What's worse, they assume you aren't interested or maybe not even qualified. So dream a little, and then find your voice.

In Stella's case, asking got her foot in the door, but she still had to prove that she could do a "man's job" in the field. Her field test, the standard for male agents, was to walk into a pub, approach any stranger, and learn as much as she could. Then she was to keep her cool when a superior officer entered and blew her cover story. "It was a completely unsuitable exercise for somebody like me, because the pub they chose was a sleazy place near Victoria Station, full of men, and not particularly nice ones," Stella recalls with a laugh. "They were leaning on the bar drinking pints in their grimy raincoats. I started to chat up a guy who was obviously surprised and thought my profession was something else!" By the time the officer entered the pub, Stella was relieved. "I felt very awkward, actually, in those circumstances and began to wonder if this was the kind of job I really wanted to do after all."

Finding your voice is not only about talking. Learning to speak up and refining your message is a form of problem-solving, and as with all problem-solving activities, preparation is important. Take time to do your research and go over what you want to convey. Be specific. You're more likely to succeed if you think through all the scenarios, visualizing what could happen in the discussion, and plan how you will overcome any resistance.

It's Your Future

There's nothing like feeling that you are in control to give you the courage to speak up, place yourself in the path of opportunities, and take the risks head-on. When you feel in control, your commitment and energy skyrocket. Better yet, you are less likely to be roiled by negative feedback or sidelined by attacks.

Ownership is also the precursor to success, so don't wait to be chosen. Find ways to create new opportunities. How? Stella had a really simple rule that kept her on the path: "I don't like working for people who I think are less competent than I am," she explains. "That's probably driven me on, because even though I was never ambitious to get to the top, I always felt I wanted to do the next job up because I could see that it wasn't being done as well as I thought I could do it." That's what taking ownership is all about.

After two years as director of counterespionage, Stella was offered an opportunity in counterterrorism. "I think the boss had some hesitation in asking me because he knew that it was not my area of expertise," she says. "But I had absolutely no hesitation in saying, 'Yes, I'd love to do it.' If somebody offers me something new and interesting, then that's what I want to do. I don't think the risk of failure occurred to me. I suppose I thought, 'If somebody's asking me to do it—they know me, they know the job—if they think I can do it, well I'm sure I can.' Obviously in the dark moments of the night you think, 'Gosh, what have I taken on here?' But it would never have occurred to me to say, 'No, I don't think I can do this.' "

In the late 1980s, MI-5 was battling the Irish Republican Army, which was using terrorist tactics to push the British out of Northern Ireland. The campaign included bombings in London and attacks on British soldiers in Germany. The job became even more challenging, Stella recalls. "About three days after I was appointed, Pan Am 103 was brought down by a bomb over Lockerbie in Scotland. I had no experience of working in counterterrorism. One of the most difficult things I had to address at that time was 'What actually is my job now?' I figured out that it was to make sure those in the field had the skills and the resources they needed and that the operations had been properly thought through. If anything went wrong, it was my job to take the flak and deal with government ministers and the prime minister. I found it quite alarming at the outset, but also extremely stimulating and very satisfying when things went right."

Clearly, Stella is a role model, even if you don't aspire to be a secret agent yourself. Consider the next milestone in your career. Do you know what you have to do to achieve it? Do you believe that achieving it is in your control? What are you doing to reach that goal? If your answers are: 'I don't know,' 'I am being held back by him/her/them,' 'It's not very likely,' 'There's not much I can do to make it happen,' we'll offer you some tactics to put all that hesitation behind you and engage the challenge head-on.

Risks Come with Opportunities

Ultimately, as Stella's story shows, engaging is about risk-taking, and often fear hovers just underneath. Choosing to act on your aspiration is seldom middle-of-the-road safe. The women leaders we interviewed took it as part of the package. Some were unafraid; they were born with (or developed) the confidence and courage to dive in; others were more circumspect, using analytic problem-solving to assess risks, make a decision, and proceed.

It's tough stuff. Stella reflects, "If everything is just too easy and too smooth, I don't think you end up with the sort of steel and the backbone you need if you are going to take a top job." When Stella was named head of MI-5, she took on an unprecedented personal risk: For the first time, the government disclosed who the director general would be. The British tabloids rushed to find out where she lived, and when they did, the family had to decamp in the middle of the night.

"That was the time when I felt most divided, because I still had my younger daughter at home," Stella says. "She'd never told her friends what I did. And then people asked her, 'Is that your mum? Fancy that.' When we had to live covertly, we didn't get mail at the house in our own name. My daughter had to work out which of her friends she could trust. That was the first traumatic moment."

Let's face it: Careers—and lives—are built on decisions that involve risk. Think of the alternative—staying on the track others expect you to take. That's fine if it's really the right thing for you, based on what you know about your strengths, what you enjoy doing, and what gives you meaning. But what if it's not? That's an even bigger risk. Harvard psychologist Daniel Gilbert, author of *Stumbling on Happiness,* researched the unique ability of the human brain to imagine what might happen under certain circumstances and to visualize the future. We tend to overestimate our potential unhappiness in downside scenarios, and this keeps us from attempting new things. Gilbert found that people who made choices and who acknowledged risk felt happier even in that downside case. If you feel like the change you're contemplating is too big a risk, ask yourself what's the worst that can happen. Then do the "premortem" and figure out what you can do to manage it.

Stella is the living example of how clarity of vision and confidence in your own capabilities mitigate risk. One of the most effective ways to reduce risk is to build expertise in an arena of your choosing. When you start from a firm foundation of subject matter expertise and experience, the risk associated with stepping into a new role or assuming increased responsibility decreases.

And as Stella realized early on, women have one more natural advantage to help them reduce risk: collaborative decision-making. "One of the first things I realized when I became director general was that it's very important to have colleagues around you who are different from you and who are not scared of you—who will give you advice without fear or favor," Stella says. "I suppose I don't feel especially convinced that I know the right thing to do on my own. Too many people in businesses work on a command and control basis. The bosses think: 'I know what the answer is, and I know this is what we're going to do.' "

Stella believes that the best thing is people who bring you diverse points of view and yet still form a team. "You choose your colleagues—not 'yes men' but a team of people who realize the importance of moving forward and achieving some kind of consensus," she advises. "Lead that team in such a way that everybody feels they have the opportunity to give their point of view. Then everybody goes away from the meeting persuaded that the decision is the right one. That's a skill you have to learn."

Many things can hold you back from engaging—upbringing, habit, discomfort with confrontation, self-doubt—the list goes on. But choosing not to engage is like having a giant boulder in your path. Chances are the uneven playing field already makes your path challenging; you don't need more obstacles in your way.

And when you do engage, you'll feel a fire burning within you to seize the day. Go ahead, light that fire.

CHAPTER 18

Stand Up, Speak Up

You cannot be afraid to be who you are. Live your values. Live your life. A woman confided to me about "sneaking out of the office" to go to her child's play and I said, "Stop right there! I have never snuck out of any place. I walk right down the center hall, and if somebody doesn't like it, too bad. Don't worry about me. I will deliver." Just stand up, do what you need to do, and smile about it. Look them in the eye and say, "If you don't like it, fire me, and I'll go find another job, because I'm talented enough and I'm committed enough."

Shelly Lazarus, chairman, Ogilvy & Mather

Many women leaders were born standing up for themselves, but a good number developed this aspect of leadership on their own. Little by little, they learned to speak up, they learned how best to influence the discussion, and eventually they learned to lead. Not only is speaking up important for your personal development, but it's part of your job. We think it is so important that we teach a course on "presence." It's not just about your voice—it's also about how you fill the room—to gain the confidence and commitment of those around you.

Why is it that so many women are reluctant to speak up? Why do they sit quietly while some guy hijacks the conversation? We are amazed by the endless list of reasons women give us:

- "I don't have anything important enough to say."
- "It's all been said already or someone else is going to say it."
- "The men enjoy talking, so let them."
- "Actions speak louder than words anyway."
- "It's not my place."
- "I'm here to listen."
- "I'm new here."
- "I'm the most junior person."
- "I get things done outside the meeting."

Baloney. Maybe that reluctance to speak masks deeper fears, such as the fear of being "found out," the fear of being ridiculed, or the fear of being found unworthy. Our first line of defense is often rationalization and evasion. Dig deeper to uncover very real fears that may have served you well—until now. If you give them power, they hurt you. Our interviews suggest that fear drives many women to set an unrealistically high bar that would stop anyone. So many wait too long to enter the conversation. (It feels a bit like double Dutch jump rope: challenging to jump in and just as hard to stay in.) Others confuse respect with remaining silent.

We know it's hard. And complicating matters is the damned-if-you-do, damned-if-you-don't problem. Often women who speak out suffer, too. They may get branded as aggressive, difficult, self-promoting, or worse. Research suggests that women often feel comfortable speaking up on someone else's behalf but have a hard time speaking up for themselves. So we wait for others to recognize what we want. Yes, we wait. Why? Because it "means more" if someone else notices without our asking, women told us.

And if you're not convinced yet, let's add more reasons to speak up! While you're waiting, men are negotiating for what they want and promoting themselves. Women are far less likely to negotiate than men; 20 percent of women have never engaged in a negotiation. In one study that compared expectations of men and women in similar roles, men expected their peak earnings to be 30 percent higher than what women expected.

Julie Daum has spent years working with the top women leaders in corporate America in her role as leader for the North American Board Services Practice of search firm Spencer Stuart. Her strength is understanding people, and what she loves to do is match people to the right roles. There is no better person to help you find your voice.

Talking with Julie

Lesson 1: It may not come naturally, but you have to speak up to be counted. "I really didn't find my voice until somebody told me I could have it. There was a senior person who believed in me, and he basically said, 'Over to you.' He gave me the right."

What was hard for Julie was figuring out the "how": "Like a lot of women, I remember thinking that you had the right to speak only if you knew the right answer—that was what was important." So, like many young women, Julie spent all her energies plugging away quietly at the work, convinced that she had to come up with the right number or the right answer.

Today, Julie can't imagine not having that voice.

Lesson 2: Find a valued way to contribute. Julie encourages us to think of a conversation or a meeting as a process of moving toward a decision. That makes it even more important to speak up and be part of the problem-solving: "People write off people who don't speak," says Julie. "If you don't take up a little bit of air time, people will assume you have nothing to contribute."

She offers this proven tactic—speak up within the first five minutes or try to be among the first six people to talk (either way works). It gets harder to speak the longer you wait. "At first this was hard for me because I'm shy," Julie says. "I used to have to make myself raise my hand and speak up. I really had to work at it."

Lesson 3: Sometimes it takes a wrong turn to discover your voice. Lots of women make false starts, and Julie openly shared hers. "I really stumbled early on, because I had gotten myself into a job where I couldn't do what I wanted to do. I had to pull myself out, but it took a couple of years to admit, 'This is wrong. I'm not happy. I'm not comfortable.' " What Julie realized is that it's easy to fall into a routine of getting up every day and going to work without your heart being in the game. Finally, she quit. She had found her voice and was able to say, "I've got to stop this. I have to figure out what it is that I want to do."

That's when she bumped into an opportunity that opened a window on what she really wanted. She took a huge cut in pay to work part-time hiring teams for a start-up. And she loved it. "I was old enough to know that it wasn't about the money. What was important was that I wanted to do something that I liked, which I felt I would be good at. And, if I was going to take time away from my family, there had to be something with meaning."

Lesson 4: Speak up for something you are passionate about. On maternity leave, Julie discovered her passion for women's leadership while watching the Anita Hill confirmation hearings in 1992. "We're the same age. I listened to what her career had been like, and then watched how these men treated her," Julie explains. "And I thought, 'I just can't believe how far we haven't come.' "

So Julie worked for Catalyst, a nonprofit organization that takes on women's workforce issues. Believing that change must start at the top, Julie wanted to help more women into the boardroom. "We just started counting the number of women. It was so incredibly small that it was a story—you know, 50 percent of the population is female but only 5 percent of board seats were held by women."

Catalyst published this research and began to help CEOs identify candidates. "That report continues to have an impact in terms of getting women in the boardroom," she says. "The numbers are still not where we'd like them to be, but they are better. And we changed the conversation. Today, boards may not have enough women, but they think about it and they talk about it."

Lesson 5: Voice is ownership. Julie recognized that no one really knows what's important to you as much as you do. If you don't say it, others will have to guess or, more likely, not think about your needs at all. "You have to own what's important to you, and then you reach out to people and say: 'I want to be able to do this. How can I make that happen here?' "

Julie remembers how easy it was for a male colleague to use his voice. "He said, 'I don't work on weekends. I'll work twenty-four hours a day, five days a week, but I just don't work on weekends.' After he said that, no one asked him to. I remember thinking, 'I would never say something like that.' "

But when it came time to accommodate the needs of her growing family without giving up her career, Julie found her voice. "I was willing to do whatever it took, but I needed certain things to make it possible. When I went to my firm and said, 'This is what I want,' their answer was 'okay.' "

Julie encourages all women to learn to speak up, even board members who have Julie to thank!

Finding Your Own Voice

You can learn to say anything that needs saying. It just takes practice. One of our favorite exercises can help you get started immediately: The next time you're in a meeting, write down the names of everyone present. Then, discreetly rate each person's comments on a scale of 1 to 5, where 5 is the most insightful comment ever made and 1 is the dumbest. Keep track for at least thirty minutes. Afterward, calculate each person's average score. We think you'll be surprised by what you find. The lesson is that the bar for speaking up isn't nearly as high as you might think. So get in there!

A second exercise can help you practice your delivery. First, pick a difficult topic: asking for something you want but are too uncomfortable to raise. You'll know it when you feel your heart rate increase. Write down what you want to say in bullet points. Then, get a friend to role-play you in the conversation.

Turning the tables lets you experience how it feels to receive your request, delivered the original way you intended. Now, switch roles and fine-tune your delivery. Don't hold back. Go to the edge in this safe environment, so you can experience what it feels like to deliver your message more forcefully. You'll develop greater comfort with what may be a challenging conversation. You're ready for it now.

The Medium Is the Message

How you say what you want to say is as important as the content. While most women have a broader emotional range than most men, it's not always appropriate or helpful to use it spontaneously. We don't mean stifling your passion or pulling your punches. Choose your tone carefully and marshal the facts to express yourself cogently and effectively.

Women who want to strike the right tone can learn a lot from the work of Marshall Rosenberg. He offers an effective way to resolve difficult situations without conflict. Imagine that Susie and Bob are working on a task force and developing recommendations for a critical product launch. Susie is sitting in Bob's office, hoping to get his sign-off on some tough issues. Bob is constantly checking his BlackBerry, taking calls, and saying hello to colleagues stopping by his office. As this continues, Susie begins to feel unsure and increasingly anxious. Her inner voice is agitating: "Susie, you are completely unimportant to this guy. He couldn't be bothered with you. Ream him out!" Holding her emotions in check but finding a way to express her needs, Susie says, "Bob, we are experiencing a lot of interruptions today and I feel frustrated. I need your full attention, because this conversation is very important to the recommendations. If you cannot focus on this topic now, let's reschedule for a time that will be better for you."

Susie has not raised her voice or criticized. She has simply shared what she has observed, noted how it makes her feel, and stated why it's a problem. Furthermore, she articulated a solution that also respects Bob's needs. In consequence, Bob is open, hears her, and responds in kind. Instead of becoming defensive and escalating conflict, he replies, "You're absolutely right. Actually, I'm waiting for some potentially bad news and I'm distracted. It would be much better if we could reschedule for later this afternoon. If you like, we can pop out for coffee to avoid interruptions."

What this example shows is how you can confront someone without allowing your emotions to take over. It is disarmingly counterintuitive: When you are able to separate facts from emotions, combining true listening and empathy, you'll find your audience less resistant. In turn, that makes it less intimidating to speak up. Try your new skills at home, too, with the hardest customers—your kids.

One final note on learning to speak up: Sometimes your best response to someone is a no. Many women leaders confess it was difficult but essential to learn this lesson in order to stay above a mounting list of commitments. Saying no is touchy, because the naysayer has the power. You worry that refusal can damage a valued relationship. Unfortunately, too many women go to great lengths to avoid no. Some say yes when they don't mean it, others say no in a hostile manner or avoid saying anything at all.

Leaders have to say no often, and negotiations expert William Ury outlines an effective approach: Start by expressing genuine interest in the asker, then say no in a clear and respectful way. Follow up with an alternative that gives both of you a chance to move on. If you do this, you leave the other person feeling good, and you've offered a way to help that doesn't commit you.

When Your Voice Is Too Easy to Find

For some women, the problem isn't finding a voice—it's finding a way to listen. An overdose of passion inspires them to keep talking. They mean to listen, but end up talking. And the effect is well-known—the more you talk, the less you hear.

If this is you, try opening up the conversation with colleagues, your senior managers, and team members, as well as people you work with outside your organization. Learn what effect you have on others. If you are ready to change, reach out to trusted colleagues. Approached the right way, they will help you spot the situations in which you lose your control. Together, you can work out a secret signal they can use in public to warn you. In the heat of the moment, that signal can be a savior.

You can also train yourself by monitoring your behavior in meetings. Keep track of how much time you take up in comparison with others. You can limit your talk-time by only asking questions—a great way to signal your openness to others and yet stay engaged. You can literally keep yourself from talking by putting your hand over your mouth when you're listening. It is a physical reminder of your intent to listen. A similar approach is to take notes, another physical activity to help you focus on what others are saying. Practice ahead of time so that, when your emotions are starting to build and you need extra support, you will be able to wait until you have considered how you want to respond.

It takes concentration to listen. You know the difference when you are really present. You are not just listening in order to respond (or checking whether that person agrees with your well-formed view). You are not just listening in order to learn, though you may be intrigued and curious. You are also listening to understand how that person feels; you are open and vulnerable. The person you're listening to will know it, and your conversation will take off: You will truly connect.

Having Presence

Why is it that some people have a "presence" even before they speak? The way you present yourself—how you move, stand, occupy space—says much more about you than what you actually say. If you don't believe us, just try this exercise. Assemble your colleagues in a room. Walk in and introduce yourself in a simple hello. Then ask them to rate your performance, ranging from 1 (a mouse just walked in) to 10 (a lioness just entered). Now try it again, but this time, choose a number you would like to represent (say, 7—bold, confident, assertive without being aggressive, or 5—poised and neutral). Don't tell your colleagues; using just your body language and those few words, see how they score you. Typically, you'll find that you gauge your presence to be more forceful than others do. In fact, what you thought was a 7 may look more like a 3 to them. You may not project the way you sound to yourself. If so, that's great feedback to help you adjust how you walk and stand, the tone of your voice, your facial expression, and so on. Of course, different situations require a reset. Matching your number to the occasion is an art, too.

So use everything you've got for a leader's presence. You may think you've crossed the line to get into the game, but you're not there until everyone else knows it, too.

CHAPTER 19

Make Your Own Luck

I remember the day I bought the business in 1999. I stood outside the major store and I just cried. I thought, "Oh, my god, what have I done? It's got this massive bank debt. What have I done?" But really, I knew what I was doing, and I knew why I was doing it—to restore that business to its peak performance. It's now the top brand for young women in Australia.

Naomi Milgrom, chairman and CEO, Sussan Group

The core lesson in engaging is taking charge and making things happen for yourself. Have you ever wondered why some people seem to be lucky? The women we interviewed all felt lucky. Looking deeper, we discovered that they put themselves in position to succeed. They opted for opportunities to develop new skills. They took risks that created more opportunities.

When we take ownership of our careers, we get lucky. People who take responsibility feel they can shape their destiny. They feel in control, and that gives them the confidence and commitment to pursue their passions, even when the odds of winning are not great. Also, when things go badly or the feedback is negative, it won't knock you down, because you know you have the power to create a better outcome tomorrow. Now, envision how you can help others gain the dignity and energy that comes from feeling in control. That's the work of leadership. Olive Darragh, head of strategy at Tudor Capital, a leading hedge fund company, is a wonderful example of someone who took control—and got lucky.

It's Your Life

Olive's start was anything but propitious. She was born in troubled Northern Ireland. The oldest girl in a family of six, she grew up at an early age "because you had no choice."

Olive treasures memories of idyllic summers on the farm. But no one could escape the political turmoil between Catholics and Protestants that erupted into violence in the 1970s. "The troubles were pretty rampant from the time I was ten," she recalls. "Until I left for university, the troubles were a huge part of our lives." By the time she did leave, more than a dozen of her friends and acquaintances had been killed. "Everywhere you went, it was just there," she says. "Awful sadness. An incredible waste of life."

Olive's parents had quit school very young to help with farmwork; hard times required it. But that gave them the determination to support their kids and find a way out of poverty. "We had no money, we didn't own land. We didn't own anything. But my mother is incredibly bright," Olive says. "When we were studying calculus in school, she went to night classes to learn calculus so she could help us."

Olive's parents imagined that she might finish secondary school and get a good job—a teller at the local bank, maybe manager one day. But Olive began to dream about getting out of Northern

Ireland and set her heart on the University of Edinburgh. "I just knew I wanted to go there. I had never even been in a city." When she was accepted and the time came to go, her parents waved good-bye at the ferry. Olive was on her own.

Two years in, she got the chance to study at the University of Pennsylvania. "I literally just got on a plane and went," Olive recalls. "To their credit, my parents said, 'Great experience. Go do it.' But the first few months were awful. I hated it."

Olive had been a top student at Edinburgh; this was different. She scored 33 percent on her first accounting exam. Determined not to fail, she told herself, "Hang on, you've just got to work this out. It's just a different way of teaching." While it bothered her, Olive figured she'd better learn it.

And she did, deciding a career in the United States could be interesting. So when Olive finished her studies in Scotland, she wrote to all the big accounting firms. "I got eight rejection letters," Olive recalls. "They said, 'If you join us in the U.K. and you do well, you can always transfer.' The top firm at the time offered me a job in Edinburgh, and I was about to accept. Then one night during dinner, the phone rang. One of my roommates answered and said, 'It's somebody from Touche-Ross in Philadelphia,' and I said, 'Yeah right,' thinking it's my mom. But he insisted. So I picked up the phone and this guy said to me, 'We got your letter, and we'll make a deal with you. You take a job here, and we'll pay for your flight. In eighteen months, if you don't like us, or we don't like you, you pay for your own flight back home.' As soon as he said that, I knew I was taking the job. And you know the joke? That man wasn't even there when I arrived. He had retired."

It seemed like a lucky break—briefly. Without U.S. accreditation, Olive could only do administrative work at the firm. Furious, she decided to take the qualifying exam, and over the next nine months, she steadily worked and studied the American system. "One day, a letter came in the mail with a big silver star on it. It looked like junk mail and I threw it out," Olive says. "Weeks later, the office manager called me into his office, and I thought, 'Ooh, he's finally going to fire me.' But he said, 'When were you going to tell us? Do you know you got the second highest score in the state?'" Olive had won the silver medal. Then and there, her responsibilities changed.

After a few years in accounting, Olive went back to school for an MBA at Harvard, then to McKinsey & Company, starting off with a thud. She wasn't a natural consultant. And as Olive thought about leaving, unexpectedly another door swung open. She took a flyer on a six-week assignment in Australia. "It was a financial institution project regarding wealthy individuals—something I knew a lot about. But it was also a huge turnaround, and the project was on its last legs." Olive recalls, "At my first client meeting, the two consultants on my new team fell asleep. That's how tired they were. So, I'm thinking, 'What's going on?' Then we turned the company around. The client was excited. My six weeks turned into nine incredible months."

Lucky again. See the pattern?

Yes, another setback. Next, Olive went to work on a project where she couldn't seem to do anything right. "It was disastrous," she winces. "The partner fired me! I went to our office manager who said, 'No he didn't. Our process doesn't work that way.'" Still in the saddle, Olive took ownership: "Whatever I'm thinking is abundantly clear. It's on my face and in what I say," she explains. "My choice was to adapt or leave, so I chose to stay. When I left, I wanted to feel good about it. I didn't want to leave feeling like I couldn't do it."

This time, the learning curve was harder: "The feedback was

about my personality," she remembers. "But the great thing was that learning to deal with it made my life better."

Better indeed. In eighteen months, Olive was elected a partner and eventually a senior partner. After nearly fourteen years there, in 2004 Olive left to manage strategy and talent at Tudor Investments. Today, she has wealth and position beyond anything she might have imagined as a girl. "My father used to say: 'Stop worrying about where you are. The best thing is to look at how far you've come.' I proved that I can do it," Olive says. "Whatever happens at Tudor, or anywhere else that I work, I'll be fine."

Olive firmly believes that ownership was the key: "You have to fail or you don't get anywhere in your life. If you're always doing what makes you comfortable, by definition you can't be developing. It's your world. It's your life. And nobody else is to blame. You decide if you're going to make the best of it."

You're in Control

Can you jump in like Olive did? We certainly think so. Ownership is what psychologists call having an internal locus of control in your life. This means you believe your destiny is up to you. The opposite is an external locus of control, believing that things happen to you regardless of your effort and behavior; events shape your life, not you.

In general, people with an internal locus can be more confident and self-motivated, less afraid to take risks. In contrast, externally focused people rely on external reinforcement (praise) for their sense of self-worth. Sadly, research also shows that women are more likely to believe their locus of control is external.

You be the judge. Ask yourself the following questions:

- When you failed to get a job or promotion, did you believe the winner had special pull?
- Have you ever negotiated your salary?
- Do you feel that in most cases, if you address an issue head-on, you can come up with a solution?

If you answered no to two of these questions, the odds are you have an external locus of control.

Here's what you can do to shift from external to internal. Start by getting some input from work associates who can help you assess what aspects of your professional situation are in your control. Your mentors—especially your sponsors—will be the most helpful. They have perspective on what actually is in your control, and it may surprise you how much is. Then ask how other people (e.g., the men) perceive their ability to shape the outcome in the same situations. Are they playing by a different set of rules that you don't know? In studies on negotiation, for example, gender differences nearly disappeared when women learned that other people were negotiating and getting a better deal. When you know the rules, you feel in control.

Now you're not waiting for others to decide your path. Think hard about where you do want to go. Use Olive as your inspiration.

For example, put yourself forward for an assignment that intrigues you. Ask yourself: Will this add to my capabilities? Does it fit with my interests? (Remember that doing just more of the same will lose its value over time.) And use that voice to ask for what you want and to say no when something does not work for you. If you focus on making day-to-day decisions consistent with your longer-term goals, you will begin to assert ownership over your own life.

Olive's story is not fairy-tale perfect. She was close to failing a number of times; her mistakes did hold her back. She tried out three careers before finding her spot. That's real life for you.

While we're talking about real life, you know—as we do—that sometimes the uphill rocky terrain isn't worth the climb. How can you avoid wasting time on the wrong organization? Look for firms where women get support. A good sign is women at the top and the presence of transparent evaluation and promotion policies. Another is benefit plans that have options clearly delineated for all to see. Yet another is an explicit process for advancing talented performers. In those companies, you have a much better chance of finding a good environment for your development. The ultimate in ownership may be choosing the entrepreneur's path—a great option if corporate life does not suit you.

Some of us get stressed trying to find the "rightest" next step, the one that will unlock our success and our happiness. Olive's story underscores that there are many good next steps, not just one right one. Let that thought go because it will only hold you back. Sometimes taking any step will bring you closer to your dreams.

One final note: Ownership goes hand-in-hand with ambition and that's taboo for many women. We prefer modesty for the most part. Some actively steer away from it, and others deny ambition altogether. Many express it only in terms of a transcendent goal, such as "serving others."

Frankly, ambition is a fine thing. Not only is it okay to recognize what you want, it's a step toward getting it. So why is it that women admire ambition in men but don't want to be seen as ambitious, too? Researchers believe it stems from early gender socialization. Traditionally, leadership has been a masculine realm and, despite the success of women in every imaginable field, our social norms reflect those outmoded values. Even today, leadership attributes tend to favor men: Leaders are supposed to be analytical, assertive, willing to take risks, decisive—stereotypical male traits. In turn, we rarely describe leaders as yielding, understanding, child-like, gentle, and creative.

We hope the concept of Centered Leadership will take hold as more women leaders succeed. Women leaders are ambitious and clear decision-makers who are self-reliant and able to take calculated risks. They speak up, they own their fates. But they're also understanding, positive, inclusive, caring, and joyful. Someday these traits will define all leaders—female and male.

By owning up to your ambition, you'll allow yourself to take ownership for success. Let go of limiting mind-sets—and you'll be amazed at the positive impact you can have.

In other words, believe in yourself. We do. That's why we wrote this book.

CHAPTER 20

Take the Step

I don't think that I'm a thrill-seeker. I'll use skiing as the analogy because I like to jump off cliffs. But I generally jump off cliffs that I'm relatively confident I'm going to land and that if I don't, it's not dangerous. There are people who like to jump off cliffs who think their skill is much better than it really is. They hurt themselves. There are people who are quite skilled but are afraid to jump. I like to be at that point where you're about to jump and your stomach is going, woo!

Shona Brown, SVP Operations, Google

When we rolled out Centered Leadership training to younger women, we gained an important new insight. Where the leaders saw almost everything as an opportunity, the young women primarily saw risks. Women leaders aren't put off by the risks that accompany opportunities to grow. Nor should you be.

The ability to take reasonable risks is an absolute requirement for any leader. You take a risk when you accept a new job. You take a risk when you step off the "standard" career progression to raise a family. When you transfer to another office for a new experience, you take a risk that you won't fit in. When you switch functions or roles, there's a risk that you may not do the new job as well. If you decide to opt out, you take a risk that you'll never have financial security. Avoiding risk is not an option: Before long, you've stalled.

While many women leaders boldly told us they were unafraid, that's just not true of everyone. Opportunities unleash fears we've kept under lock and key. So is the "prize" worth coming face-to-face with your fears? We think so.

Learning to face your fears is actually the best part of accepting opportunity. When you do, you'll find they are far less powerful than they seemed. You'll also experience the lightness of being that comes with getting back in control.

Laura Cha is a woman who knows. She rose to the top of her profession by taking on risk and becoming expert in managing it. She went on to achieve prominence by helping to bring oversight to China's nascent public securities markets—a role that friends warned her against.

Becoming a Risk Professional

Born in Shanghai, Laura moved with her family from the Communist mainland to Hong Kong in the early 1950s. According to the plan, she would go abroad for university and settle there. Laura was a dutiful oldest child, and that gave her a strong dose of cautiousness. "When I was little, I always had this fear of the unknown," she says. "I wanted to remove that fear, and the only way to do that was to go out and do something about it. That's what pushed me."

Laura married early—another Hong Kong Chinese student in college in the United States—and they settled down. "We thought we'd go to graduate school together," she says. But Laura had her first child and stayed home while her husband went to business school. Six years and two kids later, Laura got her turn; she enrolled in law school. "There was opposition from the family, not from my husband, but from my extended family. The studying itself was not difficult at all, but to cope with various other responsibilities was not easy."

Still, it proved to be her turning point. "That was probably the most important decision in my life. I really relished the opportunity even more after having kids," she says. "Before law school, whenever I had an opinion I was often not sure whether my opinion was stupid. I didn't become more confident until I became a lawyer. If you ask me, going to law school was probably the most important decision in my life."

Laura went to work for a top law firm and loved it. Then, in the 1980s, they moved back to Hong Kong so her husband could join his family business. Laura took a position in the Hong Kong office of a New York–based law firm. She helped major U.S. corporations negotiate to do business in the People's Republic of China.

So far, it doesn't sound like risky business! Many women have similar stories—long-distance travel, college, law degree, first job, second job, and then many years of hard work to make partner and a fulfilling life as a valued professional. Right?

Wrong. That could have been Laura, but in 1989, when the Hong Kong government was scrambling to restore investor confidence in its equities markets, a turn in the road presented itself.

It came in the form of a headhunter call out of the blue. The Hong Kong Securities and Futures Commission (SFC) had just been created to reform the market. Laura believed the SFC's reforms could have a huge impact, remaking Hong Kong into a credible financial market. "This was two years after our financial market was almost totally wiped out," she explains. The planned reforms might not work, and what then? At the same time, Laura enjoyed what she was doing; she had a surefire, comfortable career. Leaving was a big decision.

What would you have done?

"My first thought was 'Wow, this is a risky business.' It was a new organization, and I didn't know anyone," Laura says. "But I also thought it was an interesting opportunity to do something different." So she called up her first mentor from the San Francisco law firm. His advice startled her: "Go out and spread your wings and see the world." That helped Laura recognize her opportunity was far greater than its associated risk: "What's the worst that could happen? I could always fall back on law if I didn't like it."

So Laura signed on with the intention of staying two to three years. She wound up staying for a decade, becoming vice chairman of the agency over time. And the outcome? She helped the new agency live up to its promise.

Still, after a decade, Laura felt she'd had enough—especially of the political battles over corporate governance reforms. "In time, I decided it was very tiring to be in the public eye," she says. "I wanted to do something a little less structured, freer, so to speak. So I told the government I wasn't going to renew my contract."

Then something surprising happened: As soon as Laura's resignation was announced, she got a call from a friend in Beijing. "He said the premier wanted me to go to work in the central government. I didn't quite grasp it at that time. I thought, 'Well, okay, he wants an advisor. My friend said, 'No, no, you don't understand. You have to move to Beijing. We want you to be the vice chairman of the China Securities Regulatory Commission.' "

This opportunity came with new risks and fears. Laura would be the first non–mainland Chinese to be a vice minister in a major agency in the People's Republic, which would mean that she would have no political cover and, most likely, would be viewed with suspicion by the bureaucrats. She remembers the warnings people gave her, "You are very brave. There's so much unknown. You'll be blamed for this, you'll be blamed for that."

Would you have taken that road? Laura did. Fifty years after leaving home on the mainland to find opportunity in the West, Laura came back to bring Western-style investment markets to China. "Really, the most important thing in my working life has to be when Premier Zhu Rong Ji approached me to work there. That has to be the highlight, I would say, in anybody's career. There was risk, but I didn't look at it that way. I saw the positive would override the negative part of the venture."

Of course there was risk. Laura recalls, "I was blamed for a lot of things. But I also know that the authorities in China knew that I put my heart into what I did, I was committed, I was focused, and I tried to do a good job."

So how did Laura manage to grab these opportunities of a lifetime? "Before you recognize the opportunities are there, you have to be confident. In order to be confident, you have to be good at what you do," Laura advises. "Nothing can substitute for the substance part. If you're not there on the content, you may not be able to recognize the opportunity. Even if the opportunity arrives, it might not fall on you. And don't underestimate luck. I was at the right place in my career when the opportunity arose, and I was able to take advantage of it. I waited six years to go to law school, but when I graduated, it was at the height of the foreign direct investment in China. I joined a top law firm in San Francisco. When I came back to Hong Kong, a New York law firm wanted to hire me. Then I started doing joint ventures like the first McDonald's in China. I made my way up, a step at a time."

Laura has had her share of bad luck, too, including serious illness, but she stays focused on the upside. "I'm just very excited by opportunities. I don't look upon a job as tiring or demanding. I look at it as challenging and try to do my best," she says. "I kind of radiate the positive energy out. Years ago people asked my husband, 'Your wife works so hard. How do you cope with it?' And my husband said, 'It's worse if she doesn't work so hard!' Work for me has to do with fulfillment, gratification, self-realization. I like to think I've had the best of all worlds at different times of my life."

Why It's So Hard to Take Risk

Just to set things straight, when we talk about risk, we're not talking about bet-the-company decisions. Nor are we suggesting that women leaders must throw the dice to determine where their careers should go next. We're talking about the risk and the fears inherent when you're challenged to leave your comfort zone behind. If you haven't heard the term before, it's where "you know what you know" and "you don't know what you don't know." In other words, everything is familiar and that gives you comfort. Take one step beyond, and you begin to feel uncomfortable.

For the most part, women exercise more caution than men. According to one study, roughly one in three women believes that risks do not translate into professional success. In our own research on Centered Leadership, we found that women are more reluctant to take risks than are men.

There are many good reasons why. Women are less likely to have powerful sponsors in the organization to give them "air cover," and they receive less support from colleagues, too. It's still hard to find other supportive women, particularly in senior positions. So it's understandable that many women may be reluctant to leave the safety of their comfort zone behind.

Let's cross the line on this one together.

It's still true that reward is proportional to risk—nothing ventured, nothing gained. If success isn't enough to motivate you, consider personal growth. Basic human learning theory says that you grow by exposing yourself to new challenges. That doesn't happen without a willingness to step into your "learning zone." What happens when you cross into this new territory? It's scary! It's the place where your fears reside—perhaps fear of failure, of being judged, of losing control, of getting hurt. It's the place where you'll make more mistakes. But it's also exhilarating! It's the place where you develop, you experience the thrill of newness. You're alert.

Staying in your comfort zone will inevitably bore you over time. Step into the learning zone and resist your desire to head back to comfort, and you'll have expanded leadership capacity.

That's why we included lots of stories of wrong turns, mistakes, setbacks, and outright failures from women leaders, to remind you that valleys (along with peaks) are normal and an essential part of the growing process.

How Do You See Opportunity?

What struck us in the interviews was how often women leaders bumped into opportunities. They weren't just luckier than the rest of us. Some had what scientists call a prepared mind. Being prepared helped them see possibilities where others didn't. Even better, these women made their own luck by engaging; open to their futures, they pursued them. They understood their choices and, rather than standing still, paralyzed by uncertainty or frozen by fear, they decided on a path and took it.

So we kept asking the women leaders we met, "How did you know that was an opportunity? What gave it away?" Their answers helped us develop a different approach for spotting and assessing opportunities. Start with the upside. Most of us approach risk assessment by listing what can possibly go wrong. We're pros at filling out that list.

Flip this around. First imagine the very best that could happen. Write it down and make it tangible—what you will learn, what skills you will build, what options you will have, what new people you will meet. Then talk to five people who know something about that opportunity, and ask them to imagine the best that could come out of it. If you don't know five experts, that's okay. Think about how someone you admire would approach this opportunity. What would Thomas Edison or Steve Jobs say about the upside? This will give you more ideas, and you should write them down. Only when you've really given the upside its due can you judge whether the next part is going to be worth it.

Risk and fear are natural companions to opportunity; the upside is a bit frightening and that's natural. Identify your fears and write them down: "I'm afraid I'm going to blow it. People will realize I'm a fraud. They will make fun of me. I might lose my job and I'll never find another one." Go ahead, give those fears a name.

Up until now, they have served a useful purpose: They protected you. Those fears helped you plan ahead, work hard, avoid the downside. But to fight them is to give them power. Instead, get to know them, identifying what behaviors they feed and the consequences of those behaviors. Thank your fears for how they've helped you, recognize when and how they hold you back, and put them in their place. You're the boss. Take a deep breath. You're free.

Now you're ready to understand the real downside outcomes of your opportunity, undistorted by fear. Imagine how you would mitigate each downside possibility. It might even help to write it down. Look right in the eye of the worst-case scenario. Only you can determine whether it's worth taking on.

On Your Way

Okay, you're ready for opportunities, and you're eager for some real-life confrontations—you're ready to face risk and fears.

One way to practice is with small ones. Learning to ask for what you want is perceived as a risk by many women. So try asking outside of work, where the outcome doesn't matter. For example, the next time you're in a store, ask for a discount (and not just because that sweater is missing a button). Practice asking everywhere. The actual discount is not what you're after; it's risk-taking. Though it's uncomfortable to do at first, you'll soon get the hang of it.

Now you're ready to take on professional risks. If it doesn't quite feel that way, start by taking stock of your knowledge. You know more about your own strengths and abilities than anyone else. What do you know about yourself that will help mitigate potential risks? What knowledge and what strengths can you build on to turn a brand-new opportunity into something that feels achievable? Talk to others, too. The more people you touch base with, the better off you'll be, gaining insights you don't see yourself.

If taking a professional risk still fills you with anxiety, take a chance in an area where you feel more comfortable. A step out in your own department can help you build the confidence to try for bigger opportunities. As Laura told us, few things trump expertise. When you develop a strong base of knowledge in an industry or in a particular discipline, your self-confidence soars. One male sponsor at our firm told us that, in his observation, women who "owned" an area of expertise were much more willing to put themselves on the line and grew more successful with each risk they took. That's exactly what Laura did.

We recognize that it may be daunting to become an expert from a standing start. But you can get there if you set out with passion for your topic, a willingness to invest the time to learn, and some creativity. Choose a valued arena that interests you. Then make it your business to learn as much as you can. Knowledge builds competence, competence builds reputation, and reputation opens doors.

The Risk of Being Risk Averse

Deep down, you know that staying on course with the status quo is actually not safer than moving ahead. In terms of psychological well-being, "climbers" do better, despite the dangers of falling, than the people who stick to the safety of the low ground.

Try this exercise. Envision sitting in that rocking chair on your front porch, years from now. Will you regret what you didn't do? We genuinely hope you won't have any painful regrets, though we all have a thousand small ones. Gandhi once said, "We stand in a circle whose circumference is bounded by the circle of our own fears." It's time to push the boundaries now.

And if nothing else works, ask yourself what our women leaders ask themselves: What's the worst that can happen? Measure your heart rate. And then make a decision and get going.

CHAPTER 21

Weathering the Heights

From the beginning of our leadership project in 2004, we have counted Andrea Jung as a key supporter. As CEO of Avon Products, she is one of the world's most high profile women business leaders. With a passion for helping women everywhere, she has led Avon's transformation since becoming CEO in 1999. And when performance dipped, she showed remarkable resilience. The bold, growth leader transformed herself and re-emerged to lead the turnaround.

Defining Moments

I had a very disciplined childhood. There were high expectations, but they were always wrapped in a tremendous amount of nurturing. It was a wonderful way to grow up. For example, when I had piano lessons, it was sixty minutes a day of practice—fifty-nine was not good enough. Our mother put a kitchen timer next to the metronome to make sure.

The thought that you don't just quit in the middle of things was instilled early on. In my first job at Bloomingdale's, where I started in a retail training program, the work was menial—changing hangers, really stockroom work. By Thanksgiving, most of the others in the program were looking to do something else. I remember calling home and saying, "This is just not fulfilling, and I feel like I'm not using my education whatsoever, so I'm thinking about quitting and doing something else." I remember my mom's reaction—no different from when I was on that piano bench: "We don't quit in this family. You haven't even given it a chance. You can learn from this. It may be boring, but you have to start at the bottom to make your way up." I didn't quit, and the rest of my time there became the first chapter in my success. You don't give up, and through hardship or ennui or bad bosses you learn. Perseverance counts.

I learned to work for my own goals. That's another thing my parents taught. In the fourth grade, I remember walking by an art store. I saw a set of 120 colored pencils in a blue velvet box, and I wanted them. But we didn't have a lot of money, and it was not Christmas or my birthday. My mother told me, "If you get straight A's and keep working hard, you can have those pencils." I worked like crazy, and I got those colored pencils. That high bar, setting high standards, is something that I owe to my parents.

By my very early thirties, I realized that what I was doing probably didn't have the purpose and the growth that I wanted. So when I had the chance to make the switch to Avon, it wasn't about a title or a bigger company. At the time, I can tell you, not a single person could believe I was making that move—no one in my family, nobody in my peer group, nobody in the industry. I had been in luxury retailing and was probably going to run one of those companies. Back in the early 1990s, Avon had a much more downscale image with this alternative distribution model, and it was struggling. It seemed more than a little risky.

The original things that propelled me to choose Avon were cerebral: It was a global company. It was a different sales channel.

It was a turnaround, something I had not done before. But that turned out to be only 10 percent of it. What I didn't realize at the time was that 90 percent of why I took the job was the emotional aspect—the purpose of the company, how the business model could change the lives of women around the world. Understanding the larger social role of the enterprise was a defining moment for me. When you get out to the developing markets and see the impact, the opportunity that the work can provide if we do it right, it's very motivating. It's very satisfying, whether we've had a good quarter or a bad quarter. It's clearly what keeps me here—the idea that the enterprise has an ability to make a difference.

One of my strengths, an inherent part of my DNA that has really helped me, is I am not afraid. You know, I always had that courage, being a little girl who wasn't afraid of much. So making a bold career jump like that never scared me. I think it excited me. I was not 100 percent sure it would be right, but I knew the learning would be. I just didn't think I could lose, even if the job didn't work out in the end.

There are so many people—young women getting into their thirties—who stay with a career when it's really not their passion. For me, taking that one risk relatively early and moving to Avon and finding a job with purpose changed my life. If you don't love your work, don't keep doing it. Find something different.

Sponsorship, Sponsoring

In the early years here at Avon, I saw so much that needed to be done, but it wasn't in the area I was in. There's a time when you see an opportunity that's bigger than the role you're in. You can complain about it over drinks with people you work with, or you can do something about it. That decision can be career-defining for young people. It was for me. We had a quasi-global agenda, but it was not well constructed. I was in a domestic marketing role, and I realized I was going to have to do two jobs. I would also define how we should take on international growth, forcing globalization of brands across an organization where everything was very decentralized. It was extremely unpopular, and I knew the "antibodies" would come out and kill the concept.

I worked many nights at home just figuring out how to present my ideas. I also needed to find a way to let management know there was this opportunity. Luckily, because Jim Preston [then CEO and chairman] was such a great sponsor, I did get heard and they wanted to understand more.

Jim was a man ahead of his time. When I first met him, he had a little plaque behind his desk that showed four footprints: barefoot ape, barefoot man, wingtip shoe, high heel. The idea is the evolution of leadership. I remember thinking, "Do you really mean that?" Even at Avon, most of the people in the executive suite were men. Early on he said to me, "You know, one day a woman will run this company—a woman *should* run this company." Jim helped me advance; he's been a mentor ever since. He stuck his neck out for me. Jim believed that I could see things and do things that he could not, and so he was willing to take a bet on me. Without his air cover, I wouldn't be here. On the day I became CEO, Jim gave me that plaque. It sits behind my desk now, in the same place.

I have to keep reminding myself how lucky I was to have a sponsor. I tell myself, "If somebody didn't take a risk on you when you were thirty-nine years old, you wouldn't be in this job. Hey, you weren't perfect. You didn't know everything. But he believed you could figure it out." I don't think we take enough bets on people early enough. If you can't accelerate things for the next generation, you're going to be behind the times.

Today, people write to me and come and see me on things that have nothing to do with the job they're in. Someone in legal just had an opinion about a brand issue that was spot-on. The fact that she took the time to draft a white paper was great. You've got to do your regular job in the day and then be accountable to follow through if somebody says, "Okay, help us figure it out." Taking ownership is not just saying, "This is what you all should do," but "This is how I can help you" or "Here's how we can get this done." You have to have passion and courage enough to believe. That's taking ownership, in a true way, for the enterprise's success.

Adapting to the New Realities

Avon was a $3 billion company when I joined in the early 1990s and not much more in 1999. Then suddenly we were at $8 billion. It's very different to run an $8 billion company: different kinds of people, capabilities, processes, thinking, and strategies. Execution is just wholly different. We were trying to run ahead of ourselves, and it caught up to us. So by 2005, the business had outgrown our capabilities, our investment strategies, and our processes. We had to change everything. That was challenging for the company but particularly challenging for me as the leader.

I remember distinctly, in the fall of 2005, speaking to an executive coach. He basically put a two-by-four to my head and reminded me that a CEO in my position usually gets the ax—most people who can effectively orchestrate a turnaround of the magnitude we faced come from the outside, because outsiders are objective enough to take apart the things that need to be taken apart. It was eight o'clock on a Friday night. He told me to go home and assume that the board had fired me and had then called a recruiter and rehired me Monday morning as the turnaround expert. "Can you make the necessary decisions about people, about strategies you yourself launched, about the organization structure that you yourself designed?" he asked. "Can you start again with a white sheet of paper? If you can't do that, you'll probably be fired anyway in a few quarters." Very few people can do that.

It's just in the nature of who I am to look forward, not back. Whether it's a personal disappointment or a professional disappointment, I don't spend a lot of time thinking about what went wrong. I hope I spend just enough time to learn from it, but I don't dwell on how we got there. What difference does it make? We will never see it again. So, being forward-looking is what matters to me. Do I have a plan? Do I have a solution?

So, Monday morning I came in and did what he suggested. It was going to be brutal, as it related to some extraordinarily difficult people decisions—friends, trusted long-service leaders. In fact, we took out nearly 30 percent of management in four months. I went around the world and faced thousands of associates before I knew who we were going to let go. I felt that I had to tell them why and assure them that we were going to be fair in the process. We were going to restructure the company first and then see who had the needed competencies.

I will tell you one thing: I was never afraid of losing my job. I was only afraid of letting the company down. That probably made a big difference: I had a clean, pure agenda. Also, I'm so optimistic, I never worried about whether the turnaround would actually work or not. But it was the hardest thing I've ever done. I actually got walking pneumonia because of the emotional and physical drain. But slowly, e-mails came in that said things like, "Your message was really difficult to swallow, but you had a lot of courage to come out face-to-face to see us. You're doing the right thing for the company. I hope I'm one of the ones that make it, but if I'm not, I'm going to be a fan of this turnaround because I think it's the right way to go." That was an inflection point for me.

Stepping Up to Lead

How do I feel about becoming a leader? I remember that my father was interviewed by CBS when I became CEO. When the television crew was set up in Mom and Dad's home and the anchor asked, "Did you always know? Was she always like this?" His answer—right there on nationwide TV—was "Absolutely not. I never would have thought, with her personality, that she would be able to be a successful leader." We grew up in an Asian culture where the very fine line of assertive versus aggressive is deep. We had no such thing as "constructive conflict" or even "energetic dialogue" at the dinner table. My father could not imagine that his respectful Asian daughter, whom he had trained and groomed, would be able to have the persona of the stereotype CEO, the man who closed plants and fired people.

When I first went into business, I did have a tough time. It's countercultural for me to be the most energetic person at the meeting. It's countercultural to assert yourself. Through most of my thirties and forties, I had to work on it, to have a seat at the table and have a point of view. I think I have found a sweet spot that feels like I'm still me. I think I'm very assertive now, but I don't think I'm overly aggressive—maybe a moment here or there.

When was my turning point? I'd say it was when the company was in trouble, in 1998. I was not selected to be the CEO, but I stayed because I knew that people needed me in this transition.

My decision to stay was not for the title, not for the job, but because I knew I could help keep the organization together, grounded, aligned, and motivated. That was huge. I knew I was a leader whether I had the top job or some other job. This was the first time, in a meaningful way, that I knew leadership carried privilege and the responsibility of helping people through tough times. I realized that I should follow my compass and not my clock. Passion for Avon, and not for my career, trumped all.

I still have things to work on. It's a constant process of reinvention, a constant process of self-improvement. It's human nature to want people to point out the things you do well. Having people who honestly tell you the truth is critical. When I look at CEOs who have failed, I really always see a lack of self-awareness. If someone isn't going to give you a self-awareness shot in the arm every so often, you can't grow and get better. So that's what I try to look for in my network.

I'm a good listener now, but I had to work on that. I tend to want to have a point of view early, but I realize sometimes that shuts people down. So I got coaching on this. As a leader, the minute you open your mouth, people are going to just say yes, and then you won't actually hear nuances or other thoughts. You'll never know anything but your own point of view. So, try to be the last one to speak. Using that, I have been able to judge the nuances. Sometimes I arrive at the same decision I thought I would make when I came in. But sometimes it's 180 degrees away. You really can't just think you have to go from A to B to C. There is no perfect strategy. There is no one answer. There's never a picture-perfect answer in that linear framework. I think I'm intuitive and by nature flexible, but I build capability by good listening skills.

You can manage a lot of people, but to lead you have to inspire, not intimidate. Have passion and compassion. This concept of continuous change and transformation is critical for leaders in the twenty-first century. The differential for success will be having the combination of IQ and EQ inspiration—the ability to pick the best people, motivate the best people, not look backward, not worry about yourself. If you put that all together, you end up with leaders who truly have the right goals. Great leaders.

What's Core

I also have two kids, and that matters a lot to me. I'm a single mother, and they know that I'm trying doubly hard. And they try doubly hard to let me know they think I'm a pretty great mom. I remember once I got an invitation to be the only woman at a CEO reception at the White House. It was the day that my daughter was going away to summer camp for the first time. She just didn't want to do it. And I figured, "George W. will never know or care if I'm there. But Lauren will always remember, either way."

So you make it work. I have some regrets, but they're only small ones. I'm pretty lucky, I guess.

PART FIVE

Energizing

CHAPTER 22

Energy in Your Toolkit

I just love a debate. The best thing that happens is when the first-year lawyer comes and starts arguing with you on a legal proposition, and he holds his own sentence for sentence. And they see that bubbliness in me when that happens. My enthusiasm is quite infectious. It's just fun to be a lawyer.

Zia Mody, founder, AZB and Partners

Meaning, framing, connecting, and engaging are all in your toolkit now, ready for you to use on your leadership journey. But you're not going anywhere if you're too exhausted to move. Leading requires extraordinary commitment, no matter what field you choose. The work hours are long and spill into nights and weekends. Add in parenting and home responsibilities—over 90 percent of working women say they still assume more of these responsibilities than their spouse—and you see why constant pressure is our reality today. One recent study of professional women by the Work Life Balance Centre found that 26 percent feel that they need to be available 24/7 to respond to job-related issues; 14 percent work with or manage people in different time zones; and almost 20 percent feel pressure to stay extra hours in the office for face time. No wonder that, after starting the day with a full tank of energy, so many of us crawl into bed without an ounce left; all we wish for is uninterrupted sleep. What steals your energy away week after week? Maybe you think it's just dreaming to hope that you can break this cycle.

We can't turn sand into gold, and we can't find the twenty-fifth hour in the day. But we can help you think about your personal energy reserves—what fills them and drains them. We can also help you redesign your schedule with these factors in mind. It takes courage and discipline and even some energy to make it happen. But once you start operating this way, you'll get paid back with a great return.

It all starts with a more productive view of work-life balance. Most women tend to assume that being out of balance is the cause of energy issues, because conventional wisdom says that home time is restorative and work time is draining. So when you meet other working women, the question on your mind is how they get it all done. In reality, it's not so black-and-white. The right kind of work can be exhilarating—when you're so engrossed that you lose track of time. And the wrong kind of family time can be debilitating. Just ask anyone who has tried to juggle screaming toddlers, barking dogs, a dinner that is burning, and a needy spouse! You have energy ups and downs at work; you have them at home, too.

A second assumption is worth challenging: Other women have somehow found work-life balance—you just haven't cracked the code. Rest assured; there is no code. What did women leaders tell us about balance? "It's a myth!" No one is in balance. Indeed, it's not about being in balance but about coming more into balance when you're way off. Some women confided that it's about not letting anything drop to the floor.

We appreciate that the question of having a personal life within the very demanding expectations of leadership is a real question for many women, and in particular, for young mothers. So if there is no such thing as balance, what then? The women leaders we met don't give up sleep, they don't give up home life to devote all their time to work, and they do take vacations. So how do they do it?

It's time for a fresh start. Let go of the notion that you can reach a steady state where you're in total control. Replace it with managing your actual energy flows—within a personal framework of what is important to you.

By reframing the challenge this way, you're replacing an insoluble problem (obtaining a work-life equilibrium state) with a very solvable one (managing your energy reserves). This approach offers a big payoff: never running on empty. That's when you're most vulnerable, most likely to make bad choices, and when you lose the joy of leadership. Energy plays a huge role in your success.

Julie Coates is the general manager of BIG W, a 150-store retail division of Woolworth's in Australia that employs thirty thousand people. She's also the mother of three active girls and was training for the marathon at the time of her interview. Julie could easily be consumed by her work schedule. Instead, she succeeds by treating her energy as an asset that she invests and grows.

The Energizer

Julie was born on a dairy farm, another 24/7 kind of business. "I'm the oldest of four, and I guess I always worked hard," she recalls. "There was always more to be done. My father told me that I could do whatever I wanted in my life when I was eight or ten years old. It was just up to me. Being a farmer was the first thing I wanted to do. Then I wanted to be a teacher, and I became one. There was a period when I wanted to be Australia's first female prime minister. But I ended up in retail, and I love the everyday emphasis on results." What Julie also loves about retail—what gives her energy—are the people, whom she says are "salt of the earth." She likes working with them and figuring out how to motivate their personal best.

Other sources of energy? "My daughters, for starters," she says. "Also, I've been married to the same person for twenty-one years. I'm comfortable and happy with my personal life. Achieving also gives me great energy." What saps Julie's energy? "If I don't feel like I'm making progress, I can slow down pretty quickly. As long as I'm achieving things, I keep going. I'm happy when I'm busy!"

And she was. During her six years as head of human resources, Julie helped lead a radical reorganization that resulted in closing two-thirds of the distribution facilities, a challenge that required sustained energy along with real people skills. "The first thing I'd talk about is changing the lives of four thousand people without making anyone redundant," she says. "We closed sheds. We opened sheds. But we really looked after the people. I'm proud of that because it was the right thing to do."

From there, Julie became chief logistics officer and immediately ran into a huge problem that would take the next two years to solve. "We had just opened our largest distribution center in Brisbane to move 2 million grocery cartons a week. We turned it on, and it didn't work," she says. "Imagine the impact—our stores would grind to a halt. And no one was taking responsibility."

Julie realized she needed to work out how she was going to manage this giant new job. "When I took over, my predecessor told me, 'You're going to have to get used to your phone ringing all weekend. There are lots of issues and lots of problems.' And I thought, 'I won't be able to sustain that, so I need to fix it.' We had to find the cause of the problems," Julie recalls. "What they're ringing up about shouldn't happen in the first place! But at the beginning, not many people lined up to help. I had to get my senior team to step up and help solve the problems."

The first few months were stressful, and Julie remained anxious, working very hard to demonstrate that she could do the job. Pulling the team together proved to be the turning point. "We went to the edge of the abyss, and then it got better much more quickly. We started talking about a partnership for performance. How do we work together? What is it that we expect from one another?" she says. "Someone said to me that one of the important things I did was talk to the whole team about needing to get on the bus. They had a choice, but they needed to make their decision quickly, because if they weren't committed, I'd put them off the bus. I moved on a couple of people fairly decisively when they let the team down. I'm pretty good at tough decisions. That comes from growing up on a farm."

Her experience with solving the logistics problem showed Julie how much energy she derives from working with a team to solve hard problems: "I don't know the answers, but I do know how to get the answers through others. The bigger the problem, the more energetic I get about pulling people in to solve it. I think women are more open to say, 'I don't know,' and 'Someone else has a good idea,' and 'How do I get the best out of my team?'"

In 2008 Julie was promoted to the general manager of BIG W. She followed the outgoing leader for a month to see how he managed the demands of the job. He did it by powering through a grueling schedule. "Given my family commitments, it was something I couldn't possibly sustain," she says. "He was in the office by 6:30. He worked very long hours six or seven days a week and attended functions after work. When I was shadowing him, we were catching planes, getting into cities after midnight. Regularly."

Julie pulled out her energy management tool—redesigning the job. "I thought about what would work for me and how I could achieve the same outcome," Julie says. "I needed to make some structural changes in the schedule. For example, Mondays were tied up with three hours of a management meeting, then three hours of a trade review, in which some of the same things were discussed. I talked to the finance manager about what we could do differently. At the same time, I saw an opportunity to reinvest in more strategic team time."

Julie's schedule is still demanding, but it frees up the time for her family and personal fitness. "I start work most days at 8:00 a.m. and have dinner with my family Fridays, Saturdays, and Sundays. I do spend one weekend day visiting stores, but since my girls love to shop, I bring them along, and in that way still have some family time." Julie seems to be thriving. "People say to me, 'I don't know how you do it.' But energizing is almost a self-fulfilling prophesy. The busier you are, the more you can do. The more energized you are, the more energized you become."

Another part of Julie's energy management is to find ways to preserve the energy she has. Like many high achievers, Julie is well organized. Even as a young woman, she made life plans around the demands of a career and motherhood. "My children are four years apart to ensure that life was a bit easier for us and that I wasn't feeling that I couldn't do it," she explains. "Also, I could probably sustain a small country for what I spend on their support. But if I'm honest about it, I would say it's worth it, because I want to work. I get bored easily. If I didn't work, I'd probably drink or spend too much time trying to feel fulfilled in other ways!"

Knowing What Makes You Stop and Go

It would be marvelous to be like Julie, naturally overflowing with energy despite the grueling hours. But what if you're not? We'll show you how to identify your own sources and uses of energy—and how to protect and replenish your reserves day to day. Edy Greenblatt's research points to four sources of energy that you can put to use: physical, cognitive (or mental), psychological (or emotional), and social (or spiritual). Here are some questions you can use to gauge your own energy state:

- **Physical: Your basic stamina and drive.** How much energy do you have right now? Could you go work out? Do you eat healthy, regular meals? Do you explicitly take good care of yourself? If you do, you've taken on an essential task for leaders; many women feel guilty attending to their needs—and that's plain wrong-headed.
- **Cognitive: Your mental activities.** How easy is it for you to stay focused? What kind of mental activities most excite you? For example, if valor and zest are core strengths for you, your brain may whir with joy when you lead a heated meeting.
- **Psychological: Your emotional moods.** What sparks anxiety, fear, or stress for you, and what makes you want to dance for joy? Some of us enjoy competition; others find it draining. Many of the women we met cited a common emotional drain—watching colleagues sit quietly through a meeting, then happily engaging in hall politics after.

- **Social: Your relationship to others, your core values.** Do group activities energize or drain you? Do you use your strengths on a regular basis? Are you living your purpose? A woman politician said she found that the travel and grueling daily schedule was not draining because she was working on her goal to improve the lives of citizens.

Sometimes the four dimensions of energy work together, but they're often at odds: For example, you may be physically drained after a long run but brimming mentally—buzzing with fresh ideas and feeling emotionally serene. Research shows that if you're getting little sleep, you can actually improve your focus with a quick walk or workout. Similarly, you may feel brain-dead after a day of back-to-back meetings, but socially refreshed because of your impact on your team. Getting ready for a speech may exhaust you emotionally, but you'll feel a surge of adrenaline-fueled energy when you're connecting with the audience.

If these examples don't represent you, that's not surprising. There are only a few universal energizers. At the top of that list is sleep—a good night's sleep is restorative for everyone. Please remember that the next time you try to convince yourself that you can get by without it. How much is enough? The best advice we can offer you is to pay attention to what your body tells you. For example, during our waking hours we're programmed to respond to what scientists call ultradian rhythms. These are cycles of alertness and fatigue, which for most people last about ninety minutes. When a cycle ends, a quick break will refresh you. This is why taking breaks is good for you and why sitting for long periods tires you out. That's a "gimme"—something you can put into action today.

Learning to identify your sources and uses of energy is a worthwhile exercise. Edy teaches a practical approach: Take a closer look at four recent situations—two where you were clearly energized and two where you were drained. For each situation, jot down the physical, cognitive, emotional, and social circumstances. Sometimes we miss the clues—was it quiet or noisy; were you with new people or old friends; were you inside or outside; were you talking or thinking? Get to know your personal patterns for what stops you and what makes you go.

Fill Up on Energizers

You can sprinkle your day with energizers that don't take up much time and begin to see a difference right away. We can't prescribe what will work for you, but here are some ideas:

- Learn yoga and build a simple exercise or two into your work-day routine. Many women leaders turned to yoga to bring their lives more into harmony and help them handle periods of severe stress.
- Take a quick walk down the hall or outside several times a day. For many of us, sunlight is energizing. Try looking out the window or going outside to feel the warmth of the sun. A social break may be refreshing. In either case, changing your venue for even a few moments may restore you.
- Play your favorite music when you need to call on your passion for an intense activity like writing. One leader told us she blasted opera music to help her finish a white paper for the committee on the arts she was chairing.
- Bring fresh flowers to work. And take the time to really look at

them more than once. This one came from a woman who derived pleasure from the variety of her blooms. It's not surprising that one of her strengths is appreciation of beauty.

- Perform an act of kindness for someone who doesn't expect it, or express gratitude to someone who has helped you. Psychologists have evidence that proves what we intuit: kindness and gratitude are among the strongest boosters of fulfillment. Try it and see if you have a new spring in your step.

It's okay if you don't see yourself in any of these ideas. Make your own list, and add to it as you recall more daily activities and experiences that fill you up with energy. The list itself takes energy, but living it will refresh you.

Minimize the Drains

The most important energy-preserving tactic that women leaders shared is establishing your priorities and sticking with them. You can save a lot of energy, time, and anxiety by having a set of rules, rather than reinventing your schedule daily in the heat of the moment. An example is deciding ahead of time to exercise daily. That way, you won't have to waste time agonizing over the decision each day. In effect, you're turning exercise into a habit. Habits are automatic, and that in itself conserves energy. With the time you save, you can build more energy-generating activities into your schedule.

Communication is critical in making this work. Share your customized work schedule with your team and colleagues. Tell them where the boundaries are, and they will respect them. Many working mothers establish a rule about being home for family dinners without interruption from coworkers. Once you set and practice your rules, your colleagues may adopt them, too. You might even adapt company culture, as Julie did when she redesigned meeting agendas and changed everyone's activities.

Of course, there will be times when you choose to make the exception, breaking your rules to accommodate emergencies and unexpected events. The key words are *choice* and *exception.* If you make these exceptions truly exceptional and stick to your plan, you'll be amazed how much energy you can save.

One of the biggest risks to maintaining energy is the 24/7 pace of business, abetted by cell phones and BlackBerrys. Think about it. Are these work tools in your bedroom? Are you sneaking peeks on a regular basis? Do you have a Pavlovian reaction to your cell phone ring? These are habits you may no longer even notice. And what you think of as productivity boosters may be draining your energy and making you far less productive. When you fragment your time through ongoing e-mailing, texting, and phone calls, you not only lose concentration, you lose control of your schedule. Your to-do list remains undone, because others are hijacking your time on matters that may be far less important. Do not mistake urgency for importance.

Once you kick the always-on habit, you'll be much more productive. One retail operations executive told us how she did it: "I used to keep my BlackBerry next to my bed, and I checked it first thing," she says. "I realized that I was thinking about what those e-mailers wanted—not about the people and the issues I should have focused on. So I stopped." Now she avoids e-mails until she is ready. "I have a good hour before I get in, when I can plan and when I am offline," she says. "Everyone knows that if it really is an emergency, they should phone." You really can set the rules, and your team will respect them.

Time management consultant Julie Morgenstern recommends

several strategies for taking back your time. Here are a few to get you started:

- Turn off the mail alert on your computer and check e-mail only at specified intervals during the day and never before you've made your own plan for the day.
- Try to create blocks of time in your calendar for different types of work—for meetings, calls, and, most important, uninterrupted stretches for concentrating on high-level thinking and analysis or for writing. Remember, the quality of your ideas and your management is a necessary part of leading. It's great to be responsive, but no one will promote you on the basis of your e-mail skills!
- Turn off your cell phone and put your PC to sleep when you join conference calls. We learned that an executive who took up this best practice significantly improved her relationships with her team within months; by focusing on the calls, her direct reports felt she was actively listening and joining in the problem-solving. They noted that she showed greater caring and demonstrated real value-added—just by this one change!
- Set a rule for all meetings: no gadgets—because even the silent ones interrupt when the light turns from green to red; who can resist not checking under the table? Whether you mean it or not, receiving messages from others during the meeting is a clear signal that the people in the room are less important to you. If you must take a call, let others know ahead of time.

Finally, stop multitasking. Yes, it seems like the only way to get through life these days. And, like most women, you're probably great at it. Contrary to your intent to fit everything in, psychologists have found that multitasking is highly counterproductive.

When you drop what you're doing to answer your e-mail alert or phone, you incur "switching" costs, as your brain moves from one type of activity to another. Switching takes energy and makes you less effective. Also, scientists say it takes you twenty minutes to get back to the level of concentration you had before the interruption. That saves hours if you are willing to take charge.

Multitasking can even be dangerous—literally—if you do it while driving. Scientists have found that even using a hands-free phone distracts your attention and slows response times. Sure, everybody does it. You see busy executives at the wheel and on their cells every morning. They're flirting with disaster on the highway, and they're de-energized before they walk in the door.

Schedule Redesign: The Right Mix

Schedule redesign is another important tool to preserve your energy resources. Edy Greenblatt created this tool by observing employees at a Club Med resort. Like many of us are tempted to do, they lumped all the draining tasks into a single day-part to get them out of the way. But they used up so much energy that they were tapping into their "reserves" before the afternoon. Greenblatt taught them to mix sources and uses of energy for a more productive and enjoyable day. What's more, this insight was a key to reducing attrition.

It's what Julie essentially did as she entered each new position. So, if your day has a similarly draining effect on you, break it down activity by activity to see what's happening to your hourly energy level. Redesign your own daily sequence with restorative intervals, and you'll feel less like quitting.

As you start to actively manage your energy reserves, keep in mind that you can build capacity for each kind of energy source. If you have ever trained for a sport, or worked hard at dance or yoga, you know that by pushing yourself a little beyond your limits you build capacity—as long as you rest between workouts. The same holds true for other kinds of energy.

Your energy will always go up and down, and that's normal. With a little bit of active management, however, you'll be in control and not the other way around—a nice change in itself.

And if that sounds like a pretty good deal, it is—for you and everyone around you.

CHAPTER 23

For a Quick Recovery

When I leave at night, it's done. I shut down. I find I need some time with no voices to relax. I call that my recovery time. I detox and get the stress out by having quiet for a while. It's typically on airplanes now, or it may just be in the evening, reading by the fire with my husband.

Jane Fraser, managing director, Citigroup

Recovering from the unpredictable is one of the biggest challenges to managing your energy. Setbacks happen, many beyond your control. Wouldn't it be great to know you have the resilience to bounce back quickly?

We've all had weeks like this: A family celebration is coming up, so you work feverishly to clear the decks, and at the same time you plan a memorable evening. It would all have worked out, except that your boss just threw you a critical problem on a tight deadline. And without notice, she calls an emergency meeting the night of your dinner. Let's pour on a bit more stress: It wasn't in your plan, but your baby has a bad cold and has been keeping you up at night. Your in-laws are on their way for a five-day visit. Forgetting everything you learned about energy management, you tell yourself you'll catch up on life later. Suddenly, work has no zest.

Sound familiar to you? When adverse situations happen, you burn energy to face them, often running down your reserves. And while you know that recovering from the valleys is what makes or breaks a leader, you're exhausted and the steep hill facing you is formidable. The last thing on your mind is throwing yourself into a new plan. You're just not ready. Soon, you're wondering whether it's time to opt out. Tears begin to flow.

Let's reframe this! With energy, you have resilience. And with resilience, you'll quickly get back to a place where you're feeling strong and enjoying life again. It's what helps you sustain yourself so that you can make a difference.

Yifei Li is a woman leader who exudes resilience. She showed us how to recover at a pace we didn't think possible. A talented athlete, she started her career in business with tremendous physical strength and stamina. Eventually, she became a groundbreaking media executive in Asia, bringing MTV to the region. And recently, she took up a new challenge, setting up Asian operations for a leading U.S. hedge fund.

Physical Strength Builds Resilience

Growing up in Beijing, Yifei Li loved to "do everything," she says. Perhaps that's why she was singled out by the Beijing Sports Institute for special training. "About a hundred students were selected to test, and they eliminated seventy the next day," she recalls. "A few days later, another twenty-three had to go. The remaining seven became martial arts team members. At nine, I was on that team." The martial arts training and competitive experience instilled a strong discipline that Yifei carried through to adulthood. It was her foundation to handle the ups and downs of life.

Making the martial arts team did not mean Yifei had truly arrived. "For three years, I was the tea lady," she says. "I was on the bench. I was not really a competitive person, timid and shy. But sitting on that bench and watching other people win, hearing the applause, and seeing the standing ovation, it was quite inspiring. I thought, 'Hmm, that's a good feeling. Maybe I should try harder.' So I tried harder!"

At thirteen, Yifei became a national champion in rainbow sword, an ancient Chinese discipline. In the ten years she held that title, she learned to recover from losing, in addition to enjoying the wins. "The frequency of losing gave me balance," she explains. "I was always the national champion throughout college, because everyone else was amateur. But then at the national professional level, I lost a lot, because I wasn't training as much as before. That helped me maintain the perspective that training is the key to winning and that no one wins all the time."

Yifei's training helped her accept wins and losses without feeling defeat. She used that mind-set to recover from business setbacks later on in life: "I don't believe in rejecting myself," she says. "I think the world provides opportunity for all of us. We just have to say yes to ourselves. And if there's a chance that people will say no, then I just continue to say, 'Yes, you can do it.' And in the end, usually you can." She told us of a Chinese saying: "If God has given you this life, then you should really make good use of it." She certainly does.

Yifei actively trained herself to turn worrying into a positive force. "I have a little habit. Every time I'm paranoid, I write it down on a list called 'Why am I worried?' The moment I write it down, I realize, 'You know what? Just take action on it!' " For example, Yifei was worrying about a deal that she had not closed. After putting it on her list, "I picked up the phone and called. I took action to delete my worry—that is great therapy for me."

Yifei's resilience served her well when things went unpredictably sour. There was the time when she planned a concert at a two-thousand-seat stadium in Wuhan, starring a popular Korean boy band—and ten thousand students showed up. Disaster was brewing. "The party secretary of the school was really worried," she recalls. "He decided to cancel the show half an hour before the band was scheduled to go on! That meant a big financial loss to us. It meant a blow to our reputation. On top of this, we were afraid of protest and escalating violence. I called anyone who might be able to change the decision. But I couldn't save the concert. That was the first time in my life that I couldn't fix the issue on the spot. I had a big sense of loss and failure."

Once Yifei realized she could not find an immediate solution, she went to the hotel to sleep. "You know Scarlett O'Hara's famous line, 'Tomorrow is another day'? When I sleep, I don't think about anything. And then by the time I wake, I feel better. I'm mentally strong and can deal with the issues." True to form, the next day Yifei came back with a remedy. She told the authorities, "We will plan a bigger event, exclusively for this boy band and in a stadium with ten thousand seats." She got approval and even signed up new sponsors to foot the extra expense. She converted what had been a professional disaster and personal disappointment into a success that set her up for even better things.

Yifei, like other women we met, draws power from her close relationships. Having emotional support is critical at times of stress and helps Yifei restore her energy and optimism. She credits her husband with giving her the strength to bounce back: "Sometimes when I feel like I'm not able, he will say, 'Oh, absolutely, you can do it.' He reminds me of a very famous saying from Confucius: 'When God is giving you a big burden, he usually first dirties your body; he works hard your mind and gives a lot of failures to train your strength.' So whenever you meet failure or disaster, it's a time when God is going to give you big tasks ahead."

How Does She Do It?

Over time, Yifei has developed a long list of tactics that enable her to recover quickly and prevent her from running on empty. She makes sure she is physically fit, she does not say no to herself, she maintains a good support network, she systematically identifies and addresses her worries, and she always gets a good night's sleep.

Using these tools can get you through everyday setbacks, like the meeting that throws off the family dinner. But they are even more important to deploy when severe adversity occurs. The women leaders we met shared a litany of professional setbacks that take time and energy to recover from—missed promotions, a severe performance downturn, or getting fired. That's when you really need a strategy for recovery.

You don't have to be a top athlete to become an Olympic medalist in recovery. Start with your own experiences to discover what has worked for you in the past. Remember a few experiences when you were able to recover from severe adversity. They can be from your younger years, if nothing recent fits the bill. Describe what happened and what helped you recover. You might use the same energy categories to explore: physical, mental/cognitive, psychological/emotional, and social/spiritual. Remember who was around you and the roles they played, positive or negative.

Then think through one or two experiences where it took you longer to bounce back and go through the same list. Was anything different for you in these situations? As you reflect, pay attention to what helped you bounce back (or what was missing when you found that harder to do). The list may include:

- Enough sleep and attention to your physical health—a regular trip to the gym—so that you had the stamina to get through this valley
- A strong support network of family and friends who believed in you, whether the winds were blowing your way or not
- A good diagnosis of what actually happened (collected through conversations with others who counseled or coached you)
- A plan of action to recover that excited you
- The presence of influential supporters at work who were willing to help you out of your valley

Get ready for the next bout of adversity by putting these helpers in place. It's part of Centered Leadership—in fact, one of the most important parts. Anyone can look good when things are trending up; it's what you do when the chips are down that people notice and remember. And be kind to yourself. Valleys are an inevitable part of life, and figuring out how to climb out is more important than endless worrying about how you got there.

Build Recovery into Your Day

Remember to build recovery into your daily routine, too. Too many months of a draining routine will lead to burnout. You may find a challenging new assignment or a demanding schedule energizing at first. Before you know it, however, you have forgotten about energizing and your stamina and resilience are slipping away.

You may not recognize the change, because it's what everyone around you is doing. You're headed for burnout, and you'll know when the activities that normally energize you lose their power.

Often burnout creeps up on you when you're on a team and everyone's engrossed and working hard. In fact, the work may be so engaging that it's easy to forget your family; sometimes you even forget to eat and sleep. That's not good! If you're the leader of the team, try to watch out for the early warning signs—when your colleagues neglect to call home or spend too many nights in a row at the office. Perhaps the team has gotten into the habit of e-mailing late at night and early in the morning, letting work spill into weekends, and suddenly you're having a routine Sunday conference call.

Another early warning sign is catching a bad cold. Chances are you've been working a grueling schedule and dipping into your energy reserves. It goes without saying, but be the watchman to protect yourself and your team.

Here's another flag: Every single minute of the day on your schedule is booked, and your calendar is filled with the same kind of days, no end in sight. What can you do then? Put a half hour back into your schedule for free time and use it to recover.

Yifei's athletic training helped her develop resilience to bounce back from defeat. It turns out that what successful athletes learn can work for you, too. Jim Loehr, a performance psychologist, studied tennis players to understand what made some truly great. In his book *The Power of Full Engagement*, he explains how he started by watching the players during points, but he couldn't see any differences. He finally realized that the difference between great players and other pros was what they did *between* points. Some would walk slowly back to the baseline, while others would take a few seconds to focus or even to talk to themselves before play resumed. When he hooked them up to monitors, he found that their heart rates fell twenty beats or more. They were using strategic restoration techniques that gave them energy and better concentration—a winning combination.

Everyone has a different tactic for immediate restoration. It doesn't have to be physical at all. Some women leaders make a rule never to work on airplanes, using that quiet time to restore. Dare we say it? Some play hooky for an hour or two, whether it's to see their children or treat themselves to a gallery visit. Others walk the hall to meet colleagues. Think about what might work for you.

Once you begin to understand what helps you restore your energy, build those techniques into your routine. Turn these new behaviors into positive rituals. If you have a ritual that you do every day to restore yourself, in the heat of the moment it will be easier to recover. You brush your teeth every day, whether you're at a professional peak or climbing out of a valley. Make restoration your routine. If you can do that, you will never feel fully tapped out.

Training for This Marathon

We can all recall times when work took us over. It comes from wanting to do a good job, feeling responsible and accountable—not wanting to burden others. Sometimes, intense work leads to exhilaration. Often, it leads to a lost week, month, or more. It happens to all of us, but you can be ready for it.

There are dozens of ways to get ready. Here are a few:

- **Nurture and extend your support network.** Your friends and family will point out when you're sliding, even when you can't see it yourself. They're also your best safety net, but you need to keep those relationships current to be able to call on them when adversity strikes.

- **Get regular physical exercise.** We can't say it enough—it's not for fun, it's for work.
- **Make sure you are getting the zzz's you really need.** Watch your sleep patterns and don't let them get out of hand. The experts say you can't really make up for lost sleep and repeated neglect will turn you into Mr. Hyde.
- **Make sure there is some time in your week for creativity.** Julia Cameron calls this spending time with your artist child—reconnecting with your inner creative force and feeding it. Creativity comes from many sources, not just the arts. It's worth the investment to sustain your energy for the long haul.
- **Take your holidays.** It's no badge of honor to skip them. What restores you when your reserves have run low? Many of the women leaders we talked to love foreign travel. They find newness and adventure energizing. Others (particularly Australians, it seems!) love holidays on their farms, where they can enjoy peace and independence and lose themselves in physical work. Think about what kind of vacation brings you back refreshed and brimming with ideas. Then take it.
- **Try singing.** And not just in the shower, but anywhere, anytime. Being out of tune is no excuse. Belt it out when you find a song coming on!
- **Join a group.** It's one of the most energizing things you can do. Any kind of women's group works, as do religious groups, community groups, organized classes, or a group of friends you formed in school.
- **Have fun every day.** It is not an indulgence to take ten minutes to call a friend to share a joke or mini-adventure. Make it out

of the ordinary—take your team outside on the first nice day in spring. Encourage laughter in team meetings.

Your leadership journey is a marathon, with challenging hills and long stretches, along with exciting moments that come from personal and collective achievements. Yes, someone does come in first, but that's not the only goal. Enjoy your training, enjoy your endurance, and enjoy the terrain. In other words, enjoy your journey, including your own strength and resilience.

CHAPTER 24

Experience of Flow

May 4th, 1975: I still remember what I danced. There was a certain lightness of being, and there were sparks everywhere. All eight hundred people in the audience were like one. No one moved. Someone said, "We just saw light for a few moments." This is what we call *Rasa* in Sanskrit—the moment of heightened aesthetic experience. It's a flow of energy. Life is a flow, the breath is a flow, and when the flow stops, you are gone.

Sonal Mansingh, classical Indian dancer

You know the feeling. Work seems effortless. Time passes unnoticed. You're on top of the world and in the moment. You have boundless energy. And people say, "I want what she's having!" It's such a natural high—you are filling up on life itself. Once you've experienced it, you want more.

That's flow. In his pioneering, University of Chicago psychologist Mihály Csikszentmihályi observed that people in all walks of life can achieve the same altered state that athletes, musicians, and others experience when they are "in a groove." He called it flow—what an artist feels when she transforms an empty canvas or what a tennis player feels on her game. Anyone in any job can have flow, factory workers included. Flow unleashes new energy. And, because people often experience flow more at work than at home, it's what draws us to work. However, the sad truth is that most people experience flow only a small percent of the time.

But what if you could nurture the conditions for flow—not just for yourself but for your team and for many, many others in the organization? That's a surefire way to expand your energy capacity and to accomplish great things.

Linda Wolf, retired chairman and CEO of Leo Burnett Worldwide, can still recall the feeling of flow and its impact. Capping a twenty-seven-year career at the advertising agency, today she remains happily engaged, serving on several boards, including Walmart's. She shared her experiences—and the joy—of flow.

The Flow-Meister

Back in the 1950s when Linda was growing up, most dads didn't take their daughters to work. Linda's dad did, and he always talked about business in an interesting way at the dinner table. He also treated her the same way he treated her brother. Though Linda's mom wanted her to be a traditional feminine girl who would pursue traditional goals, that lesson never took hold. Linda remembers: "I think my mom would probably identify me as somewhat difficult. I was fairly independent. I didn't give her as much respect, probably, as I did my dad. Her expectations just weren't me. But in time, I realized my mother gave me life values in terms of who I am in my soul."

What Linda understood as a young girl was that she got a thrill from learning new things about the world around her—it didn't matter how obscure the topic was. "I have always had an insatiable curiosity about everything. I've just been interested in people, in places, in things, and I get a lot of energy from that," she says. "Those experiences energize me. I feel much more alive when I'm learning. Even now that I'm retired from a full-time job, I want that challenge. That's the kind of person I am. I have that curiosity that just never stops, frankly. It gets me up in the morning. I think, 'What's new today? What am I going to do differently?' "

Curiosity drove Linda to spend her junior year in college in Madrid back in 1967, though her college friends thought she was nuts to do it. "I had relatives who traveled a lot, and when I was young they shared their experiences with me. I wanted my own."

It was a growing experience. Linda recalls, "I gained an awful lot of confidence that year I spent in Europe. There was one time I was lost in France. I didn't speak the language. It was 2:00 in the morning, and cell phones didn't exist. I had no money. I had to figure something out. You go through enough experiences where you recognize you've got the capability to solve the problem or get through it. Confidence comes from that."

After school, Linda joined a market research firm in New York and eventually transferred to Chicago. She fell in love, married, and moved to Pittsburgh, where she took a market research job at H. J. Heinz. Her turning point came one year later, when Heinz offered Linda a brand-management role. A local ad agency offered her a position, too. "It was brand or account management— different sides of the same coin," Linda explains. "The woman who interviewed me at the agency tipped my decision. She was talking about account people and said, 'If you really want to be successful, you need to anticipate your client needs. You need to bring them ideas. You need to be on the leading edge of what's going on.' And I thought, 'Well, that's where I want to be. I want to be where you're taking people forward.' "

Another move, and Linda was back in Chicago interviewing with advertising agencies. Leo Burnett offered her a job and to her husband's surprise, she took it. "The people were really smart, but I thought they were pretty arrogant and took themselves a little too seriously," she notes. "They offered me less money, less responsibility. But they had a great training program, and I hadn't been in the advertising business that long. I wanted that training."

Her plan was to leave after a few years, armed with new skills. Yet she only left Burnett when she retired. "It gets back to what energizes you and what motivates you," Linda says. "I loved the advertising business from the time I got into it. I enjoyed the diversity of people, and I loved the diversity of opportunities. The thought of spending twenty years at one consumer company would kill me. It's not who I am."

The simple reason was flow, resulting from the combination of creativity, problem-solving, and competitive pitching for new business. "In new business, there was more than one occasion when I really felt flow," she says. "That, to me, was the ultimate. I loved every aspect of it. It was advertising on steroids. The whole process was compressed down to a much shorter period of time. The pressure to deliver a brilliant solution was even greater. And what got me more than anything was the team. I absolutely treasured that. There are so many multiple talents on a team, whether it's the creative people, the media people, the research people, the account people. And in new business, we would get the best of the best together. Then we would try to crack that code. That was the flow. The hours could be deadly. We could work seven eighteen-hour days, and people would say, 'You're crazy,' but it was exhilarating."

So flow became the reason Linda stayed. She described its effect to us. "Flow is much more about the joint effort as opposed to the individual one. It's challenging. It's energizing, and it's very stimulating. It's like every neuron's working, you know? Your level of attentiveness, your sensitivity to what's going on is just all heightened, because you're in the moment when it all comes together. There's nothing like it. Frankly, there are times when it's such a high that it's hard to come out when the pitch is over."

Advertising drew on everything Linda loved and on her strengths. She loved the competition; she loved setting and achieving goals. It tapped into her love of learning and curiosity; it drew on her creativity and love of a challenge. And in addition, she loved being with people.

Linda decided that pitching new business full-time would be her ideal job. "I had worked on a new business pitch and we had won some cosmetic business," she recalls. "That intrigued me, and so I volunteered to take over new business. Most people told me, 'That is not a smart career move.' Burnett didn't really feel it was necessary to focus on this area because people would knock on our door. I saw the reality that our marketplace was changing, and I told senior management I would love to run it.

"We came in with a whole fabulous business plan and everyone was really impressed," Linda remembers. That said, flow doesn't just happen. "When we went out and pitched our first year, we lost every single pitch except for one. It was devastating, and it was highly visible. In advertising, when you don't win something, it's all over the press. Not only does the outside world know, but your employees are demoralized. And it's all on your shoulders."

Flow takes a determination to build new skills in order to meet the challenge. A born competitor, Linda did not give up. "The advertising business is a tough business. Combine that with kids and a husband, and it was really tough. But I've never said, 'I give up.' It's just not in my nature." Linda pauses. "Well, I did take some moments to wallow in my sorrow. But it didn't take long to regroup. I guess I've always felt like nothing or no one is ever going to get me down. No one else is going to control me. I'm going to control myself. I'm going to solve this. How can we make this work?' " Linda was also lucky to have her top supporter at home. "My husband would tell me to get my act together and get back in the game. And most of the time, he was right!"

That's exactly what Linda did. She got mad and she figured it out. Approaching her team's failure as she would any marketing problem. She got the facts and revised how they went to market: "It was a lot of common sense. Then we went back and we won every pitch the next year, except one."

So Linda kept at it, and she and her team built new skills. "I like going to the edge every once in a while," she admits. "It's a test of your capability. One time we pitched to Walt Disney World, an account that never had an agency. We had really impressed them, but they came back and said they'd hire our creative and marketing teams but not media. I put my foot down. Our CEO worried about losing the deal, but he went with my stand. It was touch and go. Two weeks later they came around, but of course it could have gone the other way."

Becoming engrossed in a task that challenges your full abilities leaves you feeling invigorated. Taking the next risk in your development keeps flow going. But there's more. When leaders relayed their peak experiences, they first talked about a meaningful goal shared by a high-performing team selected for diverse skills. Then they went on to describe an incredible feeling of joy that has every bit the intensity and satisfaction of flow but even better—a team experience of flow. We learned that everyone cites peak experiences as the highest impact work they've ever done. It's the time when all cylinders are in sync and firing.

No wonder people who have had a peak experience feel lucky and want more of them.

Finding Your Own Flow

Flow is not only intellectually, emotionally, and spiritually stimulating, it is also physically restorative. Scientists have been able to track how brain functions change when people are in a state of flow. The brain waves you tap into bridge your conscious and subconscious, allowing your subconscious thoughts to come to the surface while giving your task-oriented, conscious mind a break. That's why it feels so different. It's also when you are at your most creative, both goal-directed and free-flowing.

Anyone can set up the conditions for flow, and it is well worth your effort. Csikszentmihályi identifies five conditions:

1. Clear and attainable goals
2. Strong concentration on a focused topic
3. Intrinsic motivation
4. Balance of the challenge with your ability
5. Immediate feedback

It's impossible to experience flow without clear goals. Of course the goal should be a stretch, but if it is truly out of reach, you'll only achieve frustration or worse. For example, Linda's goal was to win her fair share. Had she set her immediate goal to win every time, it would have been a different story. What about you? What goals inspire you and make your heart beat faster—goals you can attain but are out of reach?

Concentration allows you to tap into your deeper brain waves. Linda was easily caught up in the excitement of bringing the team together, meeting a new client, and pitching a competitive proposal. Bringing the concentration needed to achieve flow means eliminating distractions. Find a block of time and protect it from interruption. It only takes fifteen minutes to enter a state of flow.

Try as you might, it's hard to concentrate if you haven't found your motivation, tapping deep into the well of your positive emotions. Linda absolutely loved the thrill of the hunt, which unleashed her competitive spirit. Unleash your passions, and you may lose yourself in the doing.

When you haven't got the skills, flow will be elusive. Instead, you'll experience a heavy dose of frustration and disappointment as you fail to reach your goal. Linda's first year as head of new business was tough until her team built the ability to win.

Finally, you need feedback—external measures to confirm that you are performing well and that the work has impact. At Burnett, Linda knew immediately whether her team's pitch was connecting with the client—they won or lost the assignment.

Where will you find flow? Start by thinking about what parts of your job you find most satisfying—is it meeting with customers, leading a team, working on a tough problem, motivating the front line? If you're not in the right job, what would that job be? Remember back to the best peak experience you've had, and analyze what made it so. What can you do to set up the conditions for another experience like it now? What can you do to make that happen for everyone on your team?

Shelly Lazarus, chairman of Ogilvy & Mather, told us she shared the same sense of total engagement in her work. In fact, she said she enjoyed it so much that she would do it even if she didn't get paid. That's how satisfying flow can be. When you're in the flow, work is fun.

Imagine that—working for the fun of it.

CHAPTER 25

Boundless Energy

On September 11, 2001, Margaret Jackson was about a year into her tenure as nonexecutive chairman of Qantas, the Australian airline. The World Trade Center and Pentagon attacks changed everything; Margaret learned to deal with stress and uncertainty that lasted until 2007, when she stepped down.

Preparation for Leadership

I went to state school in a really small country town when I was four. I started much earlier than I should have because the school only had six students and they needed a minimum of eight to stay open. Until I was about thirty, I thought I'd had an underprivileged experience at state school, and then I realized that that school was very fundamental in forming me as a person. I went to high school by the time I was ten. In those years, I was the only one in my grade. And there were no real rules because with eight students and one teacher you didn't need any. It wasn't really until I started work that I realized that there are all these rules and regulations and expectations that you've got to do this and only this. My personality isn't like that because as a young person the world was limitless.

When I was in high school, I had a very enlightened art teacher who taught me woodwork and welding and all sorts of things that girls weren't supposed to do. And when I was a university student, I thought I was going to be a teacher, but some of my contemporaries were applying for jobs as chartered accountants. So, I thought, "I'll apply for a summer job and see if I like it." I wrote off a whole lot of letters. And I got replies, you know, "Dear Ms. Jackson, we're terribly sorry but we don't employ women." Because I was told I couldn't do it, I desperately then wanted to do it. In Australia in the early 1970s, Price Waterhouse was one of the few firms that actually employed women. So I went there first.

I think if I look back on my working life, every two or three years something new has come along. Some amazing things have happened to me. I probably have got lots of wonderful memories but they're not the ones that I remember. I think I'm the sort of person who can't really remember the sunny days. I remember the stormy days. And if I go back over my career, everything that turned really ugly or went wrong turned out to be a fantastic turning point for me in my career.

I like change, I like challenge, I like complexity. I think I'm best at complex situations that involve human drama and complexity in the environment. I like thinking about tomorrow and then helping organizations prepare for the tomorrow that others can't see. That's the thing that I get excited about.

X-treme Energy Needed

I was a nonexecutive chairman of Qantas when September the 11th happened. You wake up in the middle of the night and find out that aircraft had been used as missiles. And as a consequence of the terrible situation in the United States, we had huge security issues all over the world.

We had 3,500 passengers stranded in the United States. We had 3,500 Americans in Australia who wanted to get home. We had the Australian prime minister in Washington, and we had to get him home. On top of that it was about to be school holidays, and the football final, and our major competitor failed. On September the 12th, the second carrier in Australia ceased flying because it was insolvent. One hundred thousand Australians were stranded all over Australia. That's stress and complexity.

And as a chairman, I got to participate in that very complex set of circumstances. My most memorable moment was dealing with some of the executives. I went through the stress and the strain as they did. You're working 24/7, and it feels like there are missiles going off every five minutes. And you can't predict quite what's going to happen next. You've got politicians, the prime minister, and many ministers in various departments very concerned about everything that's happened.

I can remember in the middle of all of that, I went home one night and decided I would prune my plum tree. Now, I had never pruned a plum tree. But when I got home, that's what I felt like doing. I got out the ladder, I got the clipping shears, and I attacked this tree. When my husband came home, two-thirds of the tree was on the ground. He asked, "What are you doing?" It was then I realized I really didn't know what I was doing. I had so much built-up tension that it was a great release.

And then I thought, "That's interesting, I've used a physical thing to get rid of all this tension." I went to Sydney to talk with the executives who were also pretty stressed. So I started sharing my story about pruning the plum tree. I told them that it was okay to feel wheels spinning in your home environment as well as in your work environment. What was amazing was all these people started telling me stories, like they drove home and saw the tree that was on the left-hand side of the drive, and they thought it should be on the right hand side. Then they got out a shovel and they moved the tree. It was extraordinary how many times people told me these physical stories. As the chairman, when you share your story, you empower others to share their own. That lets out some of the tension.

Business Not as Usual

I felt exactly the same as everybody else on the planet when we saw the aircraft hitting the World Trade Center. It was just beyond belief that this was happening in our life. After that, I thought, "I'm the chairman of the airline, and the CEO and executives have all got so much to do. What can I do that's really going to help the situation, take some pressure off them, and yet be useful?" I took responsibility for all the dealings with state and federal governments, from security through to the prime minister, dealing with all of their complex issues. It was like being on a roller coaster that just didn't stop. You think, "Well, I've survived today." And then something else happens. And then something else happens.

People do scenario planning. Normally when you do scenario planning, you only do one or two catastrophes at a time. But after September the 11th, there were about twenty catastrophes. It was wave after wave after wave. What was interesting is that you just had to keep stepping up. There was no downtime. You couldn't relax. It was an unusual set of circumstances. How we dealt with it was also interesting. Normally you would make decisions in an airline very carefully, with lots of information. And you would hasten very slowly. If you're going to buy a new aircraft, you would carry out the evaluation over eighteen months. You'd have numerous board meetings and thousands of spreadsheets. You'd have the finance organized, and you would know where you're going to fly the aircraft, and so forth. But in that period, we were making decisions in weeks that would normally take months or years. We didn't actually have time to get together physically, so we used telephone conference calls extensively. And you know, we got 80 percent of the information in 20 percent of the time, and we didn't worry about the rest. We also had to have a culture that was forgiving. We didn't have a long time to decide. We needed to have a culture that would say, "You made a decision and it was the wrong one. That's okay. Move on. Make another. Don't dwell on it."

It was a very interesting experience for everybody. I can remember in the middle of all that, I went to a football match one day. And as I arrived at the stadium, the prime minister rang me over a particular drama happening. I spent the entire match in the toilet because it was the only place I could hear the mobile phone. I'd ring the CEO, then I'd speak to the minister of the transport, then to the prime minister, and then back to the CEO. Getting information, making a decision, translating the decision into action, then getting another load of information. It was a fascinating time.

But it took such a long time to end. I was chairman of Qantas for seven and a half years, and in that time there was September 11th, September 12th, bombings in Bali, bombing number one, bombing number two, avian flu, SARS, Iraq. And there were record fuel prices. There were record currency swings. There was re-equipment of the fleet and the delay of the A-380 Airbus. It just never stopped. We called it Constant Shock Syndrome. Living through that period taught me to be a different executive. You can't dwell on or ponder extensively in that environment. Then you realize you don't need to do all that pondering! You do get most of your information early on, and you have to trust your instincts. You have to trust the people around you. And if people don't rise to the challenge, then you've got to find other people who will.

X-treme Renewal

Every other stressful period that I'd been through before taught me the principles that I applied in this period. You have to eat properly. You have to sleep properly. You have to have some time out. You have to exercise.

Physical activity was really important. You have so much tension and so much energy but then you become manic. It was difficult for all of us to come down. You get so used to this manic state that coming back into calmness was tricky. But I found myself sometimes running instead of walking because it would take me fifteen minutes instead of half an hour. I'm sure I was impatient with my family, even though I was trying to be tolerant. You don't always appreciate the impact that you have on others.

I've done yoga since I was at university, and that really helped me get through that period. When I found myself getting incredibly tense, I would do yoga breathing to relax. I've had some extraordinary joyous moments of total inner peace through meditation. I actually like myself. I'm content as a person. I'm quite content to do very little. And I often think, "How did I end up doing all these things?" I was very determined. One step leads to the next. One door closes, and another door opens.

The other thing was walking. I'm a great believer in walking. There's something about the rhythm. It's almost like rocking a baby. You go for a walk and you've got a thousand things churning in your head. You're not sure what the answer is. Yet you come back from the walk and it's all sorted out.

I also like time out. I like reflective activities. I've taken a lot of photos over the years. In the last year, I've taken up painting and it's just totally absorbing. When I paint a painting, I look at it and think, "How did I do that?" It's like I don't know where it came from. And then I look at the painting and say, "Wow. I produced that." The creative process is quite fascinating. But then I think in my work life I've always been creative.

Putting It into Perspective

I had an experience in my last year as chairman that underscores this discussion. I was in the hospital, and Qantas was subject to a takeover. I did a media interview in the hospital, when I probably shouldn't have. The media coverage was quite extraordinary for the event.

Immediately after I'd done the interview I realized that I had been too aggressive. It wasn't rude language, it was just colorful. I was very tired and taking a lot of medication. When you're really sick, it's like you've chopped your legs off, and you think, "Well, yes, but I've got a job to do. I've got an obligation. I'm the chairman. I've got to do it."

I think my judgment was impaired and the journalist baited me at the beginning of the interview. Normally I would not have reacted, but he accused the CEO of certain things, which were not true. I reacted to that, and then I had this overwhelming experience of anger. All my frustration, my annoyance at my own health situation and at how the media had dealt with the takeover in general came out. Immediately after the interview, I rang the CEO and said, "I think I've just really blown up," and I acknowledged what I'd done. Then I thought, "What can I do? I've already said it. I can't ring the journalist and say, 'Don't print it,' because that's unprofessional."

The next day I read it and thought, "Oh, my god. I wish I hadn't said that." At the time I thought it would be a one-day wonder. But it didn't die. It got a life of its own. I kept thinking, "Why won't it go away?" But in another way, because I was so unwell, that helped me deal with it. I got it into perspective. I thought, "I'm still alive. It's not life-threatening." I fast-forward a few weeks and it was like, "I'm getting better. I'm still doing a good, reasonable job." And now, fast-forward over a year, and I think, "What I said was absolutely truthful." And it was very memorable. Now people say, "What you said was absolutely right." But you don't get any brownie points for being right.

What happened to me had to do with my work ethic. If I look back on my own career, I was the first woman to chair a Top 50 company in Australia. I always felt a bit of an obligation to other women; you can't let the team down. You've got to do your best. Even though I was sick, we didn't have a deputy chairman. In hindsight, I should have said, "Today's not a good day for me. The CEO or another director should do the interview."

The Final Word: Optimism

I try to see good in people. I always think that when things are going badly, I'm going through this for a reason. And then afterward the sun will shine and life will be better. I like thinking about tomorrow. I'm happy today, but tomorrow's a whole new day that hasn't been lived yet. So get excited about tomorrow.

Conclusion: Time for Action

Meaning, energizing, framing, connecting, engaging. We hope that these words are the ones you choose to put together for your own leadership journey. Because when you do, you'll feel more resilient; you will look forward to what the next opportunity will bring; you'll even feel a rush of energy.

Not sure where to start? A good place is to take inventory of what you have got. It's plenty: core strengths, a host of skills, a desire to lead, ample raw talent, more connections than you realize. You may be an optimist. You have a strong voice you can use. You have energy! You also have many hardwired advantages: an emotional core, an ability to reframe, an ability to build deep relationships, adaptability. Then there are the parts of you that are unique to you. Get those on the list.

You're already on your way. Even if you began reading this book without knowing what you know and what you don't know, you've changed. You're now self-aware. You can plan what skills you want to build. You're ready to learn. Maybe you're already practicing. As you convert these new skills into your routine, over time you won't have to consciously think about them. That's the best part—the more you use them the easier it gets. And when you put all the areas of Centered Leadership together, they will help you achieve higher impact—higher performance and success, too. There's more. Not only will others see you as an effective leader, they will also want to follow you.

The Fabulous Five

Centered Leadership also weaves together many ideas, creating a way of thinking and acting that helps any leader manage through uncertainty and change. The five arenas, in combination, reinforce each other:

- **Meaning.** Makes it possible to reframe. It gives you the courage to step out of your comfort zone and engage with others. It creates the bond and it's what propels you to speak up. Meaning makes flow possible.
- **Framing.** Unlocks the path to meaning. It creates the energy that attracts others to come on board. Framing shows you the opportunities and helps you manage the risks.
- **Connecting.** Enables you to find new opportunities that are meaningful to you. A tremendous source of energy, turning to others helps you reframe more effectively and build new capabilities. Relationships can be a source of energy, too.
- **Engaging.** Frees you to pursue meaning, to see the world differently, to reach out to others. It's liberating to make choices and own the outcome—another source of new energy.
- **Energizing.** Helps you fill the room, attract others to you, take on new opportunities and face your fears, and have more positive impact on people who drain you of energy.

Every part of Centered Leadership builds on the others and releases new energy. In effect, this becomes a self-funding model that gives you back a wonderful return—making a greater difference than you could make without it.

Start Anywhere

Where do you start? Is one place better than another? We chose the circle to graphically represent Centered Leadership because a circle symbolizes your right to start anywhere in the model and go from there. We'll share our thinking about progression with you, but we emphasize that the model works no matter where you enter. We began with meaning because it is your story that will guide you. Some women who pick up this book know their story already; if you don't, start by discovering your core strengths and ways to draw on them in what you do.

From meaning, we went to framing, because optimism is a trait common to every leader we met and one that leaders can practice more. Seeing your world without distortion is a prerequisite to success. Learn to reframe and adapt. Both are essential to leaders facing major discontinuities. And isn't that everyone today?

We moved to connecting next, because none of us gets very far without help. Coaches, mentors, sponsors, and colleagues, friends and family are all part of your world. They give you courage and confidence to venture forth. Practice reciprocity and set up a date with someone you'd like to get to know. Practice inclusivity and monitor its effect.

That brought us to engaging—where it all comes together. When fear stands in your way, try facing it directly—breathe, count to ten—and put it aside.

We put energizing last, because it is the fuel and the rush you feel when you have a peak experience. Be mindful of where you get your energy and how you use it up; it's a simple question of supply and demand.

Ultimately, you'll work your way around the five capabilities. From where you sit today, they may not all matter to the same degree. That's what we've observed from working with talented women ranging in age from twenty-three to seventy-five.

It's Time!

When you put two or more of the capabilities together, something starts to happen—a "virtuous cycle" begins to spark growth. That brings us to a really important point: *Centered Leadership is not about getting an A in every part of the model.* The last thing we ever intended was to hand you a burden. Many women grew up striving for straight A's and still look for that validation. Remember, there are no rules, no final exams in Centered Leadership.

We hope you'll keep this book nearby. Dip in at any point and revisit the ideas. Or revisit the stories from our remarkable women. We hope that more than one will inspire you. They each have something to say in their own voice, showing you that there is no one single formula, no right way.

Now it's time for you to take the step. We aren't leaving you; we're still by your side. As you head down the path, we'll be here in the pages of this book, waiting for you. And from time to time, we hope you gaze on this quote, from the writer Anna Quindlen, which says so much about your leadership journey: "The thing that is really hard, and really amazing, is giving up on being perfect and beginning the work of becoming your-self."

The world needs strong leaders now more than ever.

So, go ahead. (We're here.)

Take the step.

Methodology

This book is the product of a multi-year exploration that began with a personal quest and grew into a wide-ranging study, combining original research with the work of leading thinkers in management, organizational behavior, psychology, gender studies, sociology, and biology. It started with direct observation—video interviews with women leaders around the globe whose stories guided us—and it continued with academic research that confirmed those insights. That provided the basis for a new leadership model, which we verified with original survey work and which now underpins our internal Centered Leadership development program.

We are grateful to all the women and men at McKinsey & Company who devoted time and energy to collaborate on the analysis. We are indebted to the professors and gurus we met and the ones we met only through their works. And we are indebted to more than one hundred amazing women leaders who participated in our video interviews over the past five years.

Centered Leadership's Underpinnings

Centered Leadership did not arise in a vacuum. When we searched for answers to why the women we interviewed shared certain traits and behaviors, we began with well-established thinking on management and leadership. We recognized that we needed to place our observations into the context of the great body of research about leadership. We saw that the traditional requirements and attributes of leadership—a strong desire to lead, vision, ability to build a great team, and so on—applied to our women. But we also saw that the clusters of traditionally male traits that are associated with leadership do not explain the sense of meaning and connectedness that made some women extraordinarily effective leaders. That pushed us to explore newer thinking on leadership and organizational behavior that considers the power of the "softer" aspects of leadership, such as empathy. To understand the optimism, commitment, and courage that women leaders exhibited, we turned to the leaders of positive psychology. (For a look at our proprietary study, please see the chapter following.)

Many of the thinkers represented here had significant impact on how we defined and refined Centered Leadership. They are also acknowledged throughout the preceding chapters and in the endnotes. Their thinking is helpful in understanding what Centered Leadership is all about and explaining why the model works.

As you dive deeper into Centered Leadership, we encourage you to look to these sources, too, for deeper understanding.

Leadership. We began our exploration by reading up on the works of Ronald Heifetz and Martin Linsky. They stress the importance of the adaptive mind-sets we saw in our interviewees. We also looked at some of the recent work on leadership by academics such as Peter Senge and Otto Scharmer, who explained the importance of authenticity and clarity in organizational relationships. In addition, we drew wisdom from the works of Rosabeth Moss Kanter and Debra Meyerson.

Positive psychology. We began our exploration of optimism with Martin Seligman, the "father" of positive psychology. We also studied contributions to the field by Tal Ben-Shahar, Mihály Csikszentmihályi, Barbara Fredrickson, Daniel Gilbert, Jonathan Haidt, Sonja Lyubomirsky, and Christopher Peterson, all of whom helped us grasp the science that explains how optimism and happiness are determinants of success. Carol Dweck's work on the importance of mind-sets further crystallized the concept of framing. And we recognized in our women the essential role of learned optimism, which Seligman teaches.

Search for meaning. For our understanding of meaning and its role in fostering the commitment to achieving leadership and building optimism, we also looked to Viktor Frankl along with the positive psychologists. They taught us that women (and men) can choose to be more optimistic and happier by learning what is truly meaningful to them and by choosing to deploy their core strengths. This perspective was extremely important for us, because it encouraged our team to think of ways of moving to action and how to teach Centered Leadership through formal training, self-study exercises, and coaching. We coined the term "positive framing" to encompass learned optimism as well as the ability to reframe—to see the world with expanded vision, as Senge and Scharmer prescribe.

Energy. Part of our exploration involved the links between outlook and energy. We observed that successful women leaders seemed to have extra energy, which they seemed to derive from the work itself. Extraordinary energy helps women leaders cope more successfully with the conflicting demands of business, family, and social roles. Seligman and Haidt gathered the evidence to show how happiness enhances physical health. We also studied research that showed how it was possible to actively monitor and adjust personal energy levels. We found this in the work of Jim Loehr and Tony Schwartz, and from Edy Greenblatt and Leslie Perlow. We also learned from Mihály Csikszentmihályi's research on flow, a positive mental state that arises when a person fully engages his or her core talents in challenging activities toward an ambitious goal. The research of McKinsey's Organization Practice on workplace peak experiences affirmed and complemented this work, helping us connect the dots between energy and performance.

Gender differences, evolution and biology. We looked for reasons why the careers of women seem to unfold differently than those of men. Inevitably, this led us to gender studies, biology, evolutionary theory, and medical research. Louann Brizendine, a specialist and practicing clinician in neuropsychiatry, and Michael Gurian, a family therapist and author, provided insights into our brains and why there is an elevated risk of depression in women. Shelley Taylor's work explained how, at a fundamental, hormonal level, women have different responses to stress and social interaction that can be traced to evolutionary adaptations. That helped refine our thinking on the nature and importance of relationships that our interview subjects talked about. We recognized the importance of emotions and belonging in our leadership model—why success depends on harnessing, rather than suppressing, emotions. We found the abilities to develop deep, authentic connections enhanced the success of women leaders. We continue to study how inclusiveness is emerging as a leadership trait that will serve organizations well in today's more complex and challenging environment.

Networking/bonding. Our experience teaching women had taught us the importance of networks, which led us to the work of

Monica Higgins and Herminia Ibarra, which helped focus our approach. In addition, Roy Baumeister's provocative theory as to why men are more adept at business networks got us thinking about ways to help women leverage their natural relationship-building instincts. Finally, the work of Shelley Taylor opened our eyes to the power of plugging into communities, with their multiplier impact.

Risk-taking. The art of engaging is something that all successful women leaders must master, but it is a very tricky subject. The aggressive behavior and self-promotion that can propel a young man can leave a woman stranded—labeled as too pushy. Linda Babcock and Sara Laschever helped us figure out where the invisible lines are drawn. Paul Stoltz's work on adversity helped us understand how risk and learning are interrelated. Research by Marshall Rosenberg and Deborah Tannen also helped crystallize our thinking around more effective communication. Along with engaging comes risk. The women we knew were utterly fearless (yet clear-eyed) about risk, and Daniel Gilbert's work helped us see why.

The Best Resource of All: Women Leaders

In 2004 we began conducting interviews with women leaders for our video archive. We met women who head up major organizations in business or the public and social sectors, women on their way up, and women in developing markets who are entrepreneurial pioneers with missions to push the edge of social norms. In 2008 we began to conduct interviews with male leaders in order to test the resonance of our leadership model and recognize differences in how to teach it to mixed audiences. (Our heartfelt thanks to those brave men who participated early!) Today, our video archive houses well over one hundred interviews from across markets as diverse as Argentina, Australia, Canada, China, France,

India, Israel, Japan, Jordan, Kazakhstan, Kenya, Mexico, Nigeria, Peru, South Africa, the United Kingdom, the United States, Uganda, Vietnam, and Zimbabwe. We continue to conduct new interviews to dig deeper, finding new experiences and stories that push our thinking in particular on how these women developed, and begin to understand if and how men and women leaders differ. Though our interview findings are qualitative in nature, the stories, personal insights, and tips are powerful teachers that, combined with the academic research, can help you turn your own self-discoveries into action and personal growth.

Throughout our exploration, we never forgot that women are neither a segment nor a homogeneous group. That's one reason why we continue our interviews and why we included the stories of so many women leaders in this book. We welcome you to weave a tapestry that combines traits of women whose stories and experiences speak to you. Each has something to say in her own voice. Listen and you will learn that there is no fixed path to leadership. We believe, however, that the Centered Leadership model gives you the compass to find your own way.

TABLE I

The amazing women leaders

The women	Their lessons
Amina Agbaje	1. It all begins with meaning
Georgia Lee	2. Your own happiness equation
Ann Moore	3. Start with your strengths
Gerry Laybourne	4. A sense of purpose
Alondra de la Parra	5. Dreamcatcher
Emma Fundira	6. A matter of framing
Shikha Sharma	7. The practice of optimism
Ellyn McColgan	8. Moving on
Christine Lagarde	9. Ready for change
Eileen Naughton	10. The journey, not the destination
Amanda West	11. A path to belonging
Anne Mulcahy	12. Your organization as family
Denise Incandela	13. Reciprocity forms relationships
Carolyn Buck Luce	14. The tapestry you weave
Ruth Porat	15. On the shoulders of sponsors
Shirley Tilghman	16. Member of the tribe
Dame Stella Rimington	17. Crossing the line
Julie Daum	18. Stand up, speak up
Olive Darragh	19. Make your own luck
Laura Cha	20. Take the step
Andrea Jung	21. Weathering the heights
Julie Coates	22. Energy in your toolkit
Yifei Li	23. For a quick recovery
Linda Wolf	24. Experience of flow
Margaret Jackson	25. Boundless energy

Our Research Survey

This chapter is for those who hunger to learn more about the science underlying Centered Leadership, including our survey research methodology and findings. In the following pages, we describe the statistical research we developed and conducted to validate the model. We're excited that our model appears to hold across geographies, industries, and tenure. The results confirm differences between women and men, but these differences are not big; the model holds up for men as well as women. We're delighted that this early research points to a correlation between Centered Leadership capabilities and professional success and satisfaction.

As we stated at the outset, our research is ongoing, and we will continue to test the model and findings to validate this correlation and derive further insight that can help you accelerate your leadership development.

Survey Methodology and Process

We started with the goal of challenging our hypothesis that Centered Leadership capabilities correlate with professional success and satisfaction. We knew from early observation that Centered

Leadership released tremendous positive energy, but we didn't know whether it would lead to higher performance over time. Given the newness of our model, we were seeking a way to get an early read in order to bring these insights to you.

In addition, we set a secondary goal of validating Centered Leadership as a performance model that would work as well for women as for men (or better). We wanted quantitative evidence for whether women actually lead differently than men. And we wanted some help in answering questions that we always field, like "How do women leaders differ from their male counterparts?" and "With advancement, do women simply become more like successful men?"

So we developed an initial battery of questions that measure Centered Leadership practices for each part of the model and mixed these with questions about overall measures of success and satisfaction. We worked with a team of research experts to ensure that our questionnaire was robust and impartial.

We then tested each question using a sample that spans age groups, tenures, geographies, and positions. We spent five months in prototype testing, revising the survey as we went. Of course, we wanted to make sure the questions were understandable in the same way by different people.

We also wanted to make sure that each question would yield statistically valid data. We weeded out questions overly correlated to others; we added new questions to round out our understanding of each set of Centered Leadership practices. We did all that with the constraint that even patient people won't devote much time to an online survey. That's why we collapsed parts of the model to simplify the survey tool.

After more than 200 test runs, we had validated the basic questions. Then we began to develop a formal research approach to understand if, and how, Centered Leadership varied across cultures, industries, and tenures. Once we finished creating the survey, we recruited a worldwide sample of male and female executives using *The McKinsey Quarterly* online research panel, a pool of thousands of qualified respondents.

With a good response rate (30 percent), nearly 2,000 people participated in the survey (1,938 to be exact); in return for their time, they received a short summary of the findings. The population was 72 percent male, 34 percent C-level executives, 41 percent senior managers, and 25 percent mid-level managers. They were evenly distributed according to tenure, industries, and functions. They came from every part of the world: 35 percent from North America, 28 percent from Europe, 12 percent from Asia/Pacific (excluding China), 6 percent from China, and 7 percent from India. A total of 12 percent were from Latin America and other developing markets. They represented a range of companies by size as well. Of course, by its nature this is a self-selected sample of *Quarerly* readers who are in business.

Survey Findings

By October, we had our first data set and began sorting the findings. Three intriguing findings arose from the data, which we hope to explore with further research.

1. Centered Leadership appears to have validity across the sample. Matching our qualitative evidence from interviews, we saw that Centered Leadership has relevance across geographies, industries, and functions, taking variations into account. As Figure 2 shows, results from North America and Western Europe look

Figure 2.

Centered Leadership Apears Relevant Across Regions

Average practice score; 1 = lowest, 6 = highest
(e.g., European respondents scored an average of 4.5/6.0 on Meaning)

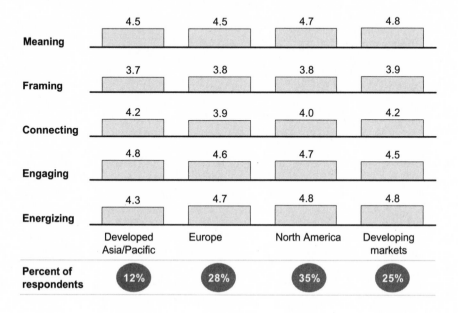

almost identical, with more variation in other regions. Each score corresponds to the simple average of several questions related to that component of Centered Leadership. At the bottom, you see the percent of respondents from each part of the world. There are some interesting twists that will take further research to explain: For example, respondents from developed Asia/Pacific markets showed lower scores on Meaning practices but high scores on Connecting practices.

We saw similar results when we compared scores across company size, functions, and industries. Nothing in the data suggests that Centered Leadership skills are more relevant or more common

Figure 3.

Similar Centered Leadership Scores Across Tenures

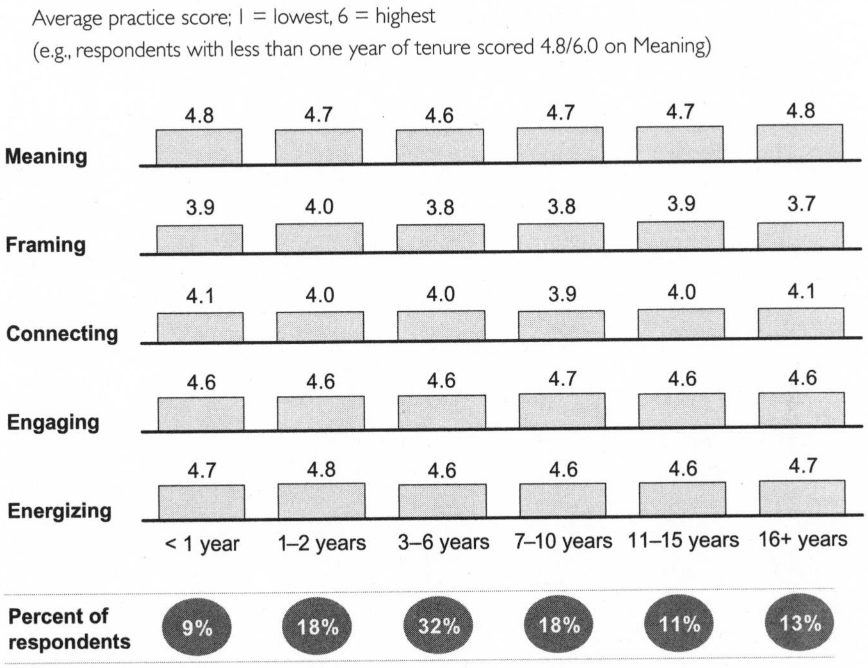

Average practice score; 1 = lowest, 6 = highest
(e.g., respondents with less than one year of tenure scored 4.8/6.0 on Meaning)

	< 1 year	1–2 years	3–6 years	7–10 years	11–15 years	16+ years
Meaning	4.8	4.7	4.6	4.7	4.7	4.8
Framing	3.9	4.0	3.8	3.8	3.9	3.7
Connecting	4.1	4.0	4.0	3.9	4.0	4.1
Engaging	4.6	4.6	4.6	4.7	4.6	4.6
Energizing	4.7	4.8	4.6	4.6	4.6	4.7
Percent of respondents	9%	18%	32%	18%	11%	13%

in one place versus another. In general, variations in geography, company size, industry, or function were not statistically significant.

In addition, Centered Leadership can be practiced at any career stage, as Figure 3 suggests. Here we had hoped to see a progression in skills from early tenured to late tenured men and women. Looking more closely, we did see a loose correlation with position in the company, but not as much as we had expected. This finding led us to hypothesize that until men and women explicitly practice Centered Leadership skills, they won't use them in day-to-day leadership. In other words, mind-sets alone do not build the skills.

2. Correlation to performance and satisfaction. Just as we expected from our interviews and our research, Centered Leadership appears to have a significant correlation with self-reported performance, success, and satisfaction. According to our statisticians, Centered Leadership's correlation with performance, success, and satisfaction passes the chi square test for this sample (determines the degree to which two variables are independent).

Take a look at Figure 4, and here's what you'll find: A higher percent of the people who scored the highest on use of Centered Leadership practices (in this case, the top 20 percent for each of the five components) report high success, satisfaction, and performance versus those who scored the lowest on the same practices (the bottom 20 percent). For example, take Meaning: 80 percent of the top scorers on practices rate themselves as high performing versus 60 percent for the bottom quintile on Meaning practices. These differences are significant.

Please note that performance, success, and satisfaction are self-reported; we plan to continue our research to validate this correlation with other samples. When you focus on the difference between the bottom and top quintiles—not the absolute numbers—you see the strength of the model. Every way we cut the data (by gender, by tenure), we found the same correlation.

Figure 5 takes the inverted view. It shows how the most satisfied and successful respondents (men and women combined) score higher on each of the Centered Leadership mind-sets and practices. Comparing these two groups (top 20 percent versus the rest), we're struck by the differences between the two for Meaning and Energizing. We hypothesize that the individuals who achieve greatest success and satisfaction have found flow. At least we hope so. In future research, we plan to explore which drives the other—does

Figure 4.

Centered Leadership Correlation with Performance, Success, and Satisfaction

Percent (e.g., 80% of top scorers on Meaning practices were high performing versus 60% of bottom scorers)

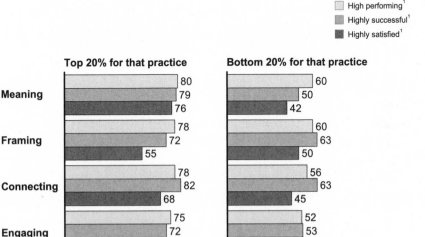

☐ High performing[1]
▨ Highly successful[1]
■ Highly satisfied[1]

Top 20% for that practice   **Bottom 20% for that practice**

	Top 20%				Bottom 20%		
Meaning	80	79	76		60	50	42
Framing	78	72	55		60	63	50
Connecting	78	82	68		56	63	45
Engaging	75	72	69		52	53	44
Energizing	90	84	73		48	49	30

[1]High performing = self-rating in top 10% of peers; highly successful = self-rating as extremely successful or successful; highly satisfied = self-rating as extremely satisfied or satisfied (top two boxes on 6-point scale)

Centered Leadership lead to greater performance and satisfaction or the other way around?

3. Centered Leadership builds on women's strengths. Our research shows that the model works for women and men. Although the results hold true for men who practice Centered Leadership—they're more successful, satisfied, and higher performing—women appear to have the advantage in Centered Leadership. Figure 6 shows that the professional women respondents practice Centered Leadership skills a bit more than their male counterparts. This is true for every element of the Centered Leadership model. We plan to dig beneath these overall numbers to understand them better practice by practice. For example, we found the greatest difference between women and men on core strengths and flow and the least differences between them on voice. Overall, women reported their highest scores on ownership and inspiration and so did men. As in-

Figure 5.

Most Satisfied and Successful Respondents Practice Centered Leadership More

Average practice score (e.g., highly satisfied respondents scored 4.9 on Meaning practices versus 4.5 for other respondents)

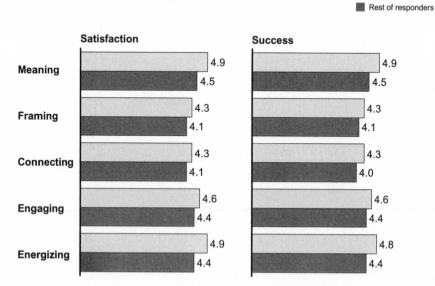

'Highly successful = self-rating as extremely successful or successful; highly satisfied = self-rating as extremely satisfied or satisfied (top two boxes on 6-point scale)

teresting, women's lowest scores were on sponsorship and moving on (avoiding rumination), the very same for men.

It's worth stopping a moment to reflect on these findings. A closer look at gender research does confirm that women are different from men on the margin, and these findings support that view. You can see women pull ahead of the men in a few critical spots: strengths and inspiration, flow, self-awareness and learned optimism, recovery, and even reciprocity (though both men and women can do better). What we don't know is if we have a selection bias from the women who responded to this survey. Did they start with an advantage in these areas or did they learn them through trial and error? And because this survey captured working women, we don't know if the women who opted out

Figure 6.

Women Outscore Men Across All Dimensions[1]

Average practice score; 1 = lowest, 6 = highest (e.g., on average women scored 4.9/6.0 for Meaning versus 4.7 for men)

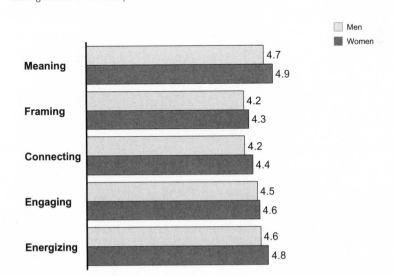

[1] All differences are significant except for Engaging

(and whose input is missing from our data) have the same advantages.

Implications

Though we are continuing to collect data and evolve the survey, you can put this survey to use in several ways. If you'd like to experiment with the current version, you can find it at www.mckin sey.com/howremarkablewomenlead.

For starters, as an assessment tool, it can help you identify your baseline: what Centered Leadership practices you regularly engage in. Many women we've talked to agree that Centered Leadership resonates, but they aren't sure where they should focus their attention first. This assessment helps you make that decision.

The earlier chapters in this book can serve as a guide, with useful tips embedded for each of the specific capabilities and practices covered in the research survey. You can also begin to understand how one practice affects another for you—you may find correlations between areas as you look at your scores.

The assessment also helps you track your progress in attaining Centered Leadership skills. As few of these capabilities are systematically taught, we don't expect many women to start with high scores across the board. But with explicit focus area by area, you will find yourself improving; the survey assessment can help you prove that to yourself.

In addition, we encourage organizations to use the survey with groups of employees to determine which skills merit specific investment in formal training and coaching. A number of companies we work with have expressed interest in cultivating Centered Leadership skills in their employees—men and women. They see these leadership skills as essential for succeeding in today's uncertain and fast-changing environment. You can administer it to men and women throughout the company to determine the division or function's baseline. Survey results can be analyzed in different ways to get a detailed picture of current institutional strengths and development needs. For example, one organization learned that their high-performing women had the lowest scores on practices across the board. Company leaders hypothesized that higher-performing women were working so hard that they didn't have time to implement the practices that link to their success and satisfaction. In effect, without intervention these talented women were headed for burnout. This insight enabled the company to target their highest performers for special support to address their issues.

The baseline assessment can also guide the design of formal customized training for future leaders. For example, front-line (and earlier tenure) managers might start with core strengths, framing, and voice/presence. As managers advance to mid-level positions, it's important to build connecting skills along with engaging. And as middle managers advance to more senior levels, meaning takes on primary importance. Every organization is different, but Centered Leadership can be parsed into a continuum of "field and forum" training curricula that builds and enhances these skills over time.

In Conclusion

Our research to date begins to validate the model in four important ways: It appears relevant across different cultures; it has a correlation with satisfaction, performance, and success; it favors inherent "feminine" strengths—strengths that women leaders exhibit; but both men and women are practicing Centered Leadership.

That said, we have much more to do. As this book goes to press, we continue to build insight to test and enhance the Centered Leadership model over time. We continue to collect additional data to understand the different baselines for men and women in companies. Even more important, we want to understand how formal training and in-the-field coaching along with self-discovery and practice can build Centered Leadership capabilities. In turn, we want to collect more data on the tangible impact of enhanced skills on performance, satisfaction, and success. And for us, the "brass ring" will be in understanding the magic that happens when two or more of the elements work together in combination.

With that in mind, which elements of Centered Leadership intrigue you the most? How can organizations use this model to accelerate the development of their talented women? What are the most effective teaching approaches? We hope you will join us in this endeavor, as we continue to evolve Centered Leadership and use it to better understand and accelerate the development of women leaders across the world and in all walks of life.

Acknowledgments

When Women Lead has many contributors. It surely has taken a village.

Our heartfelt thanks go to Dominic Barton, Ian Davis, and Michael Patsalos-Fox, leaders with the conviction and courage to steadily invest in women's leadership and in this project. Along the way, so many McKinsey friends have contributed their knowledge, opinions, time, and support—Zafer Achi, Carolyn Aiken, Manuela Artigas, Nora Aufreiter, Felix Bruck, Lowell Bryan, Beth Cobert, Laura Corb, Jonathan Davidson, Derek Dean, Sandrine Devillard-Hoellinger, Tracey Griffen, Judith Hazelwood, Liz Hilton-Segel, Tsun-Yan Hsieh, Michelle Jarrard, Scott Keller, Nancy Killefer, Eric Labaye, Anu Madgavkar, James Manyika, Anna Marrs, Tim McGuire, Monica McGurk, John McPherson, Mary Meaney, Lenny Mendonca, Mona Mourshed, Tore Myrholt, Laxman Narasimhan, Suzanne Nimocks, Gary Pinkus, Colin Price, Tom Saar, Geoff Sands, Bill Schaninger, Bruce Simpson, Kate Smaje, Lila Snyder, Ireena Vittal, Caroline Webb, and Rebecca Wei. Wow. Just writing this list has made us feel grateful.

Thanks are in order as well to a very special group of women at McKinsey—our women directors who have banded together to support women and leadership development. Every one of you has contributed to the project by the very fact that you're a senior partner and role model for so many.

An army of talented business analysts, associates, engagement managers, associate principals, and specialists also jumped in to help—thank you to Maria Arias, Elissa Ashwood, Hilary Belm, Frank Comes, Katherine Bair Desmond, Lauren Drake, Siri Eklund, Hallie Fader, David Gettman, Fiona Greig, Keri Hattich, Christy Johnson, Charmhee Kim, Rik Kirkland, Anna Carolina Koch, Mary Kuntz, Steve Lackey, Margaret Loeb, Simon London, Helen Loser, Josephine Mogelov, Laura Nilsen, Damaris O'Hanlon, Amanda Pouchot, Michael Rennie, Alexandra Ressler, Natalie Revelle, Brooke Ricalde, Humphrey Rolleston, Martin Rouse, Zeryn Sarpangal, Laura Schalekamp, Barr Seitz, Tina Shah, Barbara Stern, Heather Sumner, Nandita Surendran, Sue Treiman, Carol Weese, and Lynn Wolf. You've all been so helpful to us: publishing, filming, developing website materials, designing, interviewing, teaching, planning, and researching. Andrea Amico and Elinor Riley, thank you for your wonderful analytic and design contributions—you're a part of our McKinsey, too. On top of this, a very, very special thank-you to Kate Barrett, Rebecca Craske, Edy Greenblatt, Melissa Hayes, Johanne Lavoie, and Monica McGurk, who joined our core team, bringing fresh ideas and working side by side with us to create a living learning program.

But this wasn't just an internal project. Many, many women—and more than a few good men—opened doors, shared their networks, and gave us the gift of their insights. Thank you to every friend from outside the firm who helped to breathe life into our very big aspirations—Alysse Nelson Bloom, Charlie Cummings, Anne Fuchs, Diane Grady, Cynthia Hayes, Bob Sutton, Melanne Verveer, and Melinda Wolfe, thank you. Bill Meehan, thank you for years of mentorship to both of us. Thank you to all the sponsors we've had before the notion was even coined.

And if it weren't for the women—the amazing women who gave their time and their permission to be a part of our Living Portraits archive—we would still be at the start of our journey. Our thanks hardly seem enough. We only hope that you receive ten times over for all the help you have given us.

Giving thanks is a funny business; the more we thank, the more people we remember we still want to thank. We could go on forever, but it's time to go. Still, we are not quite finished.

We have our families to thank. Susie would like to thank her amazing husband, Russell Hamilton; her mother, Mary Cranston; her father, Hal Cranston; her brother, John; and her wonderful friends (many of whom were the inspiration for this book).

Geoff would like to thank his wife, Anne Field, and two incredible kids who keep him sane and who didn't mind that writing seemed to be a nightly and regular weekend activity.

Joanna would like to thank her husband, David, who is our team's most ardent feminist. Two special girls were—and are—the fuel for this project. Gaby and Jetta, we wish we could give you every insight that every woman taught us, but we know that you will learn your own lessons along your own journeys. We thank our mothers, too, for their gifts to us.

Honestly, we'd like to thank everyone personally and if we've inadvertently left anyone out, we apologize profusely because we couldn't have gotten very far without you. You are all mothers and fathers of Centered Leadership.

Notes

Part One: Meaning

Chapter 1 It All Begins with Meaning

22 **his hierarchy of human needs:** Maslow studied what he thought were the healthiest people to find out how human beings are motivated. His "hierarchy of needs" model holds that people are motivated to the degree that their needs are being met. The first level of needs is physiological—breathing, eating, and sleeping; next is the need for safety; the third is love and belonging; the fourth is esteem. Each need builds on the level below: Maslow observed that people are less motivated by achievement and respect if they don't have the love of their families and friends first. The highest-level need is self-actualization. It can be reached only when the other four needs have been met. It represents the highest level of human evolution or growth. Similar to how we define meaning, the motivating force of self-actualization is the ability to fulfill your greatest potential. Abraham Maslow, *The Farther Reaches of Human Nature* (New York: Penguin, 1993).

22 **the meaningful elements of the work:** In 2004, International Survey Research (ISR) asked senior-level men and women what factors made them feel most committed to their jobs. Men listed pace of career advancement, the pay and rewards associated with the job, and the balance of workload. Women had a starkly different take: They named the quality of relationships with their colleagues, a focus on delivering qual-

ity products, and communication in the workplace. In 2008 the Center for Work-Life Policy fielded a survey of women in science, engineering, and technology with similar results. The study found that 55 percent of female scientists chose their careers primarily because they wanted to make a difference in the world, compared to only 45 percent of men. The survey we fielded in 2008 in *The McKinsey Quarterly* showed that finding meaning in work is a major priority for women: Women took active steps to find meaning more often than men. Whether this phenomenon is cultural or genetic, the evidence is mounting that women who work find huge meaning in doing so. "Motivating Men and Women at Work: Relationships vs. Rewards," International Survey Research, (www.isrsurveys.com, 2004); Sylvia Ann Hewlett, et al., "The Athena Factor," *Harvard Business Review Research Report,* June 2008.

22 **the courage to plunge ahead:** Research suggests that when people are doing meaningful things, they are able to accomplish more than they thought was possible. To start with, Edy Greenblatt has shown that people can gain stamina unavailable in other situations. In addition, Tal Ben-Shahar shows that when people are focused on a specific goal, they are less distracted by the smaller day-to-day issues. Edy Greenblatt, *Restore Yourself: The Antidote for Professional Exhaustion* (Los Angeles: Execu-Care Press, 2009); Tal Ben-Shahar, *Happier* (New York: McGraw-Hill, 2007).

24 **sustained increase in happiness:** A growing body of research supports the notion that seeking higher-level goals and engaging in meaningful activities can create lasting increases in happiness. For example, researchers have found that people who engage in volunteer activities on a regular basis or who regularly express gratitude and forgiveness are happier over time. Sonja Lyubomirsky has a number of interesting works on this research: Sonja Lyubomirsky and Kennon Sheldon, "Achieving Sustainable Gains in Happiness: Change Your Actions, Not Your Circumstances," *Journal of Happiness Studies* (2006):7:55–86; Sonja Lyubomirsky, *The How of Happiness* (New York: Penguin, 2007).

24 **expert in positive psychology:** Mihály Csikszentmihályi spent years tracking people throughout their days and measuring happiness along with other life circumstances. His approach is one of the best techniques for scientifically measuring happiness. He gave subjects from all walks of life beepers and paged them at random moments throughout the day to report their level of happiness, to get a more accurate assessment than recollections would provide. He studied the corporate environment to better understand how happiness affected organizations. His research concludes that productivity and low turnover, major drivers of profitability, are connected to happiness. To read more: Mihály Csikszentmihályi, *Good Business* (New York: Penguin, 2004).

24 **set higher goals for themselves:** Barbara Fredrickson's "broaden and build" theory is based on research that concludes that people who are happy and feel comfortable are better able to learn new tasks and are more open to new ideas. This ties to Maslow's theory: When people are feeling negative or threatened, they focus inwardly and worry about their ability to continue to provide their basic needs. When people are feeling secure, they are able to extend themselves and take risks to learn. Barbara Fredrickson, "The Value of Positive Emotions," *American Scientist* 91, no. 4 (2003).

24 **as well as stamina and resilience:** Researchers looked at essays the nuns had written when they first joined the convent and evaluated the language and sentiments expressed in the essays. It turns out that the happier nuns lived an average of ten years longer than the unhappy nuns. In comparison, nonsmokers lived only seven years longer than smokers. W. V. Friesen, "Positive emotions in early life and longevity: Findings from the nun study," *Journal of Personality and Social Psychology* (2001).

In addition to living longer, happy people remain more agile and retain more muscle mass as they age. A long-range study tracked physical activity in two groups of men: those whose lifestyle choices were congruent with their core strengths and sense of meaning and those whose lifestyles were not congruent. For example, among men with generosity as a core strength, those who regularly practiced acts of kindness lived longer than those who did not. Men who lived congruent lifestyles were stronger, more likely to be able to walk up four flights of stairs, and lived longer than men who did not. For additional research, see Martin Seligman, *Learned Optimism* (New York: Free Press, 1998); Christopher Peterson, *A Primer on Positive Psychology* (New York: Oxford University Press, 2006).

24 **lower levels of stress hormones:** Andrew Steptoe, Jane Wardle, and Michael Marmot, "Positive affect and health-related neuroendocrine, cardiovascular, and inflammatory processes," *Proceedings of the National Academy of Sciences,* March 8, 2005.

24 **three forms of happiness:** Tal Ben-Shahar describes happiness as the "overall experience of pleasure and meaning." Pleasure, he writes, is an emotion that leaves you feeling happy in the moment—the glow you get from eating your favorite meal. The experience of meaning provides long-term happiness: the pleasure you get from doing something that has great intrinsic value to you. Ben-Shahar acknowledges that Seligman and Haidt place engagement as a form of happiness between pleasure and meaning; in contrast, Ben-Shahar sees engagement as a subcomponent of meaning. Tal Ben-Shahar, *Happier* (New York: McGraw-Hill, 2007).

Chapter 2 Your Own Happiness Equation

31 **too fast to stop and ponder:** Women have a hard time getting in touch with what makes them happy. In the course of training hundreds of women on Centered Leadership, one of the most common questions we heard was "What if I don't know what makes me happy?" For women who share this uncertainty, a number of exercises can help you develop more certainty. To begin with, you might talk with friends about your strengths and start to notice how you feel when you practice them. Another exercise is to think back to peak experiences you've had at work and

in your personal life with the goal of identifying and understanding the drivers underlying them.

34 **Happiness equals:** The equation is perhaps most useful as a framework for thinking about your level of happiness. The main insight is that the key variable you can manipulate is your own behavior. This is supported by the work of Sonja Lyubomirsky, author of *The How of Happiness,* who estimates that 50 percent of the differences in people's happiness can be explained by genetics (what Haidt calls the set point), 10 percent by conditions, and 40 percent by behavior. To learn more, seek out these books: Sonya Lynbomirsky, *The How of Happiness: A Scientific Approach to Getting the Life You Want* (New York: The Penguin Press, 2007) and Jonathan Haidt, *Happiness Hypothesis* (New York: Basic Books, 2006).

35 **meditation, or behavioral therapy:** A word on meditation. Based on evidence reported by psychologists and laymen alike, yoga is a simple yet powerful way in which to move toward the top of your range and possibly even raise your set point. Many women leaders told us that making yoga part of their routines had produced a long-lasting improvement in their feeling of well-being. Some went so far as to say that they were only able to sustain their grueling schedule or level of stress due to yoga. Haidt himself turned from medicine to yoga as a better personal solution for finding happiness with fewer side effects. Jonathan Haidt, *Happiness Hypothesis* (New York: Basic Books, 2006).

35 **returned to the level of happiness:** This often quoted study looked at twenty-two lottery winners, twenty-two recent paraplegics, and twenty-nine control group members to see how happiness changed over time. They found that people who experienced both winning situations and tough situations adjusted back to their original levels of happiness within several months. Brickman, Coates, and Janoff-Bulman, "Lottery winners and accident victims: is happiness relative?" *Social Psychology* 36, no. 8 (1978).

36 **"hedonic treadmill"**: The hedonic treadmill theory explains why improvements in circumstance do not have a long-term impact on happiness. The core insight is that once an improvement in conditions occurs—getting a raise, buying a new home—we quickly adapt to this new norm and then begin seeking the next achievement or acquisition. The upside is that rapid adaption serves us well when we have a decline in circumstances, too. The term *hedonic treadmill* is credited to Michael Eysenck, a British psychology researcher who likened the conventional quest to running on a treadmill. For a good summary of thinking on the hedonic treadmill, see Ed Diener, "Beyond the Hedonic Treadmill: Revising the Adaptation Theory of Well-Being," *American Psychologist* 61, no. 4 (May–June 2006): 305–314.

37 **to write daily pages:** Julia Cameron, *The Artist's Way* (New York: Tarcher/Putnam, 1992).

Chapter 3 Start with Your Strengths

44 **the twenty-four strengths:** From Martin Seligman's website, www.authentichappiness.org. This site is free but requires registration. Alternatively, you might try the Gallup strengthsfinder assessment at http://www.strengthsfinder.com. Definitions differ but the goal is the same—to help you pinpoint your innate strengths that should be building blocks for your leadership development.

45 **satisfaction with work:** Peterson describes his class assignments where students are asked to use their signature strengths in new ways on a regular basis and report back. This homework assignment seems to prove the point—using your signature strengths can make you happier. His self-administered assignment helped students discover that an ice cream break in the middle of the day was pure pleasure but hardly memorable or lasting. Sitting in on a new class was deeply satisfying for those students who shared a core strength of curiosity or love of learning. Writing a letter thanking someone and sharing it with them in person

was the most powerful satisfaction driver of the three. Christopher Peterson, *A Primer on Positive Psychology* (New York: Oxford University Press, 2006).

Chapter 4 A Sense of Purpose

50 **a million other distractions:** Ben-Shahar explains the research that shows how having a goal allows people to focus on the bigger picture. People can enjoy the process of achieving the goal more because they know what they want to do, and the small, day-to-day decisions and issues are less important and less draining. Tal Ben-Shahar, *Happier* (New York: McGraw-Hill, 2007).

51 **taking a narrow view:** The power of the learning mind-set is discussed in *Mind-set: The New Psychology of Success,* by Stanford University professor of psychology Carol Dweck. She explains how people with fixed mind-sets approach life thinking that their skills and abilities are predetermined. On the other hand, people with growth mind-sets believe that they can achieve anything that they want as long as they work hard enough. Her research shows that successful people have growth mind-sets; you have to believe in your power to grow and change if you want to succeed. People with fixed mind-sets risk sabotaging themselves by limiting their possibilities. Unwilling to try unproven tactics or to acquire new skills, they are incapable of personal growth and are unlikely to provide creative solutions. Carol S. Dweck, *Mindset: The New Psychology of Success* (New York: Ballantine Books, 2008).

52 **making three lists:** Tal Ben-Shahar, *Happier* (New York: McGraw-Hill, 2007).

53 **didn't enjoy the journey:** Haidt writes that the pleasure we feel from reaching an arbitrary career goal is really relief from stress and pressure, not joy at all. It's akin to the feeling you get when you unload a heavy backpack during a hike—and just as fleeting. Interestingly, Shikha Sharma of ICICI in India relayed a similar insight—that the happiness

she felt with each advancement did not last—as she reflected back on her career. Jonathan Haidt, *Happiness Hypothesis* (New York: Basic Books, 2006).

53 **must inspire you:** Ken Sheldon, a professor of social psychology at the University of Missouri, has studied what increases an individual's sense of well-being. His focus is on a metric he calls "self-concordance," which measures the degree to which people pursue goals that are truly meaningful. They fall into two categories:

- Goals involving growth, connection, and contribution rather than goals involving money, beauty, and popularity
- Goals that are interesting and personally important, rather than goals one feels pressured to pursue

K. M. Sheldon and L. Houser-Marko, "Self-Concordance, Goal Attainment, and the Pursuit of Happiness: Can There Be an Upward Spiral?" *Journal of Personality and Social Psychology* 76 (2001): 482–97.

53 **doesn't impress everyone else:** In his book *Stumbling on Happiness,* Dr. Daniel Gilbert presents some very interesting research showing how poorly people predict future happiness, mainly because we rely on faulty memory. We tend to remember extreme events and forget average ones, which limits our ability to imagine a happy future. For example, when we are asked about delays on our commute, we don't think about the ordinary day with minor delays. We remember the day an accident snarled traffic for three hours. His advice is to rely on the experience of others to create a view of a happy future. To imagine yourself in a different line of work, for example, talk to people who are doing what you think you want to do. Daniel Gilbert, *Stumbling on Happiness* (New York: Knopf, 2006).

Chapter 5 Dreamcatcher

57 **Ken Kiesler:** Kenneth Kiesler has been the Director of Orchestras and Professor of Conducting at the University of Michigan since 1995. He is also the founder and director of the Conductors Retreat at Medomak—the program that Alondra attended.

Part Two: Framing
Chapter 6 A Matter of Framing

66 **optimism correlates with success:** We conducted a survey of business executives from around the world, which measured Centered Leadership mind-sets and practices along with self-assessed satisfaction, performance, and success (e.g., number of promotions, position relative to peers). We found a clear correlation among these variables. Quintile analysis of the data suggests that men and women with the top scores on Centered Leadership practices feel more satisfied and more successful.

66 **taking the emotional plunge:** Brain research finds that memories are organized into groups of related incidents. This means that negative events are stored together, and remembering one negative event can set off a chain of other negative memories. This phenomenon causes the "spiraling down" phenomenon we describe. You think of a bad meeting from an hour ago, and then you remember other bad meetings you've had (over the years), then the argument with your husband a few days ago, and then that you yelled at your kids today. Before you know it, you've spiraled down, believing that no one loves you and you are about to be fired. Susan Nolen-Hoeksema, *Women Who Think Too Much* (New York: Henry Holt, 2003).

70 **through three lenses:** In his book *Learned Optimism,* Seligman describes three lenses related to optimism that people use to view a situation. The first is how permanent a situation is. Optimists see positive situations as permanent and negative situations as temporary. The sec-

ond lens is pervasiveness. Optimists see good situations as pervasive and negative situations as isolated incidences. The third lens is how personally someone perceives a situation. Optimists see positive situations as in their control but see negative events as externalized incidents out of their control. Seligman reports that people don't have consistent uses of each lens. For example, you may see negative situations as temporary but your fault. Accordingly, knowing your tendency on each of the three lenses for negative and positive situations can help you avoid the downward spiral. You can find Seligman's optimism assessment at his website: www.authentichappiness.org. Martin Seligman, *Learned Optimism* (New York: Vintage, 2006).

72 **outlook is genetically determined:** Sonja Lyubomirsky and her colleagues have researched how much of a person's happiness can be explained by genetic makeup. By running hundreds of correlations between family members and other variables, they found that 50 percent of a person's happiness level can be explained by genetics. If you find yourself feeling happy most of the time, you should thank Mom and Dad. Sonja Lyubomirsky, *The How of Happiness* (New York: Penguin, 2008).

72 **even severe depression:** Susan Nolen-Hoeksema has studied depression and anxiety in women for years and has reviewed studies from around the world to see if women's great tendency toward depression is a local phenomenon. She found that women globally are much more likely to suffer depression than men. Susan Nolen-Hoeksema, *Women Who Think Too Much* (New York: Henry Holt, 2003).

73 **creativity in problem-solving:** According to Barbara Fredrickson's "broaden and build" theory, when people feel positive emotions (e.g., joy, interest, pride, contentment) they are able to broaden their thinking and range of actions, which builds enduring personal resources. These physical, social, intellectual, and psychosocial resources last after the positive feelings go away and can help create future positive situations. In essence, positive feelings help people learn and develop, while

negative feelings cause people to turn inward. In one study, Fredrickson found that people were less likely to believe in stereotypes when they were happy, because they were more open and curious. In another, she found that groups exposed to humorous video footage were more able to collaborate on a creative solution for a hard problem, in contrast to the control groups and those exposed to depressing and sad video footage. Interestingly, Fredrickson also points out that a number of studies analyzing play in animals found that play built skills that would serve the animals at other points in their lives, providing an evolutionary explanation for this theory. Barbara Fredrickson, *Positive Organizational Scholarship* (San Francisco: Berrett-Koehler, 2003).

75 **people with flexible mind-sets:** In *Mindset: The New Psychology of Success,* Carol Dweck defines the two types of mind-sets—growth mind-sets and fixed mind-sets. People with growth mind-sets are the people most likely to succeed in life, according to her research. They see themselves as a work in progress; they believe that they can learn to do anything as long as they work hard at it with commitment. People with a fixed mind-set believe their capabilities are predetermined, and there is nothing that can be done to change their circumstances. Accordingly, they are less motivated to learn new capabilities because they don't think it will change their circumstances. Carol Dweck, *Mindset: The New Psychology of Success* (New York: Ballantine, 2007).

76 **people with growth mind-sets:** Carol Dweck, *Mindset: The New Psychology of Success* (New York: Ballantine, 2007), p. 110.

Chapter 7 The Practice of Optimism

85 **hardwired into prehistoric human brains:** Haidt beautifully describes how evolution may have caused pessimism (or at least the quick trigger for pessimism) to become a naturally selected trait. Picture our prehistoric ancestors. The ones who survived saw predators and quickly remembered how dangerous those predators were to their survival. The

pessimistic ancestors ran away from threat because they assumed the worst. More optimistic ancestors who believed that the last attack was an isolated incident were most likely to be eaten. Our optimistic ancestors were less likely to pass along their genes. And so pessimism became an easily reachable state of mind for most people. Jonathan Haidt, *Happiness Hypothesis* (New York: Basic Books, 2006).

85 **hardwired to ruminate:** Another indication that women are built to ruminate is that more blood flows to the anterior cingulate gyrus part of women's brains than to men's. This region of our brains plays little videos of things that have happened in the past. For example, when we think back to a conversation, it is the anterior cingulate gyrus that fetches that information and brings it to our consciousness. The blood flow difference means that women are replaying events from the past much more frequently than are men. This can be an incredibly powerful tool. During meeting debriefings, for example, women are much better at replaying what happened. However, the flip side is that women can get stuck replaying unpleasant experiences over and over. Several studies have found that women are more likely to "overthink" or rerun negative situations around in their heads than men. Michael Gurian and Barbara Annis, *Leadership and the Sexes* (San Francisco: Jossey-Bass, 2008).

87 **grooves in her brain deepen:** Susan Nolen-Hoeksema describes three kinds of rumination in her book, *Women Who Think Too Much*: rant and rave, life-of-their-own, and chaotic overthinking. Rant and rave rumination is when you fixate on a wrong done to you. You catalog offenses and dream up vengeance scenarios. Life-of-their-own rumination begins when you start thinking about how you're feeling in the moment, but suddenly find your thoughts have gone racing ahead—turning a thought about your fatigue into concern about a fatal disease. The third category of rumination is chaotic; all your problems and concerns just flood your mind at the same time. You don't know where to start to ad-

dress them and you feel totally overwhelmed. Susan Nolen-Hoeksema, *Women Who Think Too Much* (New York: Henry Holt, 2003).

87 **start with two techniques:** Disputation is one of the primary techniques that Seligman uses in his book. Martin Seligman, *Learned Optimism* (New York: Vintage, 2006).

90 **find greater serenity:** Psychologist Christopher Peterson ran an exercise with his college classes where he had people write forgiveness notes. In the study, he noted that "those who forgive are much more serene than those who do not and display many other positive strengths." Christopher Peterson, *A Primer on Positive Psychology* (New York: Oxford University Press, 2006).

Chapter 8 Moving On

93 **hear only criticism:** Research described in *Women Don't Ask* showed that a woman's self-worth fluctuates more in response to feedback than a man's. This difference is attributed to the fact that women are more likely to have an external locus of control—they believe that they can't control the things that happen to them. When something bad happens, like a negative review, they believe there is nothing they can do about it and feel terrible. Someone with an internal locus of control would not feel so bad because they would believe there was something they could do to change the situation. Linda Babcock and Sara Laschever, *Women Don't Ask* (New York: Bantam, 2009).

100 **predict all possible outcomes:** We use an approach to reframing based on the work of Andrew Shatte and Karen Reivich, authors of *The Resilience Factor: 7 Keys to Finding Your Inner Strength and Overcoming Life's Hurdles* (New York: Broadway, 2003). Their book suggests that people can become more resilient by changing the way they think. Shatte and Reivich suggest seven strategies people can use, providing specific exercises and examples to help people put these strategies to work in their everyday lives.

101 **from different perspectives:** Andrew Shatte and Karen Reivich, *The Resilience Factor: 7 Keys to Finding Your Inner Strength and Overcoming Life's Hurdles* (New York: Broadway, 2003).

Chapter 9 Ready for Change

104 **Adaptability is certainly a requirement:** Christine attended a private high school in the United States and has a master's degree in English. She studied law at the University of Paris and joined Baker & McKenzie in 1980. By 1999 Christine had become the first female chair of the firm's executive committee and headed the partnership until June 2005. In 2005, in the middle of a merger of New York offices with another firm, Christine was tapped to become minister of trade by Nicolas Sarkozy's predecessor, Jacques Chirac. She also holds France's Légion d'Honneur.

109 **fail to meet adaptive challenges:** Heifetz and Linsky argue that leaders need to be prepared to lead adaptive challenges—challenges for which there is not yet an answer or solution. These challenges are the most difficult, because trying to solve a problem that has never been solved before is risky. It requires taking a leap of faith, being comfortable with the risk that you might fail the first time, disturbing others as change is put in place, and discomfort. Heifetz and Linsky argue that adaptability is a requirement for success. Martin Linsky and Ronald A. Heifetz, *Leadership on the Line* (Cambridge, MA: Harvard Business School Press, 2002).

109 **"on the dance floor":** Martin Linsky and Ronald A. Heifetz, *Leadership on the Line* (Cambridge, MA: Harvard Business School Press, 2002).

111 **reach out to the opposition:** Heifetz and Linsky argue that people who think politically about personal relationships will be most successful as leaders. Specifically, they suggest six rules for aspiring leaders to use when challenged: (1) Find partners to provide protection. (2) Keep

your opposition close, since they have the most to lose. (3) Take responsibility for your role in the upheaval or disruptions being caused by the changes. (4) Acknowledge other people's loss as they change things that are familiar to them. (5) Be a role model for the change you are trying to make. (6) Accept that you will have to let go of some people to make the change work. Martin Linsky and Ronald A. Heifetz, *Leadership on the Line* (Cambridge, MA: Harvard Business School Press, 2002).

Part Three: Connecting
Chapter 11 A Path to Belonging

125 **strong networks and mentors:** Monica Higgins and Kathy Kram, "Reconceptualizing Mentoring at Work: A Developmental Network Perspective" *Academy of Management Review* 26, no. 2 (2001): 264–88.

126 **ancient survival instincts:** Women's "tend and befriend" response for reducing stress is a recent discovery. Until Shelley Taylor began researching stress, 90 percent of studies on stress had been conducted on men. When men are stressed—when their parasympathetic systems are engaged and their bodies begin to prepare for "fight, flight, or freeze"—they can help themselves calm down by releasing the aggression they feel from the increase in testosterone. A common technique is deep breathing to slow down the heart rate. Taylor's work shows that since the parasympathetic response triggers different hormones in women, they need a different mechanism for calming down. They need to be around people, and they need to care for others. Her ideas make sense from an evolutionary standpoint and have been supported through multiple research studies. Shelley E. Taylor, *The Tending Instinct: Women, Men, and the Biology of Relationships* (New York: Times Books, 2002).

126 **take care of the group:** Because women had children to care for, banding together in groups with other women and children was often

their best strategy for survival, so evolutionary biologists theorize. Women's group orientation makes sense in this context—their children would not have survived to reproduce otherwise. Shelley E. Taylor, *The Tending Instinct: Women, Men, and the Biology of Relationships* (New York: Times Books, 2002).

129 **puts women at a disadvantage:** Babcock and Laschever summarized research on women and networking in their book *Women Don't Ask.* Other sources take a different view—that women are as good as men in networking. To add to this debate, our experience training men and women from around the world supports the general conclusion that women prefer to have deeper relationships, which narrows their networks compared to men. Linda Babcock and Sara Laschever, *Women Don't Ask* (New York: Bantam, 2007).

129 **women do not allocate the time:** Ibarra and Hunter's article articulates how numerous executives they have worked with claim no time to network. It is often hard for people to see how networking can actually reduce workloads, and until you consistently invest in networking activity, you won't get any of the benefits. Although this article does not call out gender difference with respect to networking, separate research on women who work and bear the "double duty" of home and child care makes the assertion that women are more likely to feel that they don't have time to network. Herminia Ibarra and Mark Hunter, "How Leaders Create and Use Networks," *Harvard Business Review,* January 2007.

131 **Women with mentors:** One study of women of color by Catalyst found that 69 percent of women with a mentor had an upward career move in the next three years, compared to 49 percent of women without a mentor. The findings of this study have been replicated elsewhere, suggesting that mentors are an important way for women to level the playing field. Catalyst research, www.catalyst.org.

Chapter 12 Your Organization as Family

140 **women understand more:** Research reports that women are better at picking up unsaid messages than men. They read facial expressions and body postures that men don't even notice. Michael Gurian and Barbara Annis, the authors of *Leadership and the Sexes,* run an exercise where they ask men and women to write down everything they remember about the last twenty minutes of a meeting. Women routinely remember and understand much more about the dynamics in the room and what was going on than the men. Michael Gurian and Barbara Annis, *Leadership and the Sexes* (San Francisco: Jossey-Bass, 2008).

140 **additional sources of information:** Goleman's work on emotional quotient (EQ) poses that just like the IQ, a person's EQ is a major contributor to success. Essentially, EQ summarizes how well a person can read the emotions of those around him. Goleman's research suggests that people with higher EQ make better decisions than those with lower EQ. He asserts that to be a good leader, you have to have a high EQ. Daniel Goleman, "What Makes a Leader," *Harvard Business Review,* January 2004.

Chapter 13 Reciprocity Forms Relationships

144 **done in large groups:** Dr. Roy Baumeister, in a 2007 speech to the American Psychological Association, entitled, "Is There Anything Good About Men?" An enjoyable read, Baumeister's provocative speech asserts that corporate structures favor men who are hardwired to develop broad and shallow networks.

144 **women who routinely practice reciprocity:** Our research on Centered Leadership finds that women's use of reciprocity in the home does not transfer to the use of reciprocity at work. Qualitative interviews suggest one possible explanation: Women who use reciprocity with loved ones feel disingenuous using reciprocity at work. When redefined as

giving, more women see the point. What offends most often are the transactional and commercial aspects of reciprocity.

144 **the "glue that holds":** Jonathan Haidt, *Happiness Hypothesis* (New York: Basic Books, 2006).

148 **our ancestors learned:** "There is no human society that does not subscribe to this rule," Robert Cialdini says of reciprocity. It seems to be pervasive across cultures. The need to fulfill debts and match contributions may be part of what makes us human, according to a number of anthropologists and other researchers. Robert Cialdini, *Influence: The Psychology of Persuasion* (New York: Collins Business Essentials, 2007).

Chapter 14 The Tapestry You Weave

154 **well-known voice:** Carolyn Buck Luce worked in investment banking for seventeen years before joining Ernst & Young. She is also the cofounder and chair of the Hidden Brain Drain Taskforce, a public/private initiative to define second-generation policies to encourage full use of women in the workplace. They have published four articles in the *Harvard Business Review.* Carolyn also teaches a course at Columbia University.

159 **"an active interest in":** Speech by Monica Higgins to McKinsey women in New York City, January 2008.

161 **increasing the breadth:** Uzzi and Dunlap use the example of Paul Revere to illustrate the power of a diverse network. Everyone knows who Paul Revere is, but no one knows William Dawes. Both men galloped through the countryside to sound the alarm that the Revolutionary War had started. However, because Revere had a diverse network, his alarm spread more quickly and to a larger group. Brian Uzzi and Shannon Dunlap, "How to Build Your Network," *Harvard Business Review,* December 2005.

162 **planning a career transformation:** In her work, Herminia

Ibarra, director of the Insead Leadership Initiative, underscores the importance of having access to new connections for career transformations. It is important to reach out to people who are unrelated to your current workplace. It's not that people in your current job won't try to help you, but they already see you in the context of your current job. Others can help you think outside the box. Herminia Ibarra, "How to Stay Stuck in the Wrong Career," *Harvard Business Review,* December 2002.

162 **significantly more influential:** Research on the benefits of informal and formal relationships has shown that informal relationships are the more powerful career accelerators. Formal mentoring relationships (those created by an organization) are more likely to involve less motivated mentors and less effective coaching sessions between mentor and protégée. They inadvertently create a dynamic where the mentor is less likely to publicly support their protégée because the relationship is visible. Despite the fact that women have a harder time building informal relationships, research suggests it is worth the extra effort. Belle Rose Ragins and John L. Cotton, "Mentoring Functions and Outcomes," *Journal of Applied Psychology* 84, no. 4 (1999): 529–50.

163 **all possible connections:** One effective networker, Keith Ferrazzi, wrote a book describing all the techniques he uses when networking. The exercise of systematically considering your network and how it could be expanded is one of a number of exercises he describes in his book, *Never Eat Alone* (New York: Random House, 2005).

163 **It takes several interactions:** Some people have developed useful ground rules for building relationships. Ferrazzi's first rule is that people need to hear from you through at least three types of communication (for example, in person, by phone, and by e-mail) before they begin to remember who you are. His second rule is to nurture new relationships with monthly contact. His third is that transforming a work colleague into a friend requires several meetings outside the office. He also

suggests that maintaining a connection requires at least two points of contact per year. Keith Ferrazzi, *Never Eat Alone* (New York: Random House, 2005).

Chapter 15 On the Shoulders of Sponsors

167 **she calls herself lucky:** Ruth told us her sponsors included Parker Gilbert, Dick Fisher, Bob Greenhill, Eric Gleacher, John Mack, Joe Perella, and Vikram Pandit. Those in the investment banking industry will recognize these prominent Wall Street executives. Not many women leaders cited more than two sponsors, so don't worry if your list is brief.

171 **she's seen as pushy:** In one study, researchers showed subjects a variety of statements, some of which were boastful. Subjects were told to rate how much they liked the fictional person who made the statement, based on the statement itself and some other personal facts, including gender. While subjects liked the fictional boastful men and women less, they like the women 42 percent less. Linda Babcock and Sara Laschever, *Women Don't Ask* (New York: Bantam, 2007).

171 **often disdain a woman:** The sponsor's ability to provide protection for rising women leaders may be crucial. As a woman attains more power, she is likely to suffer from negative stereotyping. Research shows that assertive women are not well liked, but assertive men don't suffer the same likability "penalty." Likability does matter, because it enhances one's influence. As Babcock and Laschever point out, "The 'likability' issue can put women in a particularly tight bind because self-confidence, assertiveness, and asking directly for what you want are often necessary for getting ahead in the world." Linda Babcock and Sara Laschever, *Women Don't Ask* (New York: Bantam, 2007).

171 **toot the horn:** Don't believe this could happen to you? Take a look at this recent study: Subjects who said they believed they had no gender biases were asked to evaluate a number of leaders. They consis-

tently rated female leaders as bossier, more emotional, and domineering, even though all the male and female leaders were actors using the same script. Until there is true gender equality in senior leadership positions, keep in mind that women have a narrower band of acceptable leadership styles. Having a sponsor helps. It's comforting to know that someone is reminding others that your record as an accomplished boss doesn't mean you're "Little Miss Bossy!" Linda Babcock and Sara Laschever, *Women Don't Ask* (New York: Bantam, 2007).

171 **sponsor can be invaluable:** Mentors and sponsors can help women learn specifics that will help them navigate the politics of the organization; the norms, standards, values, ideology, and history of the organization; the skills and competencies necessary for success; the paths to advancement and hidden traps to avoid; acceptable methods of gaining visibility; and characteristic stumbling blocks. R. Burke and C. McKeen, "Mentoring in Organizations: Implications for Women," *Journal of Business Ethics* 9 (1990): 317–32.

Part Four: Engaging
Chapter 17 Crossing the Line

191 **think through all the scenarios:** Linda Babcock and Sara Laschever have spent years working on techniques that can help people succeed in asking and getting what they want. They describe the technique we mention here. Visualizing the situation and planning how it might go ahead of time decreases your stress when you are in the moment, allowing you to be more effective. Linda Babcock and Sara Laschever, *Ask for It: How Women Can Use the Power of Negotiation to Get What They Really Want* (New York: Bantam, 2009).

193 **took it as part of the package:** There are many studies on leadership that demonstrate the importance of risk taking. Heifetz and Laurie do an excellent job of describing the importance of being able to take a

risk in their discussion of adaptive leadership. New challenges are problems or issues that have no known solution or response. Solving them entails risk—you can't know that your response to an adaptive challenge will succeed. And yet, leaders who cannot respond effectively by taking the necessary risk are likely to fail. This is why learning to take risks is so important for female leaders. Ronald Heifetz and Donald Laurie, "The Work of Leadership," *Harvard Business Review,* December 2001.

194 **even in that downside case:** Gilbert's research showed that people overestimate the likelihood that taking a risk will make them unhappy, so they stay in their current situations, despite the fact that people who take risks end up happier. When elderly people are asked what they regret most in life, it is always the risks they did not take, not the risks they took. However, this inherent caution is likely a trait cultivated over thousands of years; deep-seated fears lurk underneath. Ancient people who avoided the risks of predators were more likely to live. The challenge is for people to realize that the life-or-death risks that trigger cautiousness are not the same kinds of risks we face in modern society. Daniel Gilbert, *Stumbling on Happiness* (New York: Vintage, 2007).

Chapter 18 Stand Up, Speak Up

198 **speaking up for themselves:** Despite numerous studies suggesting that women have a hard time asking for what they want, women do not have a problem asking for things on behalf of others. Mothers have no problem asking for things their children need, and business women and litigators have no problem advocating for their companies or clients. Linda Babcock and Sara Laschever, *Women Don't Ask: The High Cost of Avoiding Negotiation—And Positive Strategies for Change* (New York: Bantam, 2007).

198 **if someone else notices:** Why is it so important for women to be recognized without asking for recognition? As Deborah Tannen noted in her book *Talking from Nine to Five,* "For middle-class American

women the constraint is clear: talking about our own accomplishments in a way that calls attention to yourself is not acceptable . . . Girls are supposed to be humble—not try to take the spotlight, emphasize the ways they are just like everyone else, and de-emphasize the ways they are special." In her book *Necessary Dreams,* Anna Fels points out that these expectations continue as girls become women. Women feel like they are violating the social norms of their sex if they think of their needs or ask for recognition. Deborah Tannen, *Talking from Nine to Five: Men and Women at Work* (New York: Harper, 1995); Anna Fels, *Necessary Dreams: Ambition in Women's Changing Lives* (New York: Anchor, 2005).

198 **their peak earnings:** Linda Babcock and Sara Laschever, *Women Don't Ask: The High Cost of Avoiding Negotiation—And Positive Strategies for Change* (New York: Bantam, 2007).

202 **strike the right tone:** Marshall Rosenberg is founder of the Center for Nonviolent Communication and author of *Nonviolent Communication: A Language of Compassion.* Rosenberg's technique teaches users to express themselves with honesty and clarity but with respect and empathy for the other person. In addition, it helps the user crystallize and articulate what she wants in the situation. Practicing this form of communication is a good way for women to express themselves in an authentic way that works in professional environments. Marshal Rosenberg, *Nonviolent Communication: A Language of Life* (Encinitas, CA: Puddledancer Press, 2003).

203 **that doesn't commit you:** William Ury's book outlines a simple strategy that can debunk a common misconception that saying no has to have a negative connotation. Once you learn how to say no in a positive way, you stop trying to avoid, attack, or accommodate when you're faced with a situation where you want to say no. Who couldn't benefit from that? William Ury, *The Power of a Positive No* (New York: Bantam, 2007).

204 **you are open and vulnerable:** Otto Scharmer poses four levels

of listening: waiting to talk (when you're not really listening but actually reloading what you will say next); listening to fill in what you don't know; listening with your heart to how the other person feels; and being fully present. When you are listening with your heart and maybe your full presence, you'll show it—open body language (e.g., hands in view and relaxed), positive facial expressions, and other signals that communicate your total openness. Otto Scharmer, *The Theory of U: Leading from the Future as It Emerges* (San Francisco: Berrett-Koehler Publishers, 2009).

Chapter 19 Make Your Own Luck

207 **you have the power:** Carol Dweck's book describes how people who believe they can create their own luck—people with growth mind-sets—are energized and motivated by feedback. Failure doesn't slow them down, because they know that failure is part of learning. Dweck provides an example of children attempting to solve difficult puzzles. Children with a growth mind-set and internal locus of control loved the experience of being challenged and couldn't wait to come back for more! Carol Dweck, *Mindset: The New Psychology of Success* (New York: Ballantine, 2007).

210 **an internal locus of control:** In the 1950s, psychologist Julian B. Rotter developed the social learning theory, which states that our personalities are determined by how we engage with our society, as well as by psychological factors. According to the theory, published in 1966, people who have an internal locus of control are achievement-motivated, whilst those people with an external locus of control have the tendency to conform to others.

210 **can be more confident:** Carol Dweck, *Mindset: The New Psychology of Success* (New York: Ballantine, 2007).

211 **getting a better deal:** Although the research study we're citing here does not prove that comparative knowledge transforms an external

locus of control into an internal one, the study does suggest that women are more likely to act on their own behalf when they are explicitly told that others are doing the same thing. Researchers compared the results of male and female negotiators under a variety of circumstances. In one circumstance, the negotiators were told nothing in advance. In a second situation, they were told it was okay to negotiate if they wanted. Across all situations, male negotiators did better than women, except in the circumstance when women were explicitly told what other people had gotten in previous negotiations. Linda Babcock and Sara Laschever, *Women Don't Ask: The High Cost of Avoiding Negotiation—And Positive Strategies for Change* (New York: Bantam, 2007).

212 **women admire ambition:** In her book *Necessary Dreams,* psychologist Anna Fels talks about how women hated the word *ambition* when it was applied to them but admitted admiring this quality in men. In our own training sessions, we noticed a similar phenomenon. The women we met had worked incredibly hard their entire lives, graduating from top universities with extensive extracurricular achievements. Yet they did not want to be seen as ambitious. Anna Fels, *Necessary Dreams: Ambition in Women's Changing Lives* (New York: Anchor, 2005).

213 **stereotypical male traits:** The Bem Sex Role Inventory (BSRI) provides widely used independent assessments of masculine and feminine role perceptions in a 60-attribute survey. Published in 1974, it uses two lists of adjectives, one for male-related gender roles and another for female-related gender roles. The male-related list includes self-reliant, strong personality, forceful, independent, analytical, defends one's beliefs, athletic, assertive, has leadership abilities, willing to take risks, makes decisions easily, self-sufficient, dominant, willing to take a stand, aggressive, acts as a leader, individualistic, competitive, and ambitious.

213 **rarely describe leaders:** The BSRI includes the following adjectives for female gender roles: yielding, loyal, cheerful, compassionate, shy, sympathetic, affectionate, sensitive to the needs of others, flatterable,

understanding, eager to soothe hurt feelings, soft-spoken, warm, tender, helpful, gullible, childlike, does not use harsh language, loves children, gentle.

Chapter 20 Take the Step

219 **women exercise more caution:** Despite this perception, numerous research studies suggest taking risks is an important element of success. Experts point out that people who take risks are happier than those with a more risk-averse profile. While we believe that the ability to take calculated risks is essential to Centered Leadership, we know that it's important for everyone—even those with no ambition to lead.

220 **reluctant to take risks:** A report released by the *Harvard Business Review,* in conjunction with the Center for Work Life Balance, surveyed women with degrees in science and technology fields. More than one-third of these women (35 percent) said they thought that risks did not translate into opportunities because women don't have the same kind of support when they fail. Furthermore, women's belief that risks do not cultivate success increases with age. Sylvia Ann Hewlett, et al., "The Athena Factor: Reversing the Brain Drain in Science, Engineering, and Technology," *Harvard Business Review Research Report,* June 2008.

220 **less support from colleagues:** "The Athena Factor" relays how women interviewed reported on meetings where men arrived with a peer group ready to support them. These peers supported the man and acted as though his presentation or insights were brilliant, regardless of the reality of that situation. Sylvia Ann Hewlett, et al., "The Athena Factor: Reversing the Brain Drain in Science, Engineering, and Technology," *Harvard Business Review Research Report,* June 2008.

223 **"climbers" do better:** Paul Stoltz, an organizational consultant and author of *The Adversity Quotient: Turning Obstacles into Opportunities,* identifies three developmental stereotypes: climbers, campers, and quitters. Climbers are people who continually strive to grow, learn, and en-

large their capacity. They take risks. Campers are people who settle into comfort zones, choosing security and avoiding risk. Then there are quitters "who retired years ago, but just never bothered to tell anybody." If you're a camper, keep in mind that Stoltz's research shows that even your stable environment is constantly changing. If you don't find new opportunities and take the risks necessary to grow, you won't find the happiness you hoped that stability would provide. Paul Stoltz, *The Adversity Quotient: Turning Obstacles into Opportunities* (San Francisco: Wiley, 1999).

Part Five: Energizing
Chapter 22 Energy in Your Toolkit

237 **more of these responsibilities:** Sylvia Ann Hewlett, *Off Ramps and On Ramps: Keeping Talented Women on the Road to Success* (Cambridge, MA: Harvard Business School Press, 2007).

237 **study of professional women:** In one study of professional women in science, engineering, and technology (SET), almost 50 percent of women between the ages of thirty-five and forty-four had childcare responsibilities, and 11 percent were responsible for eldercare. The research studied women in SET to better understand the female brain drain. Compared to the data on the general population of female professionals, women in SET have it even worse: 36 percent of SET women must be available around the clock, over half of them work or manage people in other time zones, and 71 percent feel pressured to put in extensive face time. It's no wonder that 52 percent of these women end up leaving their careers at some point. Sylvia Ann Hewlett, et al. "The Athena Factor: Reversing the Brain Drain in Science, Engineering, and Technology," *Harvard Business Review Research Report,* June 2008.

238 **starts with a more productive view:** Research by Edy Greenblatt concludes that work-life balance as a notion is flawed. Her work documents how people are often energized by work and depleted by

home life. Her analysis is also supported by the work of Mihályi Cziksentmihályi, who found that people most frequently enter a "flow" state while at work, "flow" being a state where people are energized and happy. Edy Greenblatt, *Restore Yourself: The Antidote for Professional Exhaustion* (Los Angeles: Execu-Care Press, 2009); Mihályi Cziksentmihályi, *Flow: The Psychology of Optimal Experience* (New York: Harper, 2008).

239 **time for a fresh start:** The idea of managing your energy flows was also developed by Edy Greenblatt. She asserts that our energy levels are really personal resources that we can monitor and manage. Edy Greenblatt, *Restore Yourself: The Antidote for Professional Exhaustion* (Los Angeles: Execu-Care Press, 2009).

241 **"to get on the bus":** We're thankful to Jim Collins for that great phrase, and clearly Julie was influenced by him, too. Jim Collins, *From Good to Great: Why Some Companies Make the Leap . . . and Others Don't* (New York: Collins Business, 2001).

243 **four sources of energy:** Greenblatt's research supports the work of Jim Loehr and Tony Schwartz. In their book, *The Power of Full Engagement*, they also describe four primary energies: physical, emotional, mental, and spiritual. Edy Greenblatt, *Restore Yourself: The Antidote for Professional Exhaustion* (Los Angeles: Execu-Care Press, 2009); Jim Loehr and Tony Schwartz, *The Power of Full Engagement* (New York: Free Press, 2004).

244 **quick walk or workout:** Loehr and Schwartz describe energy levels as oscillating entities. They claim that learning how to increase your energy level is possible if you take an approach that respects this nature: You build capability by pushing yourself a bit harder and then taking a break. Taking a walk is one good way to restore. They illustrate this point with research showing that a quick walk can be as powerfully restorative as sleep. Jim Loehr and Tony Schwartz, *The Power of Full Engagement* (New York: Free Press, 2004).

244 **universal energizers:** Edy Greenblatt discovered universal ener-

gizers during her research on personal energy management. She learned that people have unique restoration profiles for the most part. Edy Greenblatt, *Restore Yourself: The Antidote for Professional Exhaustion* (Los Angeles: Execu-Care Press, 2009).

244 **ultradian rhythms:** These are regular intervals that researchers have observed during each twenty-four-hour circadian cycle. At the start of each ultradian cycle (of approximately ninety minutes), your alertness increases, your heart rate goes up, your muscle tension increases, and hormones move through your body. At the end of each cycle your body wants a period of rest and recovery. Jim Loehr and Tony Schwartz, *The Power of Full Engagement* (Free Press, 2004).

245 **sunlight is energizing:** Edy Greenblatt, *Restore Yourself: The Antidote for Professional Exhaustion* (Los Angeles: Execu-Care Press, 2009).

246 **With the time you save:** Jim Loehr and Tony Schwartz, *The Power of Full Engagement* (New York: Free Press, 2004).

248 **taking back your time:** Julie Morgenstern, *Time Management from the Inside Out* (New York: Holt Paperbacks, 2004) and *Never Check Email in the Morning* (New York: Simon & Schuster, 2005).

248 **stop multitasking:** Leslie Perlow's in-depth case study of a high-tech company illustrates the high cost of multitasking. Before she started working with the company, people walked into each other's offices and interrupted each other frequently. The company decided to implement a specific period of time each day when everyone was supposed to work on their own without interrupting or talking to others. Not only did productivity increase, but there was also an unexpected increase in job satisfaction. Leslie Perlow, *Finding Time: How Corporations, Individuals and Families Can Benefit from New Work Practices* (Ithaca, NY: Cornell University Press, 1997).

250 **you build capacity:** Jim Loehr and Tony Schwartz, *The Power of Full Engagement* (New York: Free Press, 2004).

Chapter 23 For a Quick Recovery

252 **leader who exudes resilience:** After graduating from an elite school in China, Yifei Li spent the decade between 1985 and 1995 in the United States, studying at Baylor University and then working at the United Nations and for law firms. In 1995, she returned to China, just when its economic boom was getting under way. For a few years Yifei worked for Burson Marsteller, the public relations firm, and then joined Viacom's MTV music network. In 2008 Yifei joined GLG Partners in China, a NYSE-listed investment firm.

256 **build recovery:** We have all had the experience of finding that something we once loved—a certain song or flavor of ice cream—can lose its attraction if we overindulge. The same is true for energy. Things that once gave you a boost of energy can sometimes become less than energizing. In energizing workshops around the world, we heard that air travel was once energizing for many who now feel drained if they fly for work each week. Diane Fassel's work reports that people need to be diligent about how they choose to energize themselves since those things become less effective once a person hits burnout. Diane Fassel, *Working Ourselves to Death* (Bloomington, IN: Authorhouse, 2000).

258 **using strategic restoration:** Jim Loehr's tennis experience has been replicated in several different research efforts. This first tennis study showed that performance and strategic restoration were correlated. Players who learned to take a quick break and relax were then better prepared to give their all on the court. A second example cited in Loehr's book was research done by the U.S. Army. The Army was trying to understand the best way to shoot down targets over a three-day period. Two teams were assigned to the task; one had the order to take intermittent naps during the three days to allow for recovery, and the other had the order to hit as many targets as possible over three days. The team that slept periodically hit more targets. Jim Loehr and Tony Schwartz, *The Power of Full Engagement* (New York: Free Press, 2005).

258 **positive rituals:** The power of rituals is that they become automatic actions, so you don't have to spend time or energy thinking about what you're doing. A ritualized behavior is more restorative than the same behavior would be otherwise because it allows maximum recovery. Jim Loehr and Tony Schwartz, *The Power of Full Engagement* (New York: Free Press, 2005).

259 **your artist child:** Julia Cameron writes about the artist in you— the childlike being that is creative, holistic, and often accessed through meditation. She recommends a tool she calls "the artist date," a block of time each week set aside to nurture your creative consciousness. Julia Cameron, *The Artist's Way* (New York: Tarcher/Putnam, 1992).

260 **laughter in team meetings:** One of our favorite lessons is Rule Number 6 from Rosamond and Ben Zander's book, *The Art of Possibility*: Don't take yourself so seriously! You don't need a whoopee cushion to make the point, but it's worth embedding Rule Number 6 into your organization's culture. Ben Zander and Rosamund Zander, *The Art of Possibility* (New York: Penguin, 2002).

Chapter 24 Experience of Flow

261 **"lightness of being":** A *rasa* in Sanskrit is a *srot,* which means taste, juice, flavor, sentiment, delight, and experience.

262 **any job can have flow:** To study when people encounter moments of flow, Cziksentmihályi developed a research methodology where subjects carried beepers around throughout the day. At fifteen-minute intervals, the beepers would go off and people would report on what they were doing and how they were feeling. From this rich data set, Cziksentmihályi was able to learn when people entered a state of flow. Mihályi Cziksentmihályi, *Flow: The Psychology of Optimal Experience* (New York: Harper, 2008).

267 **team experience of flow:** Through hundreds of executive debriefings, McKinsey's Organization Practice found that everyone has at

least one memory of a once-in-a-lifetime peak experience at work that made it all worthwhile.

267 **all cylinders are in sync:** Credit goes to Scott Keller, Carolyn Aiken, and our colleagues for their insights derived from leadership workshops over the years. They found three sets of drivers for peak experience:

- **Organizational:** An exciting and clear goal for what is expected (with explicit and specific measures), a talented team in place with diverse skills, a team leader with clear role accountability, and an effective process for working together efficiently.
- **Positive emotions:** Each team member shares the goal and brings intrinsic motivation; the team bonds, because there is mutual respect and trust; everyone immerses themselves in the work; the team feels empowered.
- **Meaning:** Shared sense of making a difference, extraordinary impact, honor and pride, a privilege to have been part of it.

267 **brain functions change:** For the large part of your waking day, your brain waves are called beta waves, operating at 14–38 Hz. When you go into flow, your brain waves are characterized by alpha waves, which operate at 8–14 Hz. In alpha states, your mind is clear and you are calm. You are able to handle new situations with ease. You are more creative. The brainwaves associated with anxiety are absent, and you can restore yourself. Anna Wise, *The High Performance Mind* (Los Angeles: Tarcher, 1997).

267 **five conditions:** Dr. Mihály Csikszentmihályi, who "discovered" flow during research on happiness, wrote this introduction to his book: "We have all experienced times when, instead of being buffeted by anonymous forces, we do feel in control of our actions, masters of our own fate. On the rare occasions that it happens, we feel a sense of exhila-

ration, a deep sense of enjoyment that is long cherished and that becomes a landmark in memory for what life should be like . . . moments like these are not the passive, receptive, relaxing times . . . the best moments usually occur when a person's body or mind is stretched to its limits in a voluntary effort to accomplish something difficult and worthwhile." Mihályi Cziksentmihályi, *Flow: The Psychology of Optimal Experience* (New York: Harper, 2008).

Index